COLUSA COUNTY F...

P9-AFZ-250

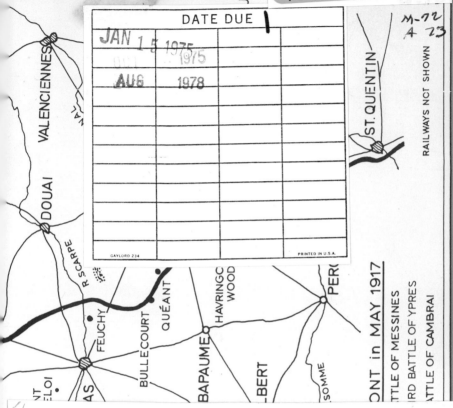

DATE DUE			
JAN 1 5 1975	1975		
AUG 1978			
GAYLORD 234		PRINTED IN U.S.A.	

M-72
A 23

ST. QUENTIN

RAILWAYS NOT SHOWN

R. SCARPE

QUÉANT

HAVRINGC WOOD

BULLECOURT

FEUCHY

BAPAUME

...BERT

SOMME

PER...

...NT in MAY 1917

...TLE OF MESSINES

...RD BATTLE OF YPRES

...TLE OF CAMBRAI

VALENCIENNES

DOUAI

...LOI

...S

51.

NO PARACHUTE

Camel pilot: the author in December 1917

NO PARACHUTE

A FIGHTER PILOT IN WORLD WAR I

Letters written in 1917 by Lieutenant A. S. G. Lee,
Sherwood Foresters, attached Royal Flying Corps

Edited by the same writer

ARTHUR GOULD LEE
Air Vice-Marshal, Royal Air Force

HARPER & ROW,
PUBLISHERS
New York and Evanston

1817

013 1862

FIRST U.S. EDITION 1970

LIBRARY OF CONGRESS CATALOG CARD NUMBER: 78-95971

To my first wife
Gwyneth Ann
who died long ago
and to whom the letters in this book
were sent
in the springtime of life

Contents

A section of illustrations follows page 74

Author's Note

The letters in this volume were written in France in 1917 when I was a pilot in No 46 Fighter Squadron of the Royal Flying Corps. Together with my flying log-book and diary, and some maps, photographs and official documents, they surprisingly survived thirty years of service life. Their travels included a trip to Istanbul in 1937, then to wartime Cairo, and, two years later, the journey back to England via the Cape. Eventually placed in storage, they were forgotten until a few years ago. Now, after half a century, I have edited them for publication.

Reading through these artless sentences of long ago, so haunted with the ghosts of smiling boys cut down in their prime, I can scarcely believe that the things they recount really happened to me. I cannot recognise myself. Could I ever have taken part in those crazy dances of death three or four miles up in the sky, flying a tiny, fragile, one-gun aeroplane, trying to kill other young men in equally flimsy craft? Could it have been me who so rashly strafed enemy trenches that I was shot down three times in nine days? Surely I could never have enjoyed such luck as to escape bullets and shrapnel by a few inches on more than a score of occasions?

But it all did happen, and in these letters the reader may share a young pilot's casually accepted routine of daily hazard. Yet they were not written with an eye to publication: a callow youngster's thoughts did not run in that direction. They were written by a husband of twenty-two to the girl he had impetuously wed in the heady atmosphere of war. They were written to satisfy, first her concern, and second his urge to describe on paper the great, great adventure. They were written in the ardour and immediacy of the hour. They contain neither heroics nor fine writing. They simply record the day-to-day happenings, in the air and on the ground, in a fighter squadron of average renown during eight months of 1917.

Perhaps my greatest surprise on going through the letters, written almost every day, sometimes twice a day, was to wonder at the stoicism of my young wife in accepting without flinching my many descriptions of risky and gruesome happenings, not least of the deaths of pilots in the squadron, some of whom she knew. But she, like the wives of fighting men in every war, quickly learned to live with fear, and without complaint.

The letters are presented as scribbled in the field on a strange assortment of writing pads and official sheets, but because twice as much material was available as I needed to produce a book of reasonable length, ruthless cutting has been necessary. Regrettable casualties among the deletions were accounts of the work of other squadrons, and of the pilots in 46 who were not in my flight. In general, therefore, the letters deal only with my own experiences.

Even these I have had to compress drastically. In addition to excluding passages of a purely personal nature, and pruning the duplications, irrelevancies and commonplaces that inevitably encumber any incautiously written chronicle, I have sometimes removed whole groups of letters that merely described repetitive patrols.

To set against these omissions there are some additions. The names of places and the location of units, of which censorship forbade mention in correspondence, have been inserted throughout. There are occasional extracts from a diary to which were confided both views that might have brought trouble from the censor and subjects too sinister for a young wife to read. There are also linking paragraphs and footnotes, as well as three appendices, to amplify the text, to make good a prentice airman's ignorance of higher service affairs, and to put the reader into the background of political and other contemporary events that affected the work of the R.F.C.

I should perhaps add that the views expressed in these appendices, and in some of the linking paragraphs, are entirely my own, and this is particularly so in Appendix C, in which the information on which I base my opinions was obtained in part from official documents only recently made available for public examination.

In the confirmation of dates, names and other factual details, and in the provision of photographs, I have received invaluable help from the following, to whom I render grateful thanks.

Air Vice-Marshal Raymond Collishaw, C.B., D.S.O., O.B.E., D.S.C., D.F.C.; Mrs Charles Courtneidge and Miss Ann Courtneidge; Wing

Commander Norman Dimmock, A.F.C.; Marshal of the Royal Air Force Lord Douglas of Kirtleside, G.C.B., M.C., D.F.C.; Marshal of the Royal Air Force Sir Arthur Harris, Bart, G.C.B., O.B.E., A.F.C.; Mrs Cicely Courtneidge Hulbert, C.B.E.; Mr S. B. Jackson, Director, Research and Development, Irving Air Chute of Great Britain, Ltd.; Major Donald MacLaren, D.S.O., M.C., D.F.C.; Mrs Cecil Marchant; Mr Herbert Wilcox, C.B.E.

I have also to acknowledge with thanks the facilities to examine official documents extended by the Keeper of Public Records, and his staff, and by officials of the Air Historical Branch, Ministry of Defence, in particular Mr W. J. Taunton and Mr E. H. Turner. For helpful aid in the search for photographs I must thank Mr Edward Hine of the Photographic Library of the Imperial War Museum, and Miss Ann Tilbury, Photographic Librarian of *Flight International*.

Acknowledgement is also paid to the following publications, which have been consulted for technical and other factual detail. *The War in the Air*, Vols iii, iv, v, by H. A. Jones, and three of the Harleyford Publications, *Air Aces of the 1914–18 War*, *Fighter Aircraft of the 1914–18 War*, and *Richtofen and the Flying Circus*.

A.G.L.

Foreword

The young airmen of the belligerent nations of the First World War, who rode their primitive flying machines high above the land-locked armies in France and Belgium, were unique in the history of mankind, for they were the first mortals ever to give battle in the vast spaces of the sky.

Among them was an even rarer breed, unique in another degree, for they waged their conflicts in a fashion that flourished for but an hour, then was gone for ever. They were the airborne warriors who engaged in single combat, like the knights of mediaeval chivalry, but wielding a winged machine-gun in place of lance and sword.

In the early days of the war, fights between the ineffectively armed two-seaters intended only for reconnaissance were rare, incidental and inconclusive. The success of the Fokker monoplane in preying on Allied two-seaters inspired the production by both contestants of a variety of well-armed and manœuvrable single-seater scouts, as they were quaintly called. These planes soon passed from tyrannising enemy two-seaters to fighting each other.

And so began the era of combat between individual pilots in single-seater aeroplanes. Because these craft were, by later standards, so slow, so small, so responsive in control, and so tight in manœuvre, a pilot could come to such close grips with an opponent that if goggles were lifted, as they often were, he might see his features, even his grimace, or when he was attacked from astern the death jerk of his helmeted head as bullets struck between the shoulders.

This was the time when air combat could indeed be tinged with something of the knightly chivalry of old, when a pilot, perhaps still in his teens, might inwardly salute his antagonist, even wave to him as they circled each other, seeking the chance to fire. And having killed, could feel pity for a fellow flyer, or, if he had gone down in flames, remorse for inflicting so gruesome an end. For now was a period, not to last for long, when enemies in the air could fight without mercy but without hate, could even respect and admire each other's skill and valour. Yet in spite of these attitudes every man fought with but one purpose—to kill or be killed.

For the most part, this saga of individual combat took place in 1916 and 1917, during the hottest spells of the first and only war of the Royal Flying Corps, aided by those squadrons of the Royal Naval Air Service which operated with the Corps in France and Belgium. It was a saga that was never to recur, for when, on the formation of the Royal Air Force in April, 1918, the brief life of the R.F.C. came to an end, so did the conditions that permitted the phase of the knightly duel.

By this time the air was crowded with hundreds of fast and lethal fighters, which operated in large disciplined formations. In the vast dog-fights that often developed, air fighting became an affair of fleeting brushes between flights of three or four planes held in tight tactical cohesion, with neither chance nor mood for knightly attitudes.

Effective as were these ordered mass engagements in terms of destructiveness, they seldom held the same fascination for earthbound watchers as the tourneys of the earlier combatants. To the soldiery bound to the slime and carnage of the trenches the occupants of the glinting specks duelling high in the heavens were as beings of another world. Forgetful of their own risks and hardships, they gazed aloft not with envy but with a shudder at the very thought of fighting in such contraptions, and generously rated the airman as the craziest of the brave.

In the homeland the expressions of admiration were more expansive and emotional. The winged striplings of the R.F.C. and R.N.A.S. were of the élite. They seemed in their secret confederacy of flight to be set apart from other fighting men, indeed from all other men. 'They are the knighthood of this war,' declared the nation's leader, David Lloyd George, 'without fear and without reproach: they recall the legendary days of chivalry not merely by the daring of their exploits but by the nobility of their spirit.'

But only occasionally were these Galahads of the air, of whatever race, scions of the knightly families of Europe. They came from every social level, from the cities and the countryside, from the streets and farms and forests of lands all over the world. The bonds that gave a unity to them all were that they flew and that they were young. For to fly and fight and die in the frail cockleshells of that day was the privilege only of audacious youth. Yet once he had taken wing in this exclusive company any fledgling with courage, skill and luck could quickly become a knightly figure, an ace, as the French called him, a flying star, to flash into the sky like a meteor, and, if he could escape destruction, to stay there, resplendent.

From among a multitude of unknown airmen drawn from all the embattled nations there emerged a constellation of champions of glittering valour and deadly talent, who were saluted both by other flyers and by non-flyers as the paladins of the aerial war. These were the men whose names, after half a century, still echo down the years, the men who vanquished their forty or sixty or eighty opponents, and sent them tumbling to death or imprisonment.

These were the men who, in 1917, included such stalwarts as Ball, McCudden, Collishaw, Bishop, Little, Mannock, Fullard among the British, Nungesser, Guynemer, Fonck, Coppens among their Allies, and among their enemies, Immelmann, Boelcke, Voss and the two Richtofens. Behind them ranged a larger but still select galaxy of lesser champions, each of whom could claim his twenty or thirty victories.

But, counting even these, the ranks of the paladins were thin. In the R.F.C. they amounted to but a small proportion of the several thousand pilots and observers and gunners who also flew and fought. These men shared all the hazards of the air war. They endured the searing tensions of daily anti-aircraft fire and of almost daily combat, often in outdated aeroplanes, knowing always that each flight could be the last, that there was no escape should their plane break a wing or burst into flames. For there were then no parachutes.

First among this legion of the unsung were those who fell, for every victory demanded a victim. Many, especially the half-trained novices and those condemned to fly ill-designed aircraft, were shot down within a few days of arriving at their squadrons. Others, though experienced and enjoying efficient machines, succumbed to foemen superior in skill or numbers. Many fell prey to the vagaries of chance, not least those hit by 'archie', or from the ground in the highly risky game of trench-strafing.

Of those who survived, the majority achieved no finer laurels than the satisfaction of seeing out their spell of perilous service before their nerve cracked under the strain. Yet it was this majority, made up of ordinary young men doing their job without thought of glory, who bore the main burden of the air war, who carried out the unglamorised routine duties—the artillery observation, the reconnaissances, the photography, the bombing, and the endless protective fighter patrols.

These men were not endowed with the superhuman fire of the headhunting aces. They attained not even the lowest ranks of the Galahads. Although they may have had their moments of triumph, their bouts of single combat, their gestures of chivalry, and even their occasional victories, they were flyers of no fame, whose proudest boast was to have been of the honourable company of the Royal Flying Corps.

This book tells, in unpretentious words, written on the day, hot on the event, of the progress from fledgling to seasoned fighter of one of these young flyers of no fame.

Heard the heavens fill with shouting, and there
  rained a ghastly dew
From the nations' airy navies grappling in the
  central blue

Tennyson, *Locksley Hall* 1842

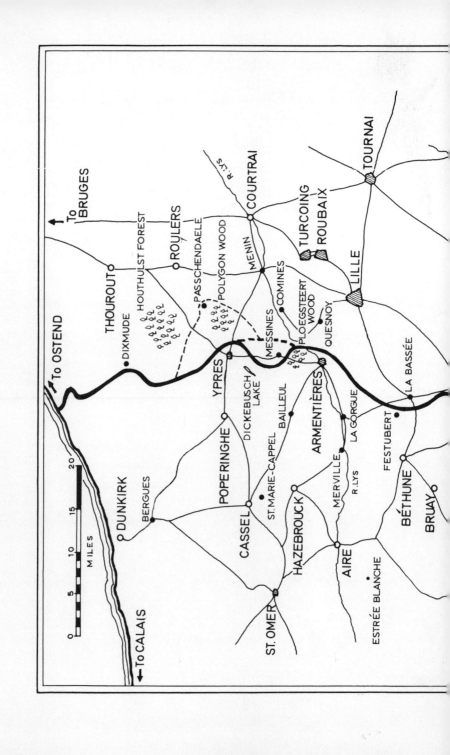

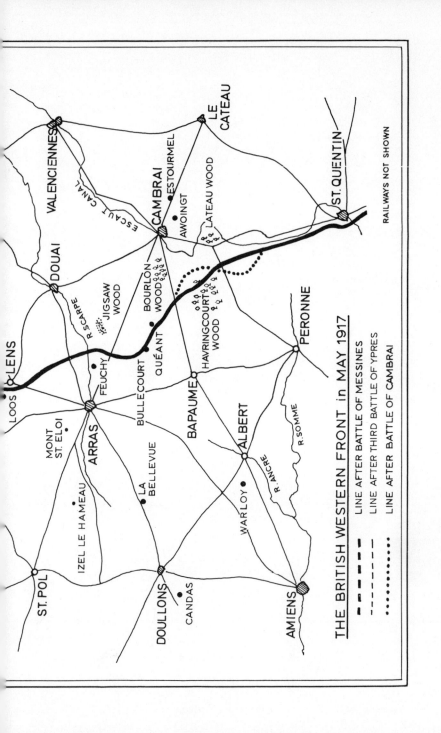

THE BRITISH WESTERN FRONT in MAY 1917

- ▬ ▬ ▬ LINE AFTER BATTLE OF MESSINES
- ‐ ‐ ‐ ‐ LINE AFTER THIRD BATTLE OF YPRES
- • • • • • • LINE AFTER BATTLE OF CAMBRAI

RAILWAYS NOT SHOWN

LENS
LOOS
VALENCIENNES
LE CATEAU
CAMBRAI
ESTOURMEL
AWOINGT
LATEAU WOOD
ST. QUENTIN
ESCAUT CANAL
DOUAI
R. SCARPE
JIGSAW WOOD
BOURLON WOOD
HAVRINGCOURT WOOD
PERONNE
FEUCHY
QUÉANT
BULLECOURT
ARRAS
MONT ST. ELOI
LA BELLEVUE
BAPAUME
ALBERT
R. ANCRE
R. SOMME
WARLOY
IZEL LE HAMEAU
ST. POL
DOULLONS
CANDAS
AMIENS

Part One

The Pilots' Pool

Historical preamble

For Britain and her Allies at the beginning of 1917 the outlook on the Western Front was sombre. In this third year of war the battle line still stretched unbroken for 350 miles across Belgium and France, from the Channel to Switzerland. The broad, shell-pitted belt of trenches and dugouts, protected by myriads of machine-guns trained on dense entanglements of barbed wire, had proved a barrier too difficult to pass by either contestant. Despite the years of ruthless fighting, and the loss of hundreds of thousands of lives, the Line had not moved more than a few miles east or west.

The last great holocaust, the Battle of the Somme in 1916, launched to lessen the pressure against the French at Verdun, had failed in its ultimate aim, although a tactically useful ridge was won at a cost of 420,000 British casualties and half as many French. And now, at the start of 1917, with four million Allied troops facing two and a half million Germans, there was no other prospect than again to assail the enemy positions with mass onslaughts of infantry, to pay the price of 'attrition' by further monstrous sacrifices in flesh and blood.

The chief British campaign planned for this year was a major break-through in Flanders, but this had to be preceded by two attacks to the south, by the French on the Aisne, in Champagne, and by the British along the Scarpe, east of Arras. In the Battle of Arras, which began on April 9th, an advance of four miles was achieved at a cost of 160,000 casualties. The battle should have ended early in May, but was pro-longed for three weeks in order to help the French, whose Aisne offensive had been bloodily repulsed, and whose troops were in a state of mutiny. The consequent weakening of French morale and manpower threw the brunt of further fighting during the year upon the British, whose response was Haig's Flanders offensive, the disastrous Third Battle of Ypres.

In contrast with the war on the ground, so far producing only deadlock, with neither contestant enjoying emphatic periods of mastery, the war in the air had seen the fortunes of the opposing forces fluctuate dramatically. Here, ascendancy rested on the relative technical efficiency of Allied and German aircraft, and as the production of higher-performance machines passed every few months from one side to the other, and back again, so did the mastery of the skies above the battlefield.

The first year of the air war saw the reconnaissance and artillery aeroplanes of the R.F.C., as of the French and German air services, carrying out their duties without serious interference. The second phase began in the late summer of 1915, when the Germans produced the Fokker monoplane, carrying a machine-gun with an interrupter gear by which it could be fired in the line of flight through the arc of the revolving propeller. With this unmatched armament the Fokker all but cleared the skies of Allied aircraft.

Not until the following spring, and later, during the Battle of the Somme, did the next phase come, when the Allies regained relative freedom of the air with the British D.H.2 and F.E.2b and 2d, which, like the pioneer Vickers 'Gun-Bus', were fighter pushers armed with a machine-gun firing from a forward nacelle, and the French 'Baby' Nieuport, firing over the top wing.

Towards the end of 1916 this advantage was lost to the Halberstadt and the Albatros D-II, both with two guns firing through the propeller arc. Early in 1917 the even better Albatros D-III arrived, and this outclassed all British fighters except the Sopwith Triplane and, at very high altitudes only, the Sopwith Pup. But both these planes had only one gun. Newer, better-armed British fighters now arriving, potentially equal to the D-III, such as the S.E.5 and the Bristol F.2a two-seater, were at first ineffective because of technical shortcomings and tactical mishandling. Later, reinforced by the Sopwith two-gun Camel, which was to come into service in July, they were to bring the odds level.

But in the Battle of Arras the German superiority was crushing, for although their pilots, led by the redoubtable Baron von Richtofen, faced over double their numbers, their D-IIIs destroyed the outdated British planes with ease. Only the Triplane, with its better climb and tighter turn, could match them. The British casualties in this battle were the most severe ever to be suffered by the Royal Flying Corps. Between March and May, 1,270 aeroplanes were destroyed or failed to return, and during one five-day period in April 75 were shot down, of whose 105 occupants, 86 were killed or missing. Not without cause did this month come to be known as Bloody April.

These heavy losses, continuing into May, consumed the reserves of qualified pilots, which necessitated replacements being rushed out from England without adequate training. These novitiates could be granted no gradual introduction to air combat, but were sent straight into action, usually on obsolescent craft, against experienced German pilots mounted on much superior planes, and were thus, with tragic frequency, shot down on their first patrols.

That the R.F.C. possessed numerical superiority in aircraft in France was a mockery, for this was one of the prime causes of technical inferiority. The Corps was being expanded too rapidly, without due regard to the capacity for production of an aircraft industry handicapped by sordid political and inter-service rivalries, by the sterilising grip of the Royal Aircraft Factory,[1] and by frequent strikes among the aircraft workers. Because too many squadrons had somehow to be equipped and maintained, quantity took precedence over quality, and the Albatros pilots continued to be presented with generous offerings of hapless prey.

It was at this unpromising hour that I arrived on the Western Front. I would have been there earlier, in good time for the Arras shambles, had I not been unfit for active service for some months as the result of injuries received in a flying accident due to incompetent instruction during training. The enforced delay gave me time to become a skilled pilot. On May 16th I was one of a group of reinforcements sent to the northern Pilots' Pool in France. From there the letters begin.

1. See Appendix A.

No 1 Aircraft Depot, St Omer,
British Expeditionary Force, France
Friday, May 18th, 1917

So far, so good! I'm at the Pool at the Depot, together with some of the fellows from Portmeadow who also crossed the Channel on Wednesday. I sent just an 'I'm here' postcard from the Hotel Folkstone at Boulogne, where we were billeted, for there was nothing much to say except that the sea was rough, and everybody, including me, was hopelessly sick. Not the cleverest way to celebrate the first time I've been out of England, nor, for that matter, my formal entry into my first war.

This depot stocks both aeroplanes and pilots (and also repairs the planes) and sends them to squadrons that suffer crashes and casualties. It is an ugly sprawling place, with scores of Bessoneau canvas hangars, and workshops, and rows and rows of Nissen huts for living quarters, among them the Pilots' Pool. Several of the chaps waiting to be posted are old friends from 66 Squadron at Filton and 40 Training Squadron at Portmeadow.

Some of the pilots who crossed with me went on by road to No 2 Aircraft Depot at Candas, near Doullons, which supplies the Southern Front. This includes the Arras sector, where R.F.C. casualties have been so heavy over the past month or so. Those kept here will go to squadrons on the Northern Front, where things are quieter, and so we'll have a chance to learn the job, and not get into trouble in the first few days.

Most pilots average 15–20 hours' flying when they arrive here, with maybe 10–12 solo, five on the type they're expected to fight on. With that amount of piloting, they can't even fly, let alone fight. I find I've done more flying than any of the others, with my 85 hours—72½ solo, 18 on Pups. My Avro crash at Filton certainly did me well by keeping me in England long enough to learn to fly properly.

Saturday, May 19th

In the afternoon the monotony of waiting around was broken by a flying job. Six of us were detailed to ferry B.E.2es to No 2 A.D. I hadn't flown a Quirk for months, and when I took off I saw in my mind's eye the nasty flat-spin crash that I perpetrated at Filton, but everything went well. There was much mist around, but I managed to find my way to Candas, and land without trouble, but of the rest, two crashed on landing, one crashed badly *en route* in a forced landing, and another, called Barlow, who lost his way and landed on what he learned was the Field of the Battle of Agincourt, also crashed when he got there. The sixth is still missing. I felt rather a cad not crashing too, because everyone is glad to see death-traps like Quirks written off, especially new ones.

The journey back in a Crossley was fun, for I bagged one of the two front seats, the other being taken by Captain Bonar Law, son of the politician, whom I'd met before. It must have been hell for the chaps inside, for the driver went like the wind, roaring round corners on two wheels and swaying madly, but I enjoyed it, and wished I'd been driving, that is if I could drive. Strange when you consider it, I can fly an aeroplane, but I've never driven a car. As it grew dark, we saw flashes of gunfire all along to the eastwards. It was thrilling to watch. The war was coming closer!

I see from yesterday's newspapers—they come only a day late, which is pretty good in wartime—that there's still no news of Albert Ball. It's now two weeks since he was missing, and people here think he must be dead, probably so smashed up or burnt that he can't be identified. He was a jolly stout fellow if ever there was one. I feel very proud that I'm a Sherwood Forester, like him.

I've just been reading about his last fight in the R.F.C. Weekly Communiqué, which everybody calls Comic Cuts, and which gives a brief account of day-to-day work in the squadrons, made up from pilots' and observers' reports. Ball's squadron, 56, gets mentioned often. They seem to be doing quite well on the new S.E.s, though the chaps here say they won't be really good until they get a more powerful engine.

I'm writing this in the ante-room after a late dinner, but I'll have to stop now as the crowd are having a booze-up, and a whale of a racket is working up. I'll either have to join them or go to bed, and as the beds are as hard as boards, it looks like drinking!

Sunday, May 20th

I didn't feel very 98·4 this morning when I woke up. The binge went on until after midnight, though I can't think why. It was one of those full-out parties that start for no particular reason and go on until the drink runs out. We had some sing-songs—one fellow produced a baby concertina—and sang things like 'When this ruddy war is over, Oh how happy we shall be' and 'The green grass grew all round' and some less delicate ones such as:

Two German officers crossed the Rhine, skiboo, skiboo.
To love the women and taste the wine, skiboo, skiboo.
Oh, landlord, you've a daughter fair,
With lily-white arms and golden hair.
   Skiboo, skiboo, skiboolby boo, skidam, dam, dam.

and so on, for lots of verses, which become more and more blue. As for skiboo, I've no idea what it means, but it's very good for yelling out at the top of your voice when you're ginned.

I went to bed with my head buzzing with all the evening's talk and songs, a mix-up of our heavy casualties and dud machines with green grass and skiboos and Albatros scouts, all flashing confusedly in a dizzy alcoholic world. The hangover this morning lasted until lunchtime.

In the afternoon I sat with the other chaps in the Pool Mess and just talked. When you're waiting day after day for the summons from the Adjutant that means a posting to a squadron there's nothing much to do except play cards or read dog-eared magazines and newspapers, but this gets boring, and so mostly we talk. About the war, of course. The air war, that is, for nobody is much interested in what happens on the ground.

And these chats give you a very different line from the soothing syrup they hand out at home. Fellows come hot from the squadrons to collect new machines, and they pop into the Mess for a drink and a meal and to see the chaps, and they tell us the unvarnished truth, straight from the cannon's mouth. About fellows we know, killed, wounded or prisoners, about the several kinds of machine they have to fly which ought to be on the scrap-heap, and how they've been shot down in droves by this Baron Richtofen and his squadron with their latest Albatros, twenty-five miles an hour faster than anything we have. That's why they bagged so many of our machines during the Arras show, especially last month. Bloody April, people are calling it.

We've got too many death-traps in service, like the F.E.8 scouts, a whole formation of nine shot down in one scrap in March, and the equally senile Martinsyde scouts, the Morane Parasols and the D.H.2s. The Nieuport and Sopwith two-seaters aren't much better, while not one of the whole breed of B.E.s has a hope in hell against the Albatros and the Halberstadt. Only the Triplane and the Pup can give them a beating. Perhaps things won't be so bad now that new machines are coming along, like the R.E.8, the D.H.4, the S.E.5 and the Bristol, but they haven't done much yet.

I'm lucky to be a Pup merchant, and also to be clear of the Arras mess-up. But it's strange that no one who goes off to Candas seems to care, each one reckons that casualties are other chaps, never maybe himself. That's how I look at it too. I hope you don't find this sort of thing depressing, but, after all, it's no good sticking one's head in the sand. Anyway, I *am* going to a quiet section of the Line.

There isn't much else to write about while I'm here at the Depot, though there'll be plenty when I get to a squadron. I'll look out for cheerful things to describe, and try to make my letters interesting. As you know, I enjoy writing, and out here it will help to pass the time. Also, I'd like to put down an account of all that happens to me. If you keep the letters, they will make a sort of record of my time in France.

May 20th (Diary)

The gloom merchants in the Mess say that even the Pup is obsolescent. It's been in service in France since October, and hasn't a chance against the new Albatros D-III, except at 17,000 feet up. The gloomers also say that the average life of a scout pilot on the Arras Front is still under three weeks. A lot of bally hot air, they're just trying to put the wind up us new boys.[1]

1. But the gloom merchants were right. The average life of a Royal Flying Corps pilot in 1916 was officially reckoned at three weeks. In the first four months of 1917, it was, because of the Arras losses, two weeks: over the whole of 1917, six weeks.

Every day a fresh batch of pilots arrives from England, but most of them go on to No 2 A.D. The newspapers say that the Arras push is now practically over, but it certainly isn't for the R.F.C., judging by the number of reinforcements going south. Something must be doing in the north too, for each day four or five pilots leave on posting. Crossley tenders arrive from the squadrons to take them, and they dash off in high spirits, just as if they were going on holiday.

I'm still waiting patiently, or, by now, impatiently, for my turn. It's an odd feeling, waiting. Somewhere, out in the squadrons, is a pilot who, today, tomorrow, will be shot down, killed, wounded or taken prisoner, and into his place, maybe into his machine, I shall move. Waiting to climb into dead men's cockpits, somebody called it, though I think this is piling it on. I may relieve a time-expired pilot who's done his six months, for that's as much as the average fellow can take if his squadron is a lot in action. If he's not rested then, he begins to crack up under the strain. I've learned all this in the never-ending discussions in the Mess.

Everybody is fed up to read about the strike of engineers, and how the production of howitzers is now held up. And we're jolly glad that some of the leaders have been arrested. It makes you sick to hear of these b——s striking for yet more money, and holding up the weapons which the men out here desperately need to fight with, especially the P.B.I., as the Poor Bloody Infantry are always ticketed, doing it all on the princely pay of a shilling a day or thereabouts. Strikers did the same last month for the R.F.C., in the middle of the Arras massacre, and held up the supply of Sopwith two-seaters (called 1½-strutters), and 45 Squadron had to fall back on even older Nieuport two-seaters, which didn't do their casualty lists any good.

I and five other merchants have just been sent for to ferry some more Quirks to Candas. It's a damn' scandal that such dangerous crocks are still being sent to France. Compared with a Pup, every variation of the B.E. is like flying a mangle. I feel darned sorry for the poor devils who have to take them up against Albatroses. It's as bad as sentencing every other man to death.

By the way, I hear that the pilot who didn't arrive at Candas two days ago crashed his B.E. into a wood and killed himself. You see what I mean when I write about fellows being sent out here to fight when they haven't even learned to fly.

Must dash off—the others are yelling for me.

Tuesday, May 22nd

I got back late last night from that blinking hole, Candas, to learn that during the afternoon I had been posted to No 1 Squadron at Bailleul, which has Nieuport scouts. The Adjutant was fuming like a bear with a sore head, sending out messages for me, thinking I was on the loose in St Omer. Eventually he sent somebody else. I would have liked to go to a famous squadron like No 1, though I've never flown Nieuports, but I'd prefer a Pup squadron, as I'm so used to them.

At breakfast the air was full of rumours about a big push coming, though, of course, nobody had an inkling where. But quite early pilots began to arrive for new machines to replace those lost in yesterday's fighting. On the Ypres front, too. They couldn't tell us much of what was happening, except that there's much more air activity now than for some time past.

Just after I'd finished that last para I was called to the Adjutant's office and informed I was posted to No 46 Squadron. The tender is already on the way, and he told me to get packed immediately, and not to forget to pay my mess-bill.

So I'll close now, and write as soon as I get to the squadron, which I've never heard of before, I'm afraid. It's stationed somewhere this side of Armentières, in what the Adj said was one of the quietest parts of the whole Line. So I can get down to the war slowly and systematically, so much better than starting with Richtofen as my tutor!

Part Two

The Ypres Front

No 46 Squadron R.F.C.
La Gorgue, France
Tuesday, May 22nd (second letter)

The day of days has come! At long last I'm with a Scout squadron in the Field in France, and feeling on top of the world.

I'm writing this after dinner, late in the evening, in bed, by candle-light, in a corner of the hut I share with three other pilots, all asleep and snoring. I can't have the electric light on as it would wake them up and they're on the dawn patrol. There's a persistent croaking from frogs in a pond just behind the hut, and another noise from further afield, the deep rumble of artillery, for we are not far from the Lines. As I write, the tremor of explosions comes to my elbows resting on the wooden frame of the bed. Through the window, eastwards, I see flashes of gunfire flooding the sky, and the glow of green and white flares fired by front-line troops, distant, of course, but very clear on a dark night like this.

I arrived about teatime, and haven't had a chance to fly yet. The squadron is a rather different set-up from what I expected, more informal, and something of a change after training squadrons in England. We're pleasantly situated alongside the River Lys, near the village of La Gorgue, with two towns within easy reach, Merville and Estaires. The Lys runs eastwards to Armentières and on into Hunland. But—there's no aerodrome! At least, nothing resembling the kind I'm used to, vast stretches of grassland like Netheravon and Portmeadow.

After a quick journey in a Crossley from St Omer to Merville we came along a cobbled, poplar-lined road until suddenly we slowed down and turned off left, past a sentry, into a cindered area surrounded by numerous huts and tents, a line of Leyland lorries, and a large wooden shed, the end one of a row backing on to the road. These were the hangars. In front of them, on a long cindered stretch which was the tarmac, stood a few Pups, attended by a sprinkling of mechanics. In the eastern background, seeming quite close, an observation balloon hung motionless, looking like an enormous vegetable marrow.

But no aerodrome. Only a wide field of potatoes. The driver had pulled up by a modest hut with oiled silk windows, a sort of overgrown packing case, with the R.F.C. ensign flying above and a gas alarm (a Le Rhône cylinder hanging from a little gallows) flanking the door. He told me this was the squadron office. As I got down I asked, 'But where's the aerodrome?' He grinned, pointed to the potatoes and said, 'There's a criss-cross of cinder tracks in the middle of that.'

I entered the hut, and found two men there, both in shirt-sleeves, one with his back to me, busily tapping away on a typewriter, the other facing me at a desk. I saluted him, but he waved me to the typist, saying, 'That's the C.O.' So I saluted his back and waited. He finished a line, turned, regarded me non-committally and said, 'How d'ye do. How much flying have you done on Pups?' When I told him nearly twenty hours, with over seventy all told, he brightened up and asked how I'd managed that. I explained I'd had crashes at Filton and hadn't been passed fit for overseas until a week ago. He muttered, 'Crashes, eh?', brightened down, and went on with his typing.

This was Major Philip Babington, M.C., and the other was the squadron adjutant, or, as they're called in France, recording officer, Captain Thompson. After I'd given him the usual cheer-me-up particulars, age, religion, favourite flowers, next-of-kin (he thought I was joking when I said I had a wife), he said I was posted to 'C' Flight, and would I report to Captain Pratt. This casual reception was, as I soon found, typical of how the squadron is run. The Major doesn't like hot air and red tape.

I've just jumped out of bed to look at a bomber passing overhead, very low, flying east, following the river I expect. His lights are on, I hope he remembers to switch them off when he enters Hunland. By George, I wouldn't have his job for love nor money.

Continuing my arrival. From the office I went along the tarmac to 'C' Flight hangar, and met Pratt, who welcomed me, checked up on my flying times and was decidedly braced thereat. He told me to take a flip next morning to get to know the aerodrome and its surroundings.

While we were chatting, a Pup arrived at 500 feet from the north, circled the field of potatoes, and made what seemed a miraculous landing among them. Two ack-emmas ran out when he circled, and now they helped him taxi in, one on each wing-tip. He drew up at the next hangar, unloaded his machine-gun (the bullets were at once picked up by an armourer), jumped down from the cockpit and started talking excitedly with several pilots who appeared from inside the hangar. Then they trooped over to the squadron office.

With me in tow, Pratt joined them. The one who had landed was a Canadian called Barrager, who'd just come off patrol, and he said he'd seen a collision at 16,000 feet over Dickebusch Lake, south of Ypres. A Pup had hit an R.E.8, its right wing had folded back, and it had gone down in a nose-dive spin. And Barrager reckoned it could have been his partner on patrol, with whom he'd lost contact ten minutes earlier.

To cut a long story short, confirmation soon came that he was right. His companion, named Gunnery, had fallen on this side of the line. His machine was crashed to matchwood, and he was killed. The R.E. got home safely.

I left them all talking about this in the office, and after watching a patrol of five come in, went over to the Mess, at the opposite corner of the aerodrome, where huts and tents are clustered alongside a farm-house, close to the river. I had tea in the dining-room half of the Mess, a long wooden hut divided into two, the other half being the ante-room. The furniture was pretty battered, but the place looked better than most, having a cocktail bar, a piano, and a good selection of Kirchner[1] wenches.

In the Mess I met more of the pilots, including two who sleep in my hut, Courtneidge and Williams. Courtneidge was one of the five I'd watched land. They'd seen no H.A.—means hostile aeroplanes: some-times E.A., enemy aeroplanes. Then I went to the hut to unpack, but discovered that the batman, called Watt, had done it already. He told me that the hut, which was wooden and roomy, not a curved-roof

1. The French artist whose drawings of glamorous near nudes were the popular pin-ups of the day.

Nissen, was quite nice except for the frogs and mosquitoes from the pond nearby, and the stench from the farmyard midden opposite.

Then he said he'd been batman to Mr Gunnery, and what a nice gentleman he was, and how he was the second gentleman he, Watt, had had killed, and how very depressing it was the way they went off in the morning, bright and hearty, and just never came back. I sympathised and said I hoped I wouldn't ever give him cause for further depression.

But all that matters is that I'm here, where I've tried and planned to come over the past two years, on active service with the Royal Flying Corps, and in a Scout squadron too, the crack cavalry of the air, as the newspapers call us. Now I'm right in the Great Adventure, of fighting the war in the air, and wondering where it will all lead to.

I suppose I ought to be excited, sleepless, imagining myself in the throes of an air fight—the swift leap through space, the rattle of guns, the dive to earth of the stricken Hun, the triumphant loops of the victor—Me! And all that kind of thing. Or else I ought to be brooding over the dangers ahead, especially after being greeted with a fatal casualty (and a funeral, which I forgot to mention I'm detailed to attend as a pallbearer tomorrow).

But to tell you the truth, apart from the thrill of just being here, I don't have any unusual emotions at all, except of anticipation of what I shall see on my first trip tomorrow, and maybe one little nagging worry—do we ever get eggs *and* bacon for breakfast?

Wednesday, May 23rd

Today I had my first two flights, I've been to the Lines, and I've seen Hun archie[1] in action. My first trip was towards midday, to get the local bearings and to practise landings. There was a home-from-home touch about the machine allotted to me, for at Portmeadow my favourite Pup was number A6187, and my grid here is A6188. This was a good omen, I thought, even though as the newest comer I'd been given the oldest crock in the flight.

1. This term, always used on the British front to denote German anti-aircraft fire, reputedly derived from George Robey's popular song, *Archibald! Certainly Not!*

It has my flight number—4—painted on the side of the fuselage and on top of the wings. Pratt is No 1, a man called Joske is 2, Courtneidge 3, and so on, in each flight. The flight is indicated by the wheels, painted red, the other flights being blue and yellow. There's also the squadron marking, two white bands painted round the fuselage just in front of the tail unit. My Pup is not too bad to fly, a bit soft on the controls, but I've asked the flight-sergeant to tighten up the rigging.

The aerodrome is a shocker, a sort of Union Jack of cinder tracks five or six yards wide, running among the potatoes and other crops. You taxi out for about 150 yards, with an ack-emma holding on to each rear interplane strut, to a cindered space in the centre some thirty yards square. The mechanics are there to stop you dropping into the drainage gullies that flank the tracks, a necessary precaution, especially in a side wind, when the Pup can be darned difficult to taxi. If you run off the track when landing, over you go on your nose with a broken prop at the least. Both Courtneidge and Williams, who've only been here twelve days or so, have had landing crashes, and they warned me to be careful.

When you get into the air you can't believe it's an aerodrome. The tricky cinder-track criss-cross makes it stand out clearly from surrounding fields, so it's bad for camouflage reasons. Apart from that, you've got a big acreage of mixed crops flanked on one side by a river lined with poplars, and on the other by a row of hangars, backed by more poplars, also telegraph poles, on the main road. Whoever picked this place as an aerodrome must have been completely off his rocker.

I flew around the district for twenty minutes, keeping the criss-cross in sight all the time, as there was a thickish haze, and it wouldn't have done to get lost on my first time up, especially with the Lines so close. It was such low visibility that I never even saw them. Then I came in and made a perfect three-pointer.[1] I did half a dozen more circuits and landings, and, fortunately, every one was good. I say fortunately, for

1. Because the Pup, in common with other aeroplanes of the time, had no brakes, it had to be landed at minimum flying speed, which meant easing down the tail to ensure that the two wheels and the tail skid touched the ground together—hence 'three-pointer'. The modern aeroplane lands in flying position, tail up, at high speed, but is pulled up by its brakes.

though I didn't know it, the Major and a bunch of pilots were watching my efforts. I gathered afterwards I'd passed. The mechanics also watched with interest. They prefer pilots who don't constantly give them landing crashes to work on.

My second go was a seventy-minute trip this evening at six, the object being to get the lie of the land behind our Lines. This time it was very clear, with only a scattering of cirrocumulus very high, and I could see for miles, as soon as I was 1,000 feet up. Pratt warned me to keep well away from the Lines, and said I should rightly have been conducted round by an experienced pilot, but nobody was available.

First thing I noticed as I climbed up was the string of observation balloons, which Pratt had warned me not to approach, as it is too easy to run into the cables. The sun was behind me, and as I got higher I could see the trenches unfolding, a wide brown belt winding roughly north and south. I went up to 10,000, and from there could pick out the belt from horizon to horizon, looking like a giant rattlesnake curving up from the south across a patchwork countryside, its flat head spread to the east of Ypres, its fang running into flooded lands towards the Channel.

I can't say how much it hit me, to be sitting up there, a couple of miles high, looking down on the battlefield, in fact on four or five battlefields, and sweeping them all in one glorious bird's-eye view. Of course, I've seen photographs of it, but they convey nothing compared with the reality, this vast country split into two by this long ugly scar, like a gigantic, dried-up river bed. To think that for three years millions of men have faced each other along hundreds of miles of no-man's-land, slaughtering each other in hordes without ever being able to break through, except for a few nibblings.

And there was I, perched up aloft, seemingly standing still in relation to the earth, for at this height you have no sensation of speed except for the rush of air past your face, and looking down on something the P.B.I. never see, their battle line of trenches and barbed wire, backed on either side by cultivated fields and villages and towns, looking quite normal, as though no such thing as war existed.

Then I started to come down to have a closer look at things, but the maze of zigzagging trenches was too confusing to disentangle, they seemed so interlocking that but for the shadowy lines of barbed wire, I couldn't have picked out no-man's-land, nor which was our front line and which the German. Lower still, I saw how the brown earth was pockmarked by millions of shell holes, many gleaming with water.

It was all so interesting to look at that I didn't realise a westerly wind was carrying me towards Hunland. Suddenly I noticed, above my level, well to the south, a bunch of black woolly balls hanging in the sky. I knew it must be Boche archie, and then I spotted their target, a group of tiny specks making eastwards. I watched until archie stopped, then, turning my gaze ahead, found an observation balloon about 100 yards away. I hastily turned in my tracks, and made for home. I was amazed at its size—100 feet long, I learned afterwards.

When I casually mentioned what I'd seen, I got a sharp tick-off from Pratt for going too near the Lines, where I would have been easy meat for a prowling Hun. I pointed out that the only machines I'd seen were the distant ones being archied, and he said that newcomers never did see anything until they were being shot at, and often not even then. I said, 'Sorry, Skipper,' very meekly, for I suddenly remembered that I'd done the trip without for a moment thinking of loading my gun.

While we were standing there talking, a Pup had appeared, circled and landed, and taxied to 'B' Flight hangar, next door. Then exactly the same thing happened as yesterday. The pilot got down, began talking excitedly, Pratt went over, and I followed. The pilot, called McDonald, had been on patrol with a man named Stephen while I'd been sightseeing. They'd met three Albatroses, had a scrap, and Stephen had suddenly dived away westwards, either hit or with a dud engine. McDonald was badly shot about, had spun to escape, and was worried about his companion.

By the time we'd reached the office, the news had come through. Stephen had been hit, had come down on this side, but had died of his wounds on the way to hospital.

I must say, to have this happen twice in two days put me back a lot. Especially following on Gunnery's funeral, which I attended before my first flip, as one of the six pallbearers. He was buried in La Gorgue cemetery, a simple ceremony taken by a Flying Corps padre, no Last Post or firing party, such as we always had at Filton and Portmeadow, just a straight burial.

I was speaking to Stephen in the Mess last evening, a jolly nice chap who thought he'd met me somewhere, though he hadn't. It was just a way to open up talking. He and another fellow called Dimmock were the ones I spoke to most, apart from my hut mates. The original members of the squadron are a little inclined to be stand-offish. Some of them have been in it since it formed in England a year ago with two-seater Nieuports, and I fancy they look on us newcomers almost as interlopers.

Of course, it may be they aren't in the mood for casual talk, having lost two fellows in two days, when the squadron hasn't had a fatal casualty for over a month. This evening the chaps who were close to Gunnery and Stephen had the pip so badly they settled down to a gloomy booze-up, so I left the Mess and went to bed early, hence this long letter. This time I'm writing with the lights on, as the other three (the fourth is a Canadian, Captain Caudwell, also a newcomer) have come to bed too, and are reading or writing.

It does seem as though this is not so quiet a part of the Lines as they said at St Omer. Everybody is being worked pretty hard, running two patrols a day per pilot. I didn't think I would have long to wait, and I was right, for Pratt has just popped his head in the doorway to warn me for patrol tomorrow afternoon. Also he wants me to go early to St Omer to collect a replacement Pup for the one lost today. Also he wants me to go to Stephen's funeral. So this is where I pipe down and hit the pillow.

May 23rd (Diary)

Gunnery's funeral was a depressing business. I've done pallbearer at so many funerals of chaps killed while learning to fly, especially at Filton, about once a week, that I thought I'd got hardened to it. But they were in coffins. For what reason I don't know, Gunnery was just sewn up in canvas, placed on a wide plank, and covered with the Union Jack. We could feel the corpse, cold and rigid, when we took him to the graveside from the trailer. It gave me quite a turn, and the others too, in fact, one of them, a very young pilot, Asher, fainted and flopped to the ground.

17

Thursday, May 24th

The Pup I ferried from No 1 A.D. this morning was a joy to fly, with smooth and willing engine, and very sensitive response to the controls, just like a spirited horse, eager to the slightest touch of rein and knee. In fact, when you get a thoroughbred Pup like this you feel as though you're controlling a living thing, as though the two of you are one creature gambolling in the air. It's something you can't convey to anybody who doesn't fly, but the Pup is really the most thrilling aeroplane, you feel you're riding the Pegasus of your dreams.

The sun shone in a cloudless sky, and life seemed good, so as soon as I was clear of St Omer I put my Pegasus through her paces. She was one of the sweetest Pups for stunting I've ever flown. Then I went on to La Gorgue, and arriving at the aerodrome, felt so full of the joys of spring that before landing I indulged once more in a few minutes' larking around.

At about 1,000 feet I did a succession of leisurely loops, some slow barrel rolls and some flick rolls, then span down to 200 feet and landed neatly off a sideslip. I felt rather braced with the flick rolls, they're a new stunt, and I'd learned the trick only a few days before leaving Portmeadow. As I glided in over the Mess huts, I saw bunches of chaps looking up and realised I'd had an audience. And when I taxied to the flight hangar I ran into another tick-off from Captain Pratt.

'Quite a nice little display you gave us,' he said. 'But it isn't your own machine. You can do what you like with your own bus, if you want to loosen it up with show-off splitassing, that's your own affair, but you'd better respect other people's, else you won't be very popular.'

I was absolutely flabbergasted. It wasn't really showing off, I was just enjoying myself in a topping new machine. It put me in an awful stew to get another roasting so soon, but I couldn't argue the toss, so I just mumbled, 'Sorry, Skipper,' once more. But then I got another shock, for he went on, 'By the way, how do you do that flick roll? I'm not up on that one.'

My tail went up at once, and I told him. Later in the Mess I explained it to the others, none of whom had done it, but simple when

18

you know how. So now I'm very full of beans—yesterday the new boy novice, today teaching them stunts.

Later, talking to Courtneidge (he's the brother of the one and only Cicely, and very like her too, and son of Robert Courtneidge, who produced *The Arcadians*) I learned something that surprised me a lot. This was that the original pilots of the squadron are in the throes of getting the hang of Pups, because until a short time ago they were still flying two-seater Nieuports, doing artillery shoots and reccos and photography. Not until early in April were they re-equipped with Pups, the observers then being posted to other squadrons. They came to La Gorgue from Droglandt, up north somewhere, only a week before I arrived, and are terribly bucked at being on single-seater fighters, but haven't yet become used to handling them, for example in stunting. Some haven't even done a spin yet. So now I feel much less of a greenhorn!

I'm writing this while sitting by the River Lys, which everybody calls the canal, because hereabouts it runs dead straight alongside the aerodrome between sloping grassy banks. It joins up with a real canal system at Merville, and large barges often pass, drawn by horses on the towpath. So far as we're concerned, river or canal, it's there for us to swim in, and that applies to the whole squadron, for the other ranks' tents are a hundred yards from our Mess and huts, under the poplars lining the banks.

I've had a topping bathe already, and half a dozen of the fellows are splashing in the water now. Occasionally, the distant rumble of gun-fire reminds us that there's a war. We are so near the Lines that we can see both British archie (white) and German (black), and with binoculars can see our artillery planes patrolling up and down. Our observation balloons seem only a few fields away, but the nearest is two miles, I suppose. Others are strung, one every three to four miles or so, on a curve that roughly marks the course of the Lines north and south of Armentières.

After coming back from St Omer this morning I went to Stephen's funeral. He was buried next to Gunnery. It was a gloomy party, nobody saying a thing. As we stood beside the grave, I heard the padre's voice, but didn't take in a word of what he said. On the way home, riding in the back of the Crossley with the other pallbearers, in complete silence, my mind drifted to the funerals at Filton, and how we marched behind the local band (I believe it was the Salvation Army), and how they always played the same slow march, the only one they knew for certain, Chopin's Marche Funèbre. Then I caught others staring at me oddly, and I realised I was quietly whistling it!

As I'm going on my first patrol after tea, I'll finish this off now, and catch the afternoon post. I'll write later about what happens. I must say, I'm longing to have a smack at the Hun.

May 24th (Diary)

The same sort of thing took place at Stephen's funeral as at Gunnery's. No coffin. But at least nobody fainted. Not a very bracing start for a newcomer to be welcomed with two funerals in two days, and especially having to handle the poor chaps' corpses.

Thursday, May 24th (second letter)

There were three of us on my first patrol, the others being Court-neidge and a tall slim fellow called Joske, who as leader had a coloured streamer on each rear strut. Courtneidge, as deputy leader, had one on his rudder. Although I'd been looking forward to the thrill of this great occasion, I was so busy getting everything ready, such as (this time!) loading my Vickers, running up the engine, and memorising Joske's instructions for signals, that before I knew what was happening, the others were taxi-ing along the track to the central take-off area.

I scurried after them, and we unstuck, as the French say, in succession, me last, and as soon as we had taken up formation, me on Joske's left rear, he started climbing full out northwards. Once this began, I was so occupied in setting the fine adjustment (the lever controlling the mixture of petrol and air according to density and humidity), and keeping exactly in formation, that I quite forgot to notice how I felt about it all.

Keeping formation is not all that easy until you have the knack, you're apt to overdo your efforts to get into position and to stay there. The Pup is so sensitive on the controls that any abrupt movement of the joystick or rudder makes her jump like a startled cat, and a ham-fisted pilot can skid off fifty yards to a flank at one moment and nearly collide with the whole formation the next. And, of course, you have to avoid getting in the slipstream of the machines in front.

The patrol height was 17,000 feet. Up we climbed, with my throttle wide open, to 6,000, 7,000, 8,000, still not halfway, and I wasn't thinking of anything much except keeping my place in this steep climb, and certainly not of Huns, when suddenly I saw three large specks in the sky ahead. They were diving towards us, and getting larger every second. My heart bounded. A Hun attack already! But Joske hadn't rocked his wings—the signal for Huns. Maybe he hadn't seen them. Should I dive forward in front and give the signal, as per instructions? But wouldn't that be a bit too cocky on my first patrol?

My heart was still thumping as though I'd run up a cliff. I looked along my Aldis telescopic sight, and could just get the outside Hun on the bead. Why didn't Joske give the signal, or fire, or do something? All he did was to climb even more steeply. Meanwhile the Huns were sinking beneath us, and in a flash had passed behind. But not before I caught a glimpse of the three pilots waving to us. They were the Pups of 'A' Flight coming off patrol!

The Pup is supposed to climb to 10,000 in twelve minutes, but we took fifteen, and it seemed far longer. You watch the rate of climb by the needle on the altimeter. 11,000. And a hundred. 200. 300. And so on, step by step to 12,000, 13,000, 14,000, like watching a kettle boil, until after nearly thirty minutes we reach 15,000. The higher, the slower. And during this time, because of the need to keep in close formation, I just had no chance to look down to earth, except in brief glimpses.

But now Joske turned east and continued the climb more easily, so that I was able to see that we were passing over the Line south of Ypres, easily recognisable because of the star-shaped citadel's walls and moat. The sky was clear and I could see for miles. To the south, a dark mass with misty smoke rising from it, which was Lille, with two more smoky masses to the north, which were Turcoing and Roubaix.

At that moment—crack! crack! crack! crack! My heart nearly stopped for good and all. A Hun firing at me! I swung clear of the others and looked behind. Nothing there. Then I heard crack! crack!

crack! again, and this time saw tracers flashing from Courtneidge's Pup. They were testing their guns by firing short bursts into Hunland. So I pooped off twenty rounds too, not awfully heroic, but maybe one of the bullets found its billet in some fat Boche well behind their Lines.

Tracers, I should explain, are special bullets, mixed one to three with ordinary, which contain phosphorus, and leave a white trail as they whizz through the air, so showing where your bullets are going, more or less—they're not all that accurate.

During the patrol, guns were fired in this way several times to stop them freezing up. They are lubricated with anti-freeze oil, of course, but that makes no odds when it's really cold, as it is at 17,000 up. I realised this when Joske eventually reached 17,500, settled level, and we began to patrol on a north–south beat on three-quarters throttle. We were on a Line Offensive Patrol, our job being to jump on any Hun scouts trying to attack our B.E.s and other two-seaters doing art-obs below. The other main kind of patrol is the D.O.P., Distant Offensive, with five or six machines or more, which goes ten to fifteen miles into Hunland looking for trouble. For me, a pleasure in store!

As the patrol drew on, the visibility grew even clearer, and I could see twenty miles or more into German territory, right to the mists of the horizon. It all looked very peaceful. Strange to think it's held by an enemy who will shoot or imprison me if I land in it.

So far, I'd not seen a single aeroplane except the 'A' Flight Pups. There weren't any Huns around—or so I thought. But just as I was taking another long look at Ypres, Joske suddenly gave the signal and began a dive. Courtneidge and I followed. It got steeper and steeper, then they started firing their guns in bursts. Their tracers were converging on something, but for the life of me I couldn't see what.

Surely this wasn't another gun test? No, Joske had signalled Huns. I stared intently ahead as the dive continued, but could spot no Hun, in fact nothing except the ground. So, not to be out of the party, I loosed off 100 rounds at a big tented camp that happened to come into my sights. It was on the German side, of course. At least, I hope so.

Gradually, Joske levelled out and turned south. As we swung round, now at 8,000 feet, I was startled to hear what sounded like the bark of a big dog. Then a quick succession of other barks. I looked towards where the noise came from, and there, about 100 yards away, was a group of soft, black woolly balls, hanging in the sky. By Jove, I thought, that must be archie. My first archie! And it was, as I knew when another salvo appeared, right ahead.

Then I realised that Joske was sliding off to the left, taking avoiding action, and I opened the throttle to catch him up. When the next bunch of woofs appeared they were off to our right, though exactly on our level. This time I saw the burst of flame at the centre of each woolly ball. Then we climbed up steeply and crossed the Lines, and after another two salvos archie gave it up. But I felt rather braced. I had actually been archied.

We were now up at 16,000 again, and Joske turned east, and tried his gun, and so did Courtneidge. I followed suit, but after twenty rounds my gun jammed. I pulled out the hammer from its retaining strap and tried to knock down the cocking handle, to force the faulty round home into the breech of the gun. But the handle just wouldn't go down, and for the next ten minutes I kept formation with my left hand while I hammered away with my right at the gun, until I became so puffed I had to stop. At 16,000 the air is rare enough for continued exertion to make you gasp.

So I followed the others around for another half-hour without a gun, which was stupid, for had we met any Huns I would have been for it. I should have dived ahead of Joske, switchbacked the machine to signal trouble, then gone home. But somehow I didn't want to end my first patrol that way. When we got back and I opened my big mouth about it, I was for the high jump again; both Joske and Pratt tore me off a strip for staying on, and being a liability had there been a scrap.

When the two hours over the Lines ended, the descent was made gradually to allow us to get adjusted to the higher air pressure and temperature. Even so, my hands tingled with pins and needles until after I'd landed, while my ears were singing for an hour at least.

You can imagine what a fool I felt when, after we reached the hangar and I'd reported my gun jam, Joske and Courtneidge started talking about the Huns we'd attacked. It seemed that when we dived we went after three Halberstadt scouts which Joske spotted over Houthulst Forest, north of Ypres, and which dived away south-east, and as they were quicker on the dive, they soon drew away. What was more, when the others tested their guns, the time I had my jam, it was because they'd seen a couple of two-seaters well to the east-wards, but on being fired at they sheered off quickly. As for me, I never saw a thing.

But apparently this happens with every new pilot. In fact, talking about it later in the Mess, Captain Heath, 'B' Flight Commander, told of a fellow in some other squadron who did the same as me, saw no Hun but fired when the others fired, and who, when they returned, was congratulated on having sent an Albatros down out of control!

Still, on the whole, I'm pleased with today's efforts. I've shown I can fly a Pup, I've clocked up my first patrol, been over Hunland, been archied, and fired at enemy scouts—not knowing they were there, admitted, but I *might* have hit one. Anyway, it was my first taste of powder. *And* I wasn't shot down!

Friday, May 25th

Because of yesterday's gun trouble I checked over the Vickers soon after breakfast, first with the Gunnery Officer, Stevens, who could find nothing wrong, then by firing into the butts. No nonsense at all. Then I took the Pup up and did proving practice against a ground target, the first time I've tried it, and it's fun. You test the gun and also your marksmanship.

Of course, you don't aim the gun, that's fixed in the line of flight, you aim the aeroplane with joystick and rudder. You dive it fairly steeply at a white square target tilted towards you in a field on the other side of the river. I did eight dives, aiming through the Aldis, and firing bursts of 20–30 shots. The Vickers worked perfectly, and when later the armourers retrieved the target my shooting wasn't too bad. Obviously the ammunition only goes dud when there are Huns about.

Today I have two patrols, one this morning with McDonald leading me and Captain Caudwell, but after an hour it was washed out through bad weather. You probably wonder why a captain should be led by a lieutenant. The answer is that when an officer transfers to the R.F.C. from the infantry, gunners, etc., his rank doesn't count, he becomes just a flying officer, with seniority dating from the date of transfer. As for my flying with 'A' Flight, the flight commanders mix their pilots to spread the work evenly through the squadron.

After lunch the clouds broke and the sun came out. Now it's darned hot, and I'm writing this on the river bank, after a swim. Although it's pretty dirty, the river is a godsend, and the chaps fool around in it with all sorts of home-made craft. Dimmock, Marchant, Joske, Luxmore and Asher take the lead in this juvenile skylarking. Of course, Asher and Dimmock are practically kids anyway, especially Asher, who looks far too schoolboyish to be killing people. Everybody calls him Warbabe, which he doesn't like at all. I suppose he's about eighteen and Dimmock not much more,[1] though because he's a six-footer, he doesn't look quite so young as Asher. They make me feel positively old at twenty-two, though not so aged as Captain Rodney Heath, otherwise Daddy, who must be at least thirty. He's an Australian, and a noted tennis player. The other Colonials, besides Caudwell and Barrager, are Joske, who's from Fiji, and Kay, another Australian.

We had a binge last evening, which started casually before dinner. Somebody was mixing some pretty potent cocktails, as we realised later. There was one drink, not deadly at all, which is prepared as a ritual before a binge dinner. It's a sort of squadron cocktail called Health and Strength, which everyone has to like whether he does or not. It's made of eggs, brandy, port and several kinds of liquor, and I found it rather cloying. We drink it at the dining-table, one foot on the chair, the other on the table, to the toast, 'Cheerio, Forty-Six', yelled very, very earsplittingly.

After dinner we had a noisy sing-song in the ante-room, with Dimmock strumming at the piano, and everyone gathering round him, bellowing to beat the band. The songs were either about women, 'She was poor but she was 'onest' kind of thing, or about aeroplanes

---

1. Norman Dimmock enlisted in the Artists Rifles at seventeen, was commissioned in the R.F.C. at eighteen, and four months later joined 46 Squadron. Asher was about the same age. Cecil Marchant enlisted at eighteen and spent eighteen months in the trenches before transferring to the R.F.C. Courtneidge, who had already done one tour in France as an observer, was about the same age as me.

and air fighting, in parodies of well-known ditties. Some I'd met before, others were new to me. The one I liked was sung to the tune of *John Peel*. It goes:

> When you soar into the air on a Sopwith Scout,
> And you're scrapping with a Hun and your gun cuts out,
> Well, you stuff down your nose 'til your plugs fall out,
> 'Cos you haven't got a hope in the morning.

Then comes the chorus:

> For a batman woke me from my bed,
> I'd had a thick night and a very sore head,
> And I said to myself, to myself I said,
> 'Oh, we haven't got a hope in the morning.'

There are several more verses—I'll write them out some time. Another song which I'd sung in England went to the tune of *And They called it Dixie Land*.

> Oh! they found a bit of iron what
> Some bloke had thrown away,
> And the R.A.F. said 'This is just the thing
> We've sought for many a day.'
> They built a weird machine,
> Strangest engine ever seen,
> But they'd quite forgotten that the thing was rotten,
> And they shoved it in a flying machine.
> Then they ordered simply thousands more,
> And sent them out to fight.
> When the blokes who had to fly them swore,
> The R.A.F. said 'They're all right.
> The bus is stable as can be,
> We thought up every bit of it ourselves, you see.'
> They were so darned slow they wouldn't go,
> And they called them R.A.F. 2cs!

R.A.F. 2cs are B.E.2cs of course. The R.A.F. is the Royal Aircraft Factory at Farnborough, which produced them, and all the other bloodsome B.E. range, including the so-called scout-fighter, the B.E.12. I've flown them all at Filton, and though they're all right for gadding around England, they're completely old rope in France. Like giving the infantry motor-driven bows and arrows.

There were lots of other songs, and we went from one to another and back again, with a terrific din going on, everyone yelling for more drinks, and the waiters whizzing round, and everybody getting more and more tight. About ten o'clock, the chaps on dawn patrol were chivvied off to bed by their flight commander, Captain Plenty, but the rest of us kept it up until after midnight.

The big consequence of the party was that it broke the ice between the old-timers and the newcomers. I had long if confused talks with Kay, Asher, Dimmock, Marchant and Pratt, and even the Major unbent enough to ask me if I knew so-and-so in the Sherwoods, which I didn't, and that ended our chat.

One of the things I realised from these talks was that the old-timers are not only learning to fly Pups expertly but they're new to air fighting. I'd wondered why nobody offered me any tips about what to do in a scrap, and the answer is that they're learning that too, even the flight commanders. In their Nieuport two-seaters they didn't fight except to defend themselves from attack, and the shooting was done by the observer while the pilot flew the machine level. Flying single-seaters is a different kettle of fish. Now they have to do the attacking, and they're learning the ropes the hard way.

Their first operational flights started only nine days before I arrived on the 22nd. Marchant told me that he and Dimmock did their first patrol on the 20th, and haven't yet attacked a Hun. So far, the squadron hasn't shot down anything, though they've hit two observers in two-seaters. So it turns out that to some extent we're all greenhorns!

I learned that Pratt only got his third pip a fortnight or so ago, but they say he's a jolly good leader in the air, and by the authority he shows (e.g. ticking me off) you'd think he'd been a captain since the Boer War. Still, I like him, he's got more go than the other flight bosses, because he's younger than them, I suppose.

I'll have to stop now, have my tea, and get ready for my second patrol at six o'clock. Marchant has just been pulling my leg about writing such long letters, but I don't care, I like writing, and it will help to pass the time out here when I'm not swimming and eating and, of course, flying. Far more interesting to me than the poker and vingte that some of the others play interminably.

Saturday, May 26th

Today I don't have a job until evening, the last patrol, and I'm taking things easy. My second job yesterday was led by Courtneidge, just the two of us. He was very braced to be flying the leader's coloured streamers at his rear struts for the first time.

We did a long climb to 18,000, turning east at intervals to warm up the guns. As before, I spotted no other machine at our height, and there was too much haze below to see anything. After an hour Courtneidge suddenly gave the distress signal, waved, and turned away westwards, leaving me on my own, with another hour to go.

After I'd become used to the situation it was good fun to be alone in a clear blue sky, three miles above that nasty belt of trenches. It made me go all dreamy. I was filled with a wonderful sense of freedom, of aloofness from the sordid earth. If only I could stay always like this, I thought, riding this obedient Pup with its willing Le Rhône engine purring at half-throttle, gliding smoothly across the sky, with scarcely a quiver, just the way you dream of flying, not in an aeroplane, not even on a broomstick, but in pyjamas, floating effortlessly through the air.

Of course, in this silly mood, I could have been jumped by any Hun that came along, but fortunately none did. After half an hour of beetling up and down between Ypres and Armentières I saw a two-seater below that didn't look like a B.E. or R.E., so dived to check up. As I gazed through the telescope, it quickly became much bigger, and the black Maltese crosses showed quite plainly. It *was* a Hun! I had to do something, quick! What am I playing at, I thought, here he is below me, in my sights, going the same way . . . I pressed the trigger and saw the tracers streaming towards him. But I'd started firing much too soon. He simply turned east, and slid away. The observer fired about fifty rounds at me, but I didn't even hear them. I continued diving and firing as he drew away, then suddenly my gun stopped.

After struggling to correct it for ten minutes until I was red in the face, I started for home, being then well east of Ypres. As I came down, I saw Hun archie bursting round a formation of six machines at my height, 12,000, well to the south, too far off for me to make out what type they were. Then archie stopped. Another bunch came up from the east, Huns, and a dog-fight began.

As I drew closer, I saw them diving and zooming like a flock of starlings. Suddenly there was a flash of red flame, and one of the specks dropped down, leaving a vertical smear of smoke. It went down like a comet, a red-yellow ball with a long black tail. Then the flame went out, and only the smoke remained.

I was so fascinated that for a moment I didn't realise that I'd seen a flamer, and that there'd been a man in it, a pilot like me. British or German, I couldn't tell. It wasn't a pleasant thing to see, even at a distance. Then, as I took my eyes off where it had fallen, and looked above, there was nothing, every machine had vanished. The whole scrap had lasted only three or four minutes.

When I got down after nearly two hours' flying I learned that Courtneidge had packed up because the Bowden control of his gun (that goes to the trigger) had broken. My jam was caused by a split cartridge case, which explained why I couldn't force it home.

After lunch some of us went to La Gorgue cemetery. The squadron carpenter had erected two fine crosses, made out of damaged props, and had neatly encircled the twin graves with posts and chains. Somebody in the village had put flowers on them, as well as on other British graves, marked by simple wooden crosses.

I've just been arranging signals with Barrager, who is leader this evening on our two-man patrol. Our conference was ended by a series of woofs! and plonks! from the east. Our archie was after a Hun with ideas of attacking our balloons, but he changed his mind, and nothing more developed. But the balloons were all halfway down, and the observers too, hanging from their parachutes, as we saw through glasses.

May 26th (Diary)

On the way back from La Gorgue, discussing Gunnery's collision, Barrager spoke of the time the machine took to get to the ground, even with one wing crumpled back. It went down in a slow flicking spin. He had a long way to go, over three miles, with ample time to escape if only he'd had a parachute. Somebody asked why we don't have them. Hundreds of lives would be saved. After all, the balloon chaps do have them, and use them often.

Barrager said there was no room in a Pup, but he's a big fellow, and has to practically use a shoehorn to work himself into the narrow cockpit. But why can't machines be made to accommodate a parachute? Every pilot would sacrifice a little performance to have a chance of escape from break-ups and flamers. It would be a great boost for morale.

Tuesday, May 29th

Sorry for the gap in my letters, but I've had no chance to write during the past two days. I had a forced landing, and only returned here early this morning. It is now afternoon, and I'm putting in a spell of writing before going for an anti-tetanus injection. I was reported as missing to Wing on Saturday evening, but this was cancelled when my message arrived next day. I hope it wasn't notified to you.

It's a longish tale, so I'll go back to the start, when Barrager and I set off at 6.30 on the late Line Patrol. It was a fine clear evening, with some masses of high cumulus cloud, and once above them, perfect visibility to the horizon. We trailed up and down the Line at 18,000 for two hours and saw no H.A. at all, and only a few of ours. We were flying north, well over the Hun side, somewhere over Houthulst Forest, and I was gazing peacefully towards the French and Belgian coasts, with the cloudless Channel like a streak of gold beyond, when suddenly I realised that Barrager wasn't there!

Afterwards he said he'd given the washout signal, then dived off alone as he wanted to shoot up a hospital behind Ypres where he had a brother, a doctor, but I never saw it, and never saw him leave, because I was formating on his left, in echelon, and my eyes were glued on the wonderful sunset. So when I came to I grasped that I was by myself again, this time at 18,000, and several miles on the wrong side of the Line. For a while I circled slowly, searching for Barrager, then I set off south-west in a half-glide.

The air was still, the engine purred, the machine slid smoothly down, I seemed to be poised in the sky, motionless. I had a strange, almost awesome, feeling of solitude. I was alone, high above the earth, like an eagle soaring. There to the west was the great red ball of the sun, sinking beneath the thin line of the horizon, which was England. It seemed very near, almost within gliding distance.

I was so wrapped up in it all that I quite forgot it was getting dark below, that a freshening wind was keeping me over Hunland, and, most important, that there was a war on. For there was a sudden rak-ak-ak-ak. My heart went into my mouth, in fact, practically out on to the dashboard. Machine-gun fire! Somebody was shooting at *me*! But where from? I looked behind. Nobody there. Then again came rak-ak-ak-ak-ak, and now tracers flashing past. Close! I could smell them, a kind of burning phosphorus. And then a startling sting in the calf of my right leg, as though somebody had wiped it with a red-hot poker. By George, did I jump!

That sting jerked me to my wits. I banked steeply over, and there, not far below, going east, was a Hun two-seater, dirty mottled green, with the black crosses edged with white staring at me from the curving top wings and the fuselage. There was an odd-looking engine exhaust stack sticking up behind the prop. The observer was still firing at me, his gun flashing, his tracers seeming to come right into my engine.

Forgetting all the tactics I'd learned from wall diagrams at training units, that a single scout should never dive on a two-seater's observer, but get under his tail, I dived on him, took careful aim through the Aldis, and pressed the trigger. I was about 200 yards away, I suppose, and 100 feet higher, and I began to overtake. My tracers and his seemed to be practically hitting one another. Then suddenly his tracer stopped. Through the Aldis I saw him apparently sit down, then slide out of sight. The pilot turned, saw me just behind, and shoved his nose down. The blighter dived so fast that although I chased him hell for leather, firing continuously, he left me standing. And then my gun jammed.

All this, from when I heard the first shots, has taken me over five minutes, I suppose, to write up, but it only took forty to fifty seconds to happen. Then he'd gone down out of sight—it was already dark in the east—and there was no sense in chasing after him when I had no gun, my leg was hurting, and I was well over Hunland. So I turned west. It was becoming obscure there too, the clouds below were closing together, and I couldn't make out where I was.

I dropped through them and was flabbergasted to find how really murky it was beneath. For a few minutes I flew along unable to pick out anything I knew in the gloom, then suddenly I spotted Ypres almost ahead, and the glint of water in the moat. To the south of it, also faintly reflecting the last of the daylight, were the two lakes, Zillebeke and Dickebusch.

During the shooting match I was too indignant at being surprised and fired at to be windy, but now I definitely was. I was in a real hole. Why I wasn't archied I don't know, but I didn't want to be, I'd already got a wound, I could feel the blood dripping down inside my flying-boot. It was so dark on the ground, with banks of evening mist forming, that I'd never reach La Gorgue. I had to find somewhere to perch, and quickly at that.

My only useful landmarks were the two lakes, and as Zillebeke was almost in the front line, I had to go for Dickebusch. And there'd be less likelihood of hitting trees in the glide-in if I landed alongside its edge. But which edge? I dived down to the lake, now a pear-shaped slab of silver in the dusk, and checked up.

Below me was a double line of twinkling gun-flashes, curving east of Ypres and down east of the lake. The drifting smoke from the guns showed the wind blowing from the north-east, and I had to land east of the water, because Dickebusch village was on the west side. I made a wide circuit over the guns, every explosion kicking the machine and sounding as though right under the cockpit, then turned round the lake for the glide in.

I missed a church spire by a few feet, then went low over the water eastwards towards the guns flashing dead ahead. For a moment I thought I was going to overshoot, and land on the business end of the guns, then I thought I'd undershoot, and drop in the lake. I actually touched down very slowly about ten yards beyond the water's edge, ran forward a dozen yards, then tipped into a shell-hole. Less than fifty yards in front were the emplacements, the guns still firing.

Within seconds I was surrounded by scores of gunners, who helped me clamber from the cockpit. The machine was on its nose, and I was dazed, having cracked my head against the Vickers butt. As soon as I stood erect, they all applauded by clapping their hands, which staggered me, it seemed such an odd reception after a crash. I felt rather like a circus performer, but it was friendly, and made me feel good. Anyway, it was so *safe* on the ground, compared with five minutes earlier.

They took me to a dugout and gave me a stiff whisky, then asked if I'd broken any bones. I said no, but I'm wounded in the leg. It was smarting a lot now, and the blood seemed to be pouring down. I sat on a box and they pulled off my sheepskin thigh boot. Then I slowly and carefully eased up my trouser. Imagine what an idiot I felt when I found not a nice blighty wound but a stupid little graze about two inches long, which had scarcely drawn blood! It shows what imagination can do. I would have put money on my boot being soaked in gore.

They put a field dressing on the scratch, and I wiped the smelly whale grease from my face, after which I had another whisky and felt better. It was now about ten o'clock. The C.O. of the battery, Major Arnold, told me I'd timed my arrival well, had I come a quarter of an hour earlier, the Huns would have seen me land, and started shelling the machine—and them too. But there were explosions enough anyway, both sides were pasting each other in the routine evening hate.

Out in the open, I looked around with much interest. This was a very different sort of war from flying. The guns of the battery were firing salvos every minute or so, casually it seemed, but there was the devil of a racket, and I gladly wore the ear-plugs they gave me. It was thrilling to be with guns in action, to see the figures of the gunners silhouetted against the flashes of flame and smoke. Eastwards, the front-line troops, British and German, were sending up star-shells, and green and white flares, Very lights and other fireworks. This was weird to watch, and it's amazing to think it goes on every night.

[The rest of this letter described my exciting two days with 'A' Battery, 190th Brigade, R.F.A., during which I had a taste of the gunner's daily round. I also had a walk with Major Arnold via Voormezeele to the front lines at St Eloi, where I was allowed to fire a couple of hundred rounds at the Boche positions opposite. Salvage of the machine by mechanics from the squadron was hindered by frequent spells of shell-fire, including gas, and so took two days to accomplish. I watched several air fights to the eastwards, and saw a flamer and two other machines shot down. Massive concentrations of troops and guns in the area indicated a coming offensive. The return to La Gorgue was made on the evening of the 28th.]

The roads were full of traffic, and it was such slow going that we didn't reach the squadron until 3.30 a.m. I found a stranger sleeping in my bed, so gathered some flying coats from the pegs and kipped on the floor. I was asleep in five seconds.

About six, Watt woke me with the news that I was orderly officer this day. He seemed to accept my sleeping on the floor as nothing abnormal. After a few appropriate remarks from me he went off to find the next for duty, and I dropped to sleep again. About eight, he woke me again, this time to give me breakfast. Finding the stranger gone, I wolfed the food, undressed, clambered into bed for another sleep, and woke again at midday.

After lunch I went over to the office to make my report, after which the C.O. tore me off a strip for staying an unnecessary day at Dickebusch, when I could have come back on the Sunday night. I suppose he was right, I'd no business to play at soldiers when there's so much flying to be done, but somehow I wanted to see old A6188 home.

While in the office, I checked up on the H.A. recognition chart, and the machine I had my set to with was a Rumpler, a high-flying photo-recco aeroplane, and one of the best the Huns possess. What a pity I didn't manage to bring it down!

May 29th (Diary)

Major Arnold was certain that a big attack is coming off. The front is filling up with all kinds of artillery. In places the field guns are lined up almost wheel to wheel. Masses of troops are moving up, and tanks too, as I saw. All this plus our intense air activity, obviously to stop the Hun seeing what we're up to, meant an offensive, he said, but if against the Messines ridge, he pitied the P.B.I., for everybody knew it was a mass of fortified trenches, concrete strong-points and impassable wire.

Wednesday, May 30th

We had a visit in the afternoon from the G.O.C. of the Flying Corps, General Trenchard, whom everybody calls 'Boom', because of his deep, gruff voice. He went round the hangars, and said a word to most of us, and seemed interested in poor A6188, still on the trailer, with several shrapnel holes in the fabric. My rigger found only five bullet-holes, but there was damage to a longeron, and the machine is going to the Depot for repair.

Caudwell was shot in the hand during a scrap and has gone to hospital. His replacement, the man who was in my bed, is Wilcox. There are two other newcomers, Lascelles, who took Caudwell's corner in the hut, and a Scot called Cameron. None of them has done much flying on Pups, about five hours each, which Marchant, who is even more outspoken than me at times, says is a damned scandal. How can chaps go up to fight experienced Huns when they can scarcely handle their machines?

I'm having a spot of trouble over my A6188, because while it was lying by the lake, some souvenir hunter lifted the dashboard watch. They are very nice watches, luminous, and keep good time, and every pilot's ambition is to win one. It is easily removed from its fitting, and when you forced-land you're supposed to take it, and put it back when you get home. But at Dickebusch I forgot all about it. Everybody thinks I swiped the thing myself, and now I wish I had, but because it's gone there's a howl from the equipment people, and I'm having to fill up forms swearing I haven't stolen it, and don't know who did. Strange, they don't mind you losing an aeroplane, but a watch, now that's different!

There's still no news about Captain Ball, I see. We all feel he must be dead, the Huns would have trumpeted enough if they'd got him as a prisoner. But it's odd they've said nothing at all.

Last night, lying awake in the still small hours, I kept thinking about the Hun observer I hit, and wondering if I killed him. If I did he's the first man I've ever killed. Being so close when I fired, and seeing him collapse, made him another human being, not just a target in an aeroplane. But I can't say it worries me terribly—after all, he started it.

Thursday, May 31st

Well, I was properly blooded today, in my first air fight. I can't say much came of it, and while it lasted I was in a complete tizzy, but it was darned exciting, and although I didn't shoot down a Hun, I definitely fired at one.

It was the early evening D.O.P., with Joske leading, and Courtneidge. Soon, at 15,000, I was looking down on Ypres and Dickebusch with no envy at all for the fellows caught there, unable to escape being shelled and shot at every day. What an existence! We turned east, still climbing, when suddenly, wuff! wuff! wuff! wuff! in quick succession. The black balls were so close, I was amazed none of us was hit. About twenty more shots followed, until the air stank of cordite.

As we drew clear, archie gave his attention to a formation of three Triplanes, or Tripes as we call them, or even Tripehounds, going east as though on a hunting affair—when they're climbing steeply in formation, their three wings give them the look of a pack of basset hounds sitting up begging. I think this crowd came from No 8 Naval at Droglandt. They've only one gun, like the Pup, but their speed and climb are far better. From what we read in Comic Cuts they're about our most successful scout.

We wandered around Hunland for over half an hour at 16,000, then suddenly Joske rocked his wings violently. Within two seconds tracers flashed among us. I looked up and saw what seemed a whole squadron of aeroplanes coming down at us, guns flashing, then they were on us, we'd broken formation, and were turning and twisting for our lives.

Things happened so fast that I have only a hazy notion of what followed. I hadn't much idea of what to do, nobody had told me a thing. I know that when the first tracers flashed past my head I banked steeply to the right, and a Hun shot by, turning the other way, thirty yards' distant, the black crosses showing under the wings. I tried to yank the Pup on to his tail, but then more tracer came from behind, close. I could smell it, the same as on Saturday evening, a peculiar pungent smell. I shoved on full right rudder and skidded wildly round and there was another Hun, red and green in front of me.

I didn't think of aiming with my Aldis, just fired and steered the tracers on to him, and they seemed to go into the fuselage below the pilot's head, but he pulled off left. More tracers passed me, another coloured Hun flashed across my front, then a Pup, more frantic ruddering, tracer stabbing everywhere, black crosses everywhere, a yellow Hun slides in front of me, I press the trigger, steer the tracer on him, he zooms up . . . then my gun stops. A jam!

Instinctively, I skidded off to a flank, grabbed my hammer, and hit the cocking handle madly. After four hearty whacks it went down. I turned back towards the fight, and to my astonishment there was nothing there. Everything had gone as though it had been a dream. Then I saw, diving down from the north, the formation of Tripes. So that was why the Huns had skedaddled! And now they were on the run south-eastwards, with the Tripehounds panting after them. By jove, what luck, the Huns were all over us.

From the moment when Joske rocked his wings had seemed at least twenty minutes, but the whole fight until my gun jammed had actually lasted less than three. It started so abruptly, and was so swift-moving and confused that I was left breathless. And now I was worried about Courtneidge and Joske. Had they been shot down? And where was I? Looking earthwards, I couldn't recognise a thing, so I turned west and started for home.

It was a relief to find the others already back. They told me we'd been attacked by six Albatros D-IIIs and both of them thought they'd scored bull's-eyes. No such hopes for me. We were all hit. I was astonished when my rigger showed me a group of eight bullet-holes in the fuselage, two feet behind my back, which is as close as I want them!

Part Three

The Battle of Messines

This afternoon, on patrol with Courtneidge, I was colder than I've ever been before. We climbed up steadily to 18,000 seeing lots of our machines on the way, but none when we got there. We sailed along the Houthulst–Quesnoy line, more or less, but the sky was empty, and there was nothing to do except stay alive in arctic cold and look out for Huns.

I searched the sky continuously, eastwards, above, below, on our level, and in rear, tipping the machine laterally and swerving slightly, to uncover the blind spots. Trying to get a view downwards, I stuck my head over the fairing of the cockpit, and the blast of the ice-cold air took my breath away, though at least it made the rest of me feel a little less frozen. But Courtneidge wasn't cold enough, for he climbed up to over 20,000, where it really was arctic, or antarctic, I wouldn't know the difference.

But after an hour of beating up and down the Hun balloon lines, with not even archie working, and the cold piercing to my innards, the patrol became a bore. The two of us seemed to be hanging on invisible cords, not moving, suspended in space. Nothing moved except Courtneidge's streamers straining at the struts, and his helmeted head turning every so often to check his tail.

I stole a glance at the dashboard watch. Holy smoke, another full hour to do! I'll never be able to last out. I'll just collapse with frost-bite or something. For heaven's sake, Courtneidge, I yelled uselessly, let's go lower and find somebody to fight—anything to end this purgatory.

But he was feeling conscientious, and we stuck out the whole patrol at the appointed height. At last he began gradually to go down, and as we descended the air became lousy with every sort of British aeroplane, all getting in each other's way, and not a single Hun to be seen. Evidently they're being crowded out of the skies.

At 3,000 he gave the washout signal. Here it was warm, and I began to recover, but the blood rushing through my half-frozen fingers gave me a stinging bout of pins and needles. I slapped my hands on my legs, beat them against my chest, clapped them together with my knees gripping the joystick. In a few minutes it worked. As soon as I could use my hands freely, I paid a quick visit to Dickebusch, dropping to fifty feet over 'A' Battery. The gunners ran about and waved, for they knew who I was. I'd told the Major and his officers I would come and see them in a new Pup No 4. It gave me quite a kick to say hello! in this way, for they'd been jolly good to me.

I passed over what was left of Voormezeele, and turned south over St Eloi, trying to find the spot where I did my little shoot, but I was moving too fast. Our troops' upturned faces were only a few yards below. I could see the shadows cast by the sun into the advanced Bosche trenches on the other side of the wire, but then I heard bullets cracking past my ear, and the rattle of a machine-gun. The dear old Hun was potting at me, so I zoomed and banked and zigzagged westwards.

Regarding yesterday's scrap, I've learned that I'm not unique in being confused, all pilots are at first, some much worse than me. The new fellow, Cameron, was up last evening on his first patrol, the late evening show, in clear weather. Towards the end of it they ran into a bunch of Huns at 15,000 over Roulers. A short, sharp fight followed, confusion reigned, then the Huns, Albatros D-IIs, not so good as the IIIs, withdrew. When the patrol returned they collected together, as usual, and started a lively talk about the fight. Suddenly Cameron, listening in astonishment, burst out with, 'Huns! What Huns? *I* never saw any. I thought you were all larking around to relieve the monotony, so I did a couple of loops, and let off fifty rounds at the moon.'

One of the other newcomers hasn't lasted long, Lascelles. He crashed during a practice flight, was severely injured, and is now in hospital. The Pup is such an easy, docile machine to handle that for anybody to crash one badly shows he hasn't yet learned to fly.

Incidentally, Watt is highly upset, having lost two more nice gentlemen, Caudwell and now Lascelles, in the past few days. He's going around looking as though he can't bear the strain any longer.

39

June 1st (Diary)

Last night I lay awake thinking of my narrow squeak in my first scrap. That group of bullet-holes behind my back, plus having a jam in the middle of a dog-fight. The odd thing is that I didn't have time to be scared, it all happened so quickly. In fact I was calm in a numb sort of way, but reacted quickly, and threw the Pup all over the sky. It's only later on, especially when you get to bed, that you begin to think about what might have happened.

Saturday, June 2nd

Did you ever hear of a frightened hawk? That was me this morning. One minute a cruel hawk pouncing on its prey, the next a fledgling, diving frantically to escape a flock of bigger and better hawks.

I was up with Joske at nine o'clock, a nice clear day with masses of high cumulus cloud floating eastwards, and we'd been ranging up and down the beat for one and a half hours at 15,000 when, east of Ypres, we saw white archie to the south, potting at a Hun two-seater going south-east, well below. Joske started to go down, and I tailed along, but we didn't catch him up until we were above Comines, six or seven miles over, at about 12,000.

Then Joske dived fairly steeply, and I saw his tracer going right at the Hun, whose observer started firing back. It was painted a sort of dappled green-brown, and I learned afterwards that it was a D.F.W. Have I mentioned that German machines are painted all the colours of the rainbow, while we are chocolate, except for squadron markings, and flight wheels?

Well, I dived with Joske, away on his left flank, feeling very tensed up as I aimed through the Aldis at the observer and pressed the trigger. After about fifty shots I saw, out of the corner of my eye, that Joske wasn't with me. Gun jam, I thought, and continued diving and firing for another 100 rounds, then suddenly my gun stopped. At the same moment the Hun plunged into the side of a cloud.

I levelled out and turned westwards. No Joske. I drew out the hammer and was banging away at the cocking handle when I heard a loud and rapid crak-ak-ak-ak-ak-ak. I saw and smelt tracers whizzing by me, and there was a splash on the instrument board as my height indicator became a tangle of metal.

I looked around, startled to death, and there, thirty yards behind my tail, was a V-strutter with a yellow spinner on the prop, his two guns flashing. They stopped, and in a split second I saw the pilot's head cocked to the side of the windscreen, checking to see if I'd been hit. Above him was a flock of other Albatroses.

Long before that split second was up I'd jerked the joystick forward and was on my way down with engine full on. I may say that the idea of turning round and fighting it out, as Ball might have done, didn't occur to me. At this height I wouldn't have had a hope against even one D-III, let alone six or seven. I didn't even have time to go into a spin, which for a few seconds would have given them a nearly stationary target. I just, in the words of the song we sang in the Mess the other evening, 'stuffed down my nose till the plugs fell out, 'cos I hadn't got a hope in the morning!'

It was a thing I could never have done in cold blood, but with bullets cracking around my head I only thought of getting away. I was scared. I was diving at such a pace that my speed-indicator needle went off the dial, and stayed there. I tried to move the ailerons to imitate a spin, but the controls were too rigid to have any effect.

Meanwhile, they were taking it in turns to dive and pot at me. Tracers flashed by in all directions, to the tune of repeated bursts of gunfire. Every burst made me cringe into the cockpit. I daren't look round again, I had to play being dead in a machine diving out of control. The wires screamed above the roar of the engine. The whole machine shuddered, as though about to break up. One shot on a bracing wire would have done it. It's a bloodsome feeling, waiting for a bullet in the back or for your wings to fold up.

It's strange how your mind works in a moment like this. Instead of yelling with fright, I thought in a detached sort of way what damned bad shooting they were making, especially the first one, yellow-spinner, who'd missed a sitting target from thirty yards.

Meanwhile I was losing height with alarming speed. The ground rushed up at me, and I knew I must level out, bullets or no bullets. At that moment, thank heaven, the firing stopped. They'd decided I was a certain goner. I pulled the throttle back very gently, and kept in the

41

dive until it was safe to ease out in a big curve. I levelled off at 500 feet, and I'd come down from 12,000.

I was five miles over. Ahead I could see the Ypres salient and the lakes. I was heaving for breath, and it wasn't because of the rarefied air. I had a splitting headache, sharp pains stabbed my ears, but I was alive, the machine was all in one piece, the engine was running. And then, the oddest thing, I went berserk, started to yell and curse with rage.

I was furious at having been caught napping, in a stupid booby-trap. I was furious at having to dive for my life like a startled rabbit. I was furious at what the troops below must have thought at my running away. I saw red, cursed all Huns and their damned Albatroses, and, like a maniac, turned back east and started to climb steeply. I just had to have a crack at somebody. I corrected the jam, fired twenty rounds, and scanned the skies for a victim. And by heck, I swore, he won't get away with it like I've just done.

I kept up this lunatic prowl for fully ten minutes, then the reaction came. I felt very sick, and to my intense surprise, threw up over the side. Just like that! Suddenly deflated, I realised I'd better get home, and turned west. Then archie woke up and let me have it. I was still only at 3,000, and was hit half a dozen times, as I afterwards found.

Back at La Gorgue, I was surprised at the warmth of the greeting from my rigger and fitter. 'We heard you'd been scuppered, sir,' they told me. And when I reached the squadron office Thompson's expression was a picture, he'd phoned Wing a quarter of an hour before to notify my regretted demise. From afar, Joske had watched my being pounced on, had seen six Huns close on my tail, followed my engine-on dive right to the ground, as he thought, and reported me as shot down north of Comines.

I told the flight-sergeant how I'd had to maltreat both the Pup and the Le Rhône, and asked him to have everything thoroughly checked up. Surprisingly, there wasn't a lot of damage, apart from the shrapnel-holes from archie. Though twelve guns had fired at me at their leisure, my rigger could only find twenty-nine bullet holes, seventeen in the fuselage, the rest in the wings.

At first I concluded that the bullet which had smashed the height indicator must have travelled right through me without my noticing it, but when I took off my muffler I found it had gone through that and my flying-coat collar.

I just couldn't understand how yellow-spinner missed me, he was so close I could have hit him with my automatic. The others were not so good either, with so many chances and no opposition. But I certainly had luck. Afterwards I worked out that I'd dropped two and a half miles in about forty-five seconds, and for forty of them I was under fire from twelve guns. So I've used up two or three of my nine lives!

Joske said he spotted the Huns as he began the dive, and gave the rocking signal before breaking off, but I never saw this as I was too busy sighting through the Aldis. He confirmed that the Huns were Albatros D-IIIs, the ones with which Richtofen and his squadron made such a killing with B.E.s and other dud machines during Bloody April at Arras, which makes my luck all the greater.

Sunday, June 3rd

Soon after I'd finished making my booby-trap report yesterday, I clicked for a new kind of job the Wing has started, a stand-by scheme with emergency calls for us to leap into the air and chase off Hun two-seaters doing artillery shoots. Luxmore and I were on this racket from 1 until 9 p.m., and we had to hang around until five before a call came. Nothing happened.

My second patrol, with Courtneidge leading me and Odell, a new chap who looks about eighteen, although he's a well-built six-footer, was also without incident, unless you can call driving down a succession of two-seaters incidents. It's a waste of time, anyway, as soon as we've gone on, they come up again and carry on with their art obs, just as ours do. But another patrol, a D.O.P. led by Pratt, had a sharp scrap, in which they got one Albatros down, but lost Cameron, miles over the Lines, not a hope of gliding to this side. That's the hell of these distant offensive jobs, if your engine's hit, or goes dud, you're a prisoner.

Newcomers like Cameron and Odell have to be pushed on patrol before they've found their feet because there's a lot of work to be done. Some pilots have been doing three jobs a day of two and a half to three hours each. In one day the thirteen pilots of the squadron did eighty-seven hours, which is quite something. The snag is that during all that time we got no Huns crashed or flamers.

From Saturday's papers I see that 713 aeroplanes, British, French and German, were shot down during May, only four less than in Bloody April. So things have been active during the month, and some were on this so-called quiet front.

The most interesting item in this report was that Baron Richtofen, who was averaging a victory a day in April, wasn't mentioned at all in the German war news during May. This may mean he's been killed or wounded. Let's hope so, although, of course, he could be on leave. Apparently there's another Richtofen also piling up victories in the Circus, as we call their squadron, because they're all so gaily coloured, and also because they seem to move up and down the whole front instead of being tied to one sector, like an R.F.C. squadron.

[Manfred von Richtofen went on leave on May 1st, having then achieved fifty-two victories. His Jasta 11 was led by his brother, Lothar, then with twenty-four victories, until he returned to the front on June 14th. The Jasta corresponded to the R.F.C. Squadron, but was smaller. Although Jasta 11 was nicknamed 'The Circus' for the reasons given, the Circus proper did not form until June 26th, when Richtofen was placed in command of Jagdgeschwader No 1 (J.G.1), comprising Jastas 4, 6, 10 and 11, and specially equipped as a mobile formation, to be moved quickly along the front as necessity demanded.]

Monday, June 4th

I was in another scrap today, and this was a real one, with a Hun shot down, the first the squadron has had confirmed since it re-equipped with Pups. Courtneidge led me and Odell on an early (7.45) O.P. In a cloudless sky, except for a sheet of mackerel cirrus very high up, we crossed the Lines opposite Lille, and went some five miles over, climbing to 20,000. By George, it *was* cold, yet somehow, this time, I rather enjoyed it.

We were now joined by a solitary Triplane, which sidled up behind

44

us, and I felt happy to see him sitting behind and above, guarding our tails. But it didn't work out that way. We had started to descend westwards towards Houthulst Forest when, at 18,000, we were suddenly bounced by a Hun formation diving out of the sun behind us. Pups don't expect to be bounced at this height, and we were more startled when the tracers flashed among us.

They should have got us in the dive, but they opened fire too soon, or weren't good shots, in spite of their twin Spandau guns. There were seven, we worked out later, all D-IIIs. My reactions are quicker now, and when I heard the rapid rak-ak-ak-ak-ak, and glimpsed the tracers whizzing by, I didn't look round to see who was doing it, but kicked the rudder sharply, skidded right, saw a red and green V-strutter flash by, then another, mostly red. It was a mad mix-up. I skidded right again to avoid the Tripe, mounting up in front of me like a lift, found a Hun crossing my front, turned after him, fired twenty shots, more tracers from behind, did a flat-turn skid, fired wildly at another Hun, deflection shot, but he zoomed up, looped and was gone. Then a Pup with a Hun behind him, I turned left after *him*, pooped twenty rounds —and the gun stopped.

I dived down clear of the fight to correct it, a stupid thing to do, for any sharp-eyed Hun could easily have picked me off, but you don't have time to work things out, you move instinctively in split seconds. I grabbed the hammer, and banged at the cocking handle, trying to force the dud round home, cursing like hell, wet with perspiration, misted goggles raised, and after one minute feeling quite whacked because of the height we were at.

Meanwhile the fight went on 500 feet above me. I saw a Hun dive off with a Pup on his tail, gun going. Then the cocking handle fell, I climbed up and went into the fight from a flank. At once a red and green Hun came for me, and we circled round each other trying to find a chance to fire. I was mildly surprised to find that I was now absolutely cool and collected. And I was tickled pink to find that all the things people had said about the Pup being best at this height were right, for I could turn inside him without losing height, while his nose kept dipping until, after three or four tight turns, I was behind and a little above him.

I'd bested him! My heart was thumping as I pressed the trigger. I was pretty close, my first burst was along the fuselage, and I edged the tracer towards the pilot. But he jerked away and twisted down under me and I lost him. But I'm sure I hit him. He had leader's streamers on his struts, too.

I climbed up, then realised we'd been having a private duel, for the rest had scattered. I saw below me the Tripe on the tail of a yellow Hun in a dive, and glimpsed another machine spinning down well below. I searched around and there was nothing in sight, so I watched the spinner until it crashed by an aerodrome west of a town—I saw the canvas hangars at the side of the field. I had a nasty feeling, thinking it was Courtneidge, but a few seconds later spotted him climbing up towards me. He came close and stuck up a thumb. It was his Hun I'd seen crash.

The Tripe had gone and so had the Huns. Presently another Pup climbed alongside—Odell. I couldn't understand it. Three Pups and a Tripe besting seven D-IIIs, it didn't seem possible. Then I remembered the height. It would have been a different story even 3,000 feet lower.

But the return to the aerodrome was very much an anticlimax. Courtneidge landed first, and with considerable surprise I watched him career right to the end of the cinder track towards the canal, tip up on to his prop, then over on to his back. Odell and I circled while he clambered clear and the mechanics pulled the machine on to its wheels and drew it aside. Then Odell, leeward to the track in his circling, went down, and you'll laugh to hear it, but he did exactly the same.

The track was now crowded with ack-emmas waving madly, and I suddenly spotted why. I looked at the effel[1] and saw that during the time we'd been away, the wind had veered right round. The others had, without checking up, landed in the direction they'd taken off, which was now down wind. I landed normally, much to the relief of 'C' Flight mechanics.

With such a small tricky aerodrome as this, there's no margin for misjudgement, especially with a machine like the Pup, whose very flat guide may fool a pilot into a too-early touch-down, which means she trundles on and on and on. Incidentally, I can't think why we don't have brakes fitted to the wheels, as on motor-cars.

1. The effel, otherwise the F.L., or French Letter, or Wind Sock, or Wind Indicator.

[The space-age reader should realise that the Pup, like other aeroplanes of the day, not only lacked brakes, but had an open cockpit, no heater, no oxygen, no parachute, no radio link with air or ground, and no compass worth the name. These deficiencies were in keeping with the construction, wooden frames braced together by wires and covered with highly inflammable doped fabric.]

Well, back to our scrap. We were all rather excited in the squadron office, making our reports. Courtneidge claimed his Hun and I confirmed it. We worked out that the town near where it crashed was Roulers. I mentioned that I thought the Triplane had sent one down too, so the R.O. rang up the nearest nauticals. Courtneidge was excessively pleased to have crashed 46's first Hun, but he didn't keep his record long, for on the late evening patrol Luxmore also crashed one, confirmed, and in the same area.

A strange thing happened while we were flying south-east, over Dickebusch, at about 8,000. I suddenly glimpsed something dark coming at me from the right, but before I could react, it had flashed past, not more than twenty yards in front of me. I jerked my head left and saw the back end of it—a big shell on its way into Hunland! There was no mistaking it, Courtneidge also saw it, and when we mentioned it later we found that other pilots had seen them too. Occasionally a machine is hit, and everything is blown to smithereens.

By the way, I noticed, while making up my log-book today, that I've now done 100 hours' solo. It seems a long, long way from that famous day at Netheravon last August when I did my very first solo, on a Maurice Farman Shorthorn, after five hours' dual.

Tuesday, June 5th

The squadron has two big D.O.P.s today. I am on the evening show, and I'm wondering whether it will be as exciting as this morning's, with nine pilots drawn from all three flights, which had a succession of fights, for the Hun was around in strength. The fiercest scrap was over Polygon Wood, east of Ypres, where Pratt had three separate combats, and got one Hun out of control, Dimmock drove down a black-and-white D-III, and Plenty and Barrager sent another down in a headlong death dive. We hope.

But almost everyone had gun trouble, and there were some close shaves. McDonald, with a jam, had to spin down 4,000 feet to get clear. Wilcox was badly shot about by three Huns, and was very lucky to throw them off. His controls were cut, and he crashed heavily on landing, and looked pretty shaken. I thought my own narrow squeak of Saturday was narrow enough, but after inspecting his machine, riddled with bullets, I yield him first place.

I see from yesterday's papers that Albert Ball's father has been notified that his son is dead. He was the greatest fighter the R.F.C.'s yet had, in a class by himself. I can't think why he wasn't given the V.C., in fact he's the kind who should be given a knighthood. After all, knighthood was originally the reward for bravery in battle, and it's a pity it isn't still.

It must be fine to have the sort of guts Ball had, to be completely without fear, to attack regardless of the odds, not giving a damn whether you're killed or not. Most of us like to try to go on living even when we have to risk our skins fighting Hun scouts far better than ours.

I wonder why everybody insists on calling us scouts? Me included. Whether British or German, we're not scouts at all, but single-seater fighters. I wouldn't have a notion what to do if I were ordered to go out and scout something.

We've had a wonderful hot summer's afternoon, wearing nothing much but towels, and lazing the hours away by the canal, swimming, reading, writing (especially me!), but now it's close on six o'clock, and I must get ready for patrol. We leave the ground at 7.15, the last evening show, and the ordained height is 18,000, which means being prepared for cold.

Wednesday, June 6th

The weather has been dud all day, with no patrols, and we've had an easy time, loafing around. Very nice too. This afternoon and evening we've had big black thunderstorms. There's been a terrific lot of gunfire up north. How the Boche infantry survive it is beyond me. But what's it all for?

My yesterday evening's job was a D.O.P. of six led by McDonald. It was a marvellously clear evening, and from 18,000 we had a wonderful view of distant England. The sinking sun threw its rays along the Channel, lighting up stretches of white cliff, and making them seem only a few minutes' flight away, though I suppose the distance was eighty miles as the crow (i.e. aeroplane) flies. I could follow the coastline from Thanet round to Dungeness. The Channel was a narrowish streak of gold, bordered this side by the line of the French and Belgian coasts, stretching from the Somme estuary to the Scheldt, and with a little imagination I could trace the faint line round to Antwerp. The Dutch islands were a dark line above the shining Scheldt, and seemed on my own level, there was no sensation of looking down.

Suddenly, McDonald gave the H.A. signal, and began a steep dive, and we followed. I took some moments to spot them, two L.V.G.s north-east of Menin, nosing towards us at about 7,000, but they saw us coming, turned about and bolted. We spread out and fired at long range, our tracers converging, but after 100 rounds, my gun stopped. Still in the dive, I tried hammering it, but with no result, so had to level out. By the time I'd remedied it, the others had gone. So I toured hazardously around by myself for an hour without seeing a thing, and went home.

It does seem darned silly not to have guns and ammo that work. We design and make a good aeroplane, we train and pay a pilot, we send him up into the air, he meets a Hun and has a fight, and after a lot of hot flying, if he's not shot down first, he gets the Hun in his sights, presses the trigger and then, after five shots, that infuriating blankness. Another jam, another priceless chance gone.

In yesterday's big fight one machine after another had to drop out to correct stoppages. We were lucky not to lose anybody, as one of the enemy formations they met was Richtofen's Circus, which had just previously given a patrol of 45 Squadron a bad time, the Albatroses waltzing round the Sop $1\frac{1}{2}$-strutters, and destroying two, sending two more down on our side, and a fifth on the other.

But it does look as though our former two-seater pilots are now finding their feet on Pups, especially Pratt, Joske and McDonald.

They're getting good scraps and driving down the occasional Hun. It was because the chaps had their tails rather up over yesterday's fights that another binge developed last evening. Marchant and Dimmock took the lead, they are a priceless pair for foolery. Marchant did a marvellous impersonation of a parson chanting the 23rd Psalm, in parody, with Dimmock striking appropriate chords on the piano. The words were so amusing I got them from him later. It's called *The Pilot's Psalm*, and it goes:

> The B.E.2c is my bus; therefore shall I want.
> He maketh me to come down in green pastures.
> He leadeth me where I wish not to go.
> He maketh me to be sick; he leadeth me astray on all cross-country flights.
> Yea, though I fly o'er No-man-'s Land where mine enemies would compass me about, I fear much evil, for *thou* art with me; thy joystick and thy prop discomfort me.
> Thou prepareth a crash for me in the presence of mine enemies; thy R.A.F. annointeth my hair with oil, thy tank leaketh badly.
> Surely to goodness thou shalt not follow me all the days of my life, else I shall dwell in the House of Colney Hatch for ever.

Of course, R.A.F. means the Royal Aircraft Factory engine. After this effort we went on to sing-songs around the piano, including *Haven't got a Hope*, *R.A.F. 2cs* and other R.F.C. specials. One of them, sung to the tune of *Hush-a-Bye, Baby*, went like this:

> Hans vos my name, und a pilot vos I.
> Out mit von Karl I vent for to fly.
> Pilots of Kultur ve vos, dere's no doubt,
> Each of us flew in an Albatros scout.
> Ve looked for B.E.s for to strafe mit our guns.
> Ven last I saw Karl, I knew he vos dones,
> For right on his tail vere two little Sops.
> *Oh, hush-a-bye, baby, on the tree-tops!*

Some of the things we bellowed out couldn't be repeated, such as 'The Parson came Home Drunk Last Night, as Drunk as he Could Be', sung to the tune of *While Shepherds Watched their Flocks*, and another, no less bawdy, variations of 'Barnacle Bill the Sailor'.

I wrote most of this letter before dinner, and am now finishing it off in bed, where I came at ten o'clock, as I've been warned for a very early patrol. (Daily patrol orders from 11th Wing, sent by motor-cyclist, don't usually reach the squadron until dinner-time, and that's why we don't know our next day's jobs until after dinner.) We've to be in the air by dawn, at 3.45, which means being called at three. I wonder why so early? The guns are still thudding away, a sort of drum-fire, as they have been doing all day.

The gunfire and the thunder seem to be a challenge to the frogs, for they're not just croaking at the moment, but practically blowing trumpets. Sometimes we put in a spot of revolver practice as they float on the pond's surface, and when you get a bull's-eye, the thing flies ten feet into the air, then falls with a flop, and lies spreadeagled, silent evermore. We did some of this during the evening, half a dozen of us, and managed to dispose of a score or more of the little devils.

June 6th (Diary)

Some of the chaps today were beefing about a G.H.Q. order that came round a few days ago, calling on all pilots and observers to show more Offensive Spirit, or words to that effect. What bally cheek! I wonder what more they expect from us fighters with only one gun, when every Hun fighter has two, and when we do practically all our fighting over Hun territory, anyway.

Thursday, June 7th

This has been a very exciting day. When the orderly awakened us at three, the front was strangely quiet compared with the racket to which we had gone to sleep a few hours before. As we dressed in the candle-light, it was pitch black outside, with none of the flickering that normally hovers over the Lines.

Then at 3.10 exactly, with no preliminary shelling at all, there came a most God-almighty roar, the deep blast of a long and terrible explosion. The sky lit up with a vivid red glare. The ground shook as it we were in an earthquake, in fact the hut seemed to jump off the ground. I've never heard such a stupendous noise before, like the thunderclap of doom. It seemed so close it could have come from just across the canal, instead of a dozen miles away, as we were soon to discover. Then as the roar ended, a hurricane bombardment began, a continuous rapid throbbing of guns, thousands of them. The hut vibrated without pause, the ground shuddered. All hell had been let loose up north.

[This was the opening of the classic Battle of Messines, the explosion, heard as far away as London, of the nineteen immense mines that had taken two years to drive under the German positions. It was immediately followed by an artillery barrage by 2,400 guns and howitzers, one to every seven yards of the nine-mile front. Under this cover, 80,000 infantry of General Plumer's Second Army advanced almost without resistance to what was left of Wytschaete and Messines. By evening they reached objectives which straightened the southern flank of the Ypres salient.]

We'd no notion what it all signified, and were eager to find out. After a quick cup of tea and a boiled egg with chunks of bread and marge (you've got to have *something* in you at this time of the morning to keep your pecker up) we dashed to the sheds in a tender, panting to get into the air and join the party. The unbroken thudding of the guns went on, coming in waves, with the ground quivering under our feet. The mechanics had already warmed up the engines, and dawn was barely breaking as we took off, with the flames of the preceding machine's exhaust as guide to getting into formation.

McDonald was leading Barrager, Williams, Odell and me. We mounted steeply north-eastwards. High above were thin streaky clouds, catching the rays of the sun well before it approached the horizon. At first, the ground seemed in darkness, but within a minute or so we saw the lights of battle right ahead, lines of flashing pin-points, the mark of thousands of guns raining shot and shell on the Boche positions.

Soon, as daylight came, and as we drew towards Ploegsteert Wood, at 13,000, we looked upon an awe-inspiring spectacle, a whole battle-field at a glance—a battle in action, but covered with a great mantle of smoke, greenish grey, with long fingers stretching eastwards under a light wind. And through the smoke, in a crescent reaching over the Messines ridge, a twinkling belt of continuous flashes which were the explosions of our shells. The whole battle front was ablaze with non-stop bombardment, a most thrilling and amazing sight.

So this, I thought, was what we'd all been working so hard for since I joined the squadron. Our job had been to prevent the Boche from tumbling to what was afoot. Now I could understand all the activity around Dickebusch Lake. How right Major Arnold had been.

Even before we arrived on the scene, the artillery spotting B.E.s were up, as well as the balloons, and quickly the air became crowded with our machines, all so busy watching the battle they constantly nearly barged into one another. Throughout the patrol, we saw only three Huns, D-IIIs, five miles over, and they slid away eastwards when we dived and fired at long range.

After two hours of patrol McDonald took us down to 2,000 feet, and at this height I could hear, above the roar of the engine, the con-tinuous thudding of gunfire and shell-bursts. I could feel them too—the concussions kept the Pup in an unbroken shudder of overlapping bumps. For a few seconds, I throttled back the engine, and the noise was staggering.

Of the infantry we could see nothing, for they were hidden under the pall of smoke. It looked a hell on earth, especially for the Germans. Even just to watch it from 2,000 feet was hellish enough for me.

We had a fine view of the group of enormous raw craters, some I should guess over 100 yards across. I knew then what had caused that stupendous roar, these mines all exploding at the same time. And they'd blown most of the dreaded Messines ridge sky high.

But it didn't take long to realise that we were at a damn' dangerous level, for shells were roaring past us every second, and in their passage throwing us about as if we'd been boats in a stormy sea. We were lucky that none of us was hit. I stopped sweating only when McDonald at last climbed up to 8,000, and led us home.

Later patrols had better luck with Huns, who turned up in force during the morning. In one fight Joske crashed an Albatros near

Comines. Other scraps were inconclusive. Unfortunately, one of our pilots is missing, Mitchell, who only arrived three days ago.

Friday, June 8th

We possessed our souls with impatience today, waiting to find out about the battle. After all, we do like to know what's going on in this war! Our only news came from the R.O. ringing up people. It seems the Army's had a roaring success, and has advanced several miles, mainly because of the mines we heard explode and afterwards saw.

When we arrived over the battlefield today there was still plenty of artillery fire, though nothing like yesterday's hullabaloo. At the end of the patrol I flew low, and as I was alone, and could fool around as I wanted, I inspected the mine craters at nought feet, in fact lower, for one was large enough for me to dip into, and do a vertically banked circle inside it, below the lip. I'd have looked silly if I'd crashed, but I didn't and it was quite fun.

Saturday, June 9th

From Friday's newspapers we learn that we took part on Thursday in a famous victory which is already named the Battle of Messines. The whole push went like clockwork, and all the papers say it's the most successful British show yet. On the ground, 5,000 Boche prisoners, and the advance made without great loss of life for us. In the air, eighteen Huns downed against six of ours missing.

We did our little bit to help, and it's good to feel that I've taken part in a full-scale land battle—or at least in the preliminaries. What I'm particularly pleased about is to have landed right by the battle area only a week ago, and to have seen something of what was afoot. If only I'd come down on the Wednesday evening! I'd have loved to see the mines go up, and the ridge, and also a few thousand Boches.

Today has been hectic. Before the main breakfast, a three-hour patrol, hit by archie, a brush with H.A., and a sight of a Hun flamer. Plus orderly dog duties. Immediately after breakfast, rushed off in a Crossley to the field cashier at Hinges, near Béthune, drew the pay money, rushed into Béthune, had lunch, did some shopping, roared back to La Gorgue, held pay parade, six francs down. Censored the men's letters, inspected their quarters and midday meal. After lunch, another three-hour patrol, archied again, another (distant) brush with H.A., and got back just in time for dinner. I definitely earned my pay today.

My first job was a dawn D.O.P. led by McDonald, and I didn't enjoy this jaunt overmuch, as he went a long way over, at 7,000, a bad height for Pups to fight, a good height for archie. We had two archie hates, and I thought they'd got us in the second, with scores of black bursts around us.

The first salvo always makes you jump. The balls of smoke appear miraculously in the sky, then you hear the woof! woof! woof! The shorter the period between seeing and hearing, the nearer the shell is to you. When they coincide you've no more interest in things! When the shells burst below or behind you get the woof! first, and that can be nerve-jerking too. But worst is to get them say fifty yards in front of you, first the flash of red flame, then the burst of smoke, then the woof!, then chunks of shrapnel tearing gashes in your wings, and maybe in you too. A second later you're flying through the smoke, which has a sharp, acrid smell, and you realise it isn't black but very dark brown.

We had no scraps, though after an hour we nibbled in on one. Barrager suddenly drew ahead, rocked his wings and pointed down. At once McDonald led us down in a shallow dive. I then saw, some way ahead, a fight in progress between five F.E.2bs (two-seaters) and eight Albatroses. The Fees were going round in a tight circle, their favourite defensive manœuvre, as the gunners then cover each other's tails, and can fire together at any too-enterprising Hun.

The Huns were diving, firing, then zooming up again for another dive. It was quite a nice little scrap to watch, with tracers criss-crossing and guns flashing, and the scouts split-assing around the circling Fees. As we drew nearer, McDonald opened fire and we followed suit. At this moment, the V-strutter which was in my sights sent out a long plume of white cloud-like vapour. His petrol tank was hit. Then there was a vivid flash, and the whole thing burst into a ball of red fire, and plunged headlong. I hated to see it—flamers do something to me.

Had we not fired at long range, we might have caught the Huns on the hop, as we were coming on them out of the sun, but when they saw our tracer and heard our bullets they sheered off eastwards. Afterwards, McDonald cursed himself for opening fire too soon. Although the flamer was in my sights, there's no doubt it was a Fee who got him, as they were shooting at close range. The Fee chaps waved to us as we swished around them, then they formed up and went off east-wards too. They still had their job to do. I'd hate to be a Fee observer, perched in the nacelle, open to the full blast of air, standing up to shoot, and liable to be tossed out when the machine is thrown about in a fight.

The second show was a high evening D.O.P. with six of us led by Captain Heath, the first time I've been with him. I much enjoyed a spell at 20,000, in spite of the cold and the thin air. It's not only that you're more or less free from the risk of being jumped, but there's always something about being so high, above the millions of people below, invisible to the naked eye on the ground. And it isn't everybody who can go up to that height and stay there for any length of time. You begin to feel the shortage of oxygen at about 16,000, and the higher you go beyond that, the deeper you have to breathe. At 20,000, you can't get enough air through your nose, and have to gulp it in lungfuls through your mouth. It's ice-cold air too. I've been up to 22,000, as shown on the altimeter—they can have errors, of course, either way—without feeling too uncomfortable, but to try to stay there for the whole patrol would be another matter, you'd faint eventually, I suppose.

[In retrospect, it seems extraordinary that in 1917–18 scout pilots were expected to patrol at 20,000 without oxygen, and that they did so without experiencing undue discomfort. Today, aircrew usually go on to oxygen at around 10,000 feet.]

Captain Heath gave the washout signal at 15,000 over the Lines and we made our separate ways home. There were some fantastic formations of alto-cumulus below me, and I was tempted to joy-ride round their pinnacles. They look so white and solid, and the bulging hills and secret valleys so inviting, you can't resist diving into them and zooming up and generally behaving like a schoolboy. And, of course, you aren't alone. You have your shadow. You see the machine on the white wall of cloud as a grey silhouette surrounded by a bright halo with a circular rainbow around it. As you fly alongside the cloudbank with the sun behind you, this beautifully coloured ghost glides along with you. If you approach the cloud to dive into it, you see the shadow and halo ahead, growing larger and larger until the very second you enter the white cliff—like having a head-on collision with yourself!

June 9th (Diary)

I keep thinking of the flamer today. The pilot jumped. He had a light-yellow flying coat, and it bellied out, momentarily checking his fall, like a parachute, so that the machine left him behind. Then he turned over and dived after it, alongside the column of black smoke. A horrid sight. I hope it wasn't me that hit him, I'd hate to get a flamer, it would be on my conscience. What a way to die, to be sizzled alive or to jump and fall thousands of feet. I wonder if you're conscious all the way down? I'd much prefer a bullet through the head and have done with it. The Hun pilot could easily have got away with it if he'd had a parachute, he'd enough time to get clear before his plane lit up.

Sunday, June 10th

No patrols today, low clouds, but a couple of chaps I knew at Port-meadow paid us a call for something to do. They're on Pups with 66, my old Filton squadron, and had hedge-hopped here from Estrée-Blanche, some twenty miles to the west. They brought news of several fellows I knew, one of them Pritt, who is another warbabe, but who's just been awarded the M.C. for shooting up carloads of German generals, well over the other side of the Lines.

I'm very glad to learn from the papers that Albert Ball has been given the V.C. He deserved it long ago, and I can't see why they have to wait until a fellow's dead before deciding he's a hero.

The papers also say that the American General Pershing has arrived in London with a staff and some troops. So the Yanks *are* coming at last! It won't be long, we hope, before they produce something pretty hot in the way of aeroplanes to replace some of the has-beens we're inflicted with now.

[A vain hope! The Americans entered the war without a single aeroplane capable of operating on the Western Front, and had to draw on the already overburdened air industries of France and Britain. American pilots and observers used Allied machines for both training and combat flying. The Liberty engine was the only notable contribution from the U.S.A.]

Tuesday, June 12th

No patrols again yesterday or today, although it's been glorious today, the heat positively grilling, and I'm becoming quite sunburnt. Of course, most of the time is spent by and in the canal. My only job was to test a new engine, replacement for one which ran very roughly and was a worry on patrol.

This new one seemed so sweet that after going up to 2,000 and flipping aimlessly around I was tempted to do some contour-chasing. I went down to the area towards Bailleul, where it's pretty level, and raced across the countryside ten feet up, lifting over trees and cottages and camps, then surging on at full throttle. Because I'd set out only to do a test, I wasn't wearing my helmet and goggles, nor, of course, flying gear, and it was fine to feel the rush of air past my temples, and my hair waving madly in the slipstream swirling around the tiny windscreen. And, of course, without my helmet, the noise of the engine was terrific.

This is the most marvellous thrill you can get out of flying, scudding along close to the ground, the feeling of speed, and especially in so smooth and docile a machine as a Pup. Everything is spinning by at ninety miles an hour. The plane's shadow skims across the fields just below. You come to a road without trees or telegraph poles, and you go down until your wheels almost touch. This flying at two feet is really intoxicating, seeing people diving for the ditch, troops scattering, lorries lurching across the road like drunks. Turning west towards Hazebrouck, I dived on a couple of staff cars, and one of them, an open tourer with red-tabbed officers, nearly went up a tree and finished in the ditch. I certainly put the gust up *that* lot. All good, clean fun, and it makes these staff wallahs realise there are dangers even in their kind of war.

Then you come back to the aerodrome, full of the joys of spring, and land perfectly, certain that flying is really worth while, but hoping that none of the red-tabs spotted your number or squadron markings. The beggars sometimes do, and then you're for the high jump. It's silly to think that this harmless high spirits could land me into real trouble, but if I did the same stunt twenty miles to the eastwards, using bullets, I'd get an M.C., like young Pritt. But somehow I don't think this is my cup of tea.

Another new man, Fleming, has arrived, who makes the seventh since I joined the squadron, of whom two are missing and one badly injured in hospital. I'm beginning to feel quite senior, and am tickled to death to find myself showing a certain air of superiority.

You ask about the frequent binges we have. But we don't have them that often, and then usually only to celebrate something, like getting a Hun. Otherwise there's not a great deal of drinking (alcoholic). I drink nothing but lime juice for meals, and the others do the same, in fact everyone has his own bottle on the table.

Usually, in the evening, after dinner, we sit outside the Mess, or more often Thompson's hut, because he has a portable Decca gramophone and a good selection of records, including all the hits of London. We lounge there, smoking hard (archie in the mosquito world war!) and fooling with Jock, a black Scots terrier, brought overseas with the squadron. He's the Officers' Mess dog, and is especially friendly with Marchant. There are several other dogs in the camp, but they're French mongrels and he has no use for them, in fact he's for ever fighting them. To us he's a casually ingratiating old thing, and he reminds us of home.

By the way, I've had to stop writing my letters in bed, as my oil lamp, dim as it is, attracts mosquitoes. We also have moths, earwigs, spiders, mice and lots of other harmless guests, but these twin-Spandau mozzies can be spiteful, and so in future I will do my correspondence in the daytime.

Wednesday, June 13th

We learned today that the squadron is to be transferred to the 10th Wing, and instead of working over Flanders, we shall patrol southwards, towards Arras. This is because, as the Messines show is over, things should be quiet on the Ypres front for a while.[1]

As I write, in the evening, the Boche is shelling nearby Estaires, and the concussions vibrate the hut continuously. Our guns are replying, so there's no lack of noise. Through it all comes the croaking of those confounded frogs. Every evening they kick up this din, real little Huns they are, deserving all they get as revolver targets. Yesterday evening Marchant and I put in ten minutes' practice, and he got five and I got four. As we ended, an ack-emma came running to report that somebody had been shot on the towpath. Marchant went to investigate, and found an A.S.C. sergeant, hit in the leg. But we couldn't have done it, because we fire in the other direction. How it happened is a mystery, but he's not much hurt, and will get some leave, so why should he worry? Or why should we?

You ask me why we carry an automatic in the cockpit. Well, it's not to use in a dog-fight when the Vickers packs up, though pilots *have* been known to try a shot. It's officially to protect yourself if you have to forced-land in Hunland, though I can't see anybody getting far with that. What they're most useful for is killing frogs.

June 13th (Diary)

Today's query from home—why do I carry a Colt in the cockpit? For the reason we all do. Not to stage a one-man battle against a platoon of Boche soldiery if forced down the other side—I'd be butchered instantly. No, it's the fear of being set alight. It's something nobody talks about, but it's at the back of everybody's mind, and each of us knows he couldn't take it. To be burned alive, however soon it's over, is the one thing we can't face. Better to use the gun and end it in a split second.

Thursday, June 14th

The 10th Wing has put us on to the standby system we briefly tried before. The idea is to cut down the amount of flying, but it hasn't taken us long to decide that we don't like it. Courtneidge and I hung

1. See Appendix B, *Trenchard's Strategy of the Offensive*.

around the squadron office from eight until twelve this morning, then again from five, and it's now six, with three more hours to go. We sit and talk and smoke and talk and smoke until we just have to get up and trot round the guard-room, the stores hut, the transport lines, the petrol dump (No Smoking!) and so on, wondering whether we shall ever again be able to enjoy the canal, and swim, and lounge in the sun.

Another change that's come upon us is that, on the order of H.Q., R.F.C., we have to stop calling Huns Hostile Aircraft (H.A.) in our combat reports. Instead we must always call them Enemy Aircraft (E.A.). Of course, this will make a lot of difference to our lives out here. My hat, do you realize we've been calling Huns *hostile* all this time! No wonder we've not shot many down. But now we know they're *enemy*, maybe we'll do better.

I see from yesterday's papers that the Boches have raided London in broad daylight. What darned cheek! They did a lot of damage too, and apparently there were no machines of ours around to have a go at the Gothas.

Gosh, it's terribly hot sitting outside the office. But no worse than when flying. Just to get into flying kit has you running with sweat. You climb gently up to the cockpit so as not to sweat more, but it doesn't work at all, and by the time you've taxied to the take-off area your underclothes are wet and sticky. As soon as you're in the air, the sweat begins to cool, and as you climb up towards the cold, it gets chillier and chillier, a most uncomfortable feeling, like being encased in an icy rubber sheet.

When you come down, gradually unfreezing, but still cold, you meet the heat haze. On Sahara days like this, especially during the middle hours, the haze can go up to over 4,000 feet. As you descend, the top of the haze spreads below you, shining in the sun like a vast silver sea. When you plunge into it, although it is only haze, it can cut down your lateral visibility to 200 yards, but once well in it, you feel the warmth, your chilliness vanishes, and you start to sweat, especially when the machine gets tossed about by the heat bumps, which can sometimes be rougher even than cloud bumps.

There is much excitement in the squadron, as some of the old-timers who've been out there six months or more are being transferred to Home Establishment, including two flight commanders, Pratt and

Heath, also Marchant, Luxmore and Thompson, the R.O., who was an observer, but will now learn to fly. After a spell of leave they'll spend some months doing flying instruction or home defence, then they'll come out here for another tour. This system gives the chaps a chance to freshen up before their nerve goes, for it's reckoned that the average pilot or observer begins to crack up after six months' active service. They're not all going on the same day, but there'll be a big farewell binge for the lot. Thompson, we're all glad to know, is leaving us his gramophone and records.

Part Four

The Vimy Front

Sunday, June 17th

I'm afraid I sent no letter yesterday, but it was in a good cause. It was my day off, and it happened to be Kay's also, and as a tender was going to Doullons, we spent the day there together, and finished up with a binge-dinner with a bunch of Sherwoods we met in the Quatre Fils. They were just out of the Line, and we all became decidedly spifflicated. Kay and I returned to La Gorgue far too late and weary to think of letter-writing.

Despite all this, I was up having my No 1 breakfast at 4.30, and on patrol at 5.0, my first over our new front, down to Arras. It was a beautiful morning, with masses of big woolly clouds, and to scud alongside them soon got rid of my hangover. There were a few Huns about, but they dived away as soon as they saw us, and we spent most of the patrol looking at the Lines, which are so very different in appearance from those up north.

From above, the Ypres salient was light or dark brown, according to recent rain, but down on the La Bassée–Lens–Arras area, the trenches show up in red and white and black as the nature of the ground changes. In the chalky areas they seem like the threads of a net curtain, an absolute maze, in which you'd think the troops could never find their way.

Today is stiflingly hot, and when we're not in the air, we spend most of our time in the canal. Lunch-time sees the Mess crowded with gents strolling round in towels, or if they wish to pretend they're in an officers' Mess, in pyjamas.

Monday, June 18th

This morning I was on another early patrol, led this time by Kay, and in two hours at 20,000, we saw not a single E.A. These very high patrols become wearisome if you meet no Huns. You are one of four, at fixed distances from each other, motionless except for slight sway-ings and oscillations, and flickers of the ailerons, plus of course, head turnings. And does one's neck ache after two hours of it!

After an hour of unceasing head turning, gun warming, being darned cold, and finishing off your slab of chocolate, your mind begins to wander, and you think about all sorts of things, such as being in a safe cushy job at the base, or on leave at home. You think of having a slap-up meal at Gatti's or the Troc or the Café Royal, and of doing a show, going to Daly's to see José Collins in *The Maid of the Mountains*, or Violet Loraine in *The Bing Boys*. Then you have to warm up the gun again, and you remember there's a war on, and you're at 20,000 feet, looking for trouble.

But in spite of the dullness of some high patrols, we flyers do at least fight our war in better style than the P.B.I. I know it may sound silly, but sometimes when you're really high, well above giant moun-tains of cloud, or billowing oceans of snow, you have a godlike feeling, you're one of the handful of human beings who may look down from the heavens on to the millions of miserable devils slaying each other in the mud and barbed wire below.

I'm writing this on standby, sitting outside the office. The one advantage of standby is that you have plenty of time for letters. I still get chaffed over writing so lengthily every day, but that doesn't worry me, I just enjoy writing. I've always had the itch to do it, and out here I have something worth while writing about. I'm taking more interest in the writing too, showing more care in describing things, for example. In a way, this is teaching me to write—it's certainly teaching me to use my eyes.

Tuesday, June 19th

A full-out farewell binge last night for the chaps going home. We were all well ginned when we trooped in for dinner, a pretty rowdy

64

affair, with everybody throwing bread at anybody, and usually hitting the waiters. After dinner there was so much speechmaking about the squadron since it started that we almost sobered up. But we soon got going again in the ante-room, with everybody yelling for drinks, and Normie Dimmock opening up on the piano, with all of us roaring our heads off until we were too hoarse to do any more bellowing. Then a rough house broke out, with everyone hilariously smashing glasses and bottles and furniture.

After doing my bit of horse-play in a wrestling match with Kay and being thrown, then pouring my whisky in the piano and tossing the glass through the window (oilskin), I suddenly realised I was on the point of passing out, so staggered off to bed and sank into slumber to the strains of the mob's loudly yelled, *'When this ruddy war is over, Oh, how happy we shall be'.*

This was but one of the numerous ditties sung. The R.F.C. regulars included a very old one we used to bawl at guest nights at Port-meadow to the tune of *The Tarpaulin Jacket*, and gaily called *The Dying Airman.*

> The Young Aviator lay dying,
> And as in the wreckage he lay,
> To his comrades all gathered around him,
> These last parting words did he say
>
> Chorus.   Take the cylinder out of my kidneys,
> The connecting rod out of my brain, my brain.
> From the small of my back take the camshaft,
> And assemble the engine again.

It goes on like this for a dozen verses, all somewhat lugubrious, and for some unknown reason the chaps enjoyed singing it. I preferred another one, *Cock Robin.*

> Who killed Cock Robin?
> 'I,' said the Hun,
> 'With my Spandau gun,
> I killed Cock Robin.'

Chorus.　All the planes in the air,
　　　　　Went a dipping and a throbbing,
　　　　　When they heard of the death of poor Cock Robin,
　　　　　When they heard of the death of poor Cock Robin.

—and so on for several verses. Altogether, it was a jolly good evening, though there'll be a hefty bill for damages. Anyway, I didn't have so bad a hangover this morning as I deserved.

Wednesday, June 20th

Quite an anxious time on patrol today, not because of Huns, but because on a six-man job led by Kay, we had two brand new pilots, and as they had never been given proper training in formation flying, their surges to and fro, trying to keep in position, gave me some jumpy moments, especially as we were flying among rain clouds most of the time.

Since Fleming arrived a week ago, we've had four new pilots, and one, Shadwell, is married, so I'm no longer on my own. Another, Ferrie, is a Canadian, short and with a cheerful grin, and another, Hughes, a lively Welshman. The fourth, Tonks, has done only fifteen hours' flying, and no formation at all, which won't help much.

There are rumours that Kay will get a flight in place of Pratt or Heath. I do hope he's given 'C' Flight, he's such a friendly, straightforward fellow, one couldn't ask for a nicer skipper.

Thursday, June 21st

Today, for the first time, I led a patrol. Certainly, I had only one fellow to lead, Odell, but I was responsible for what we did, and I must say it gave me quite a kick to see my rigger tying the coloured streamers to my rear struts.

We had an early standby call while still in the middle of our No 1 breakfast, when the phone rang, and the tender arrived within seconds. The engines were running, and we were off very quickly. I led the way towards Lille, and soon spotted the Hun, an L.V.G. beating up and down the Line at 4,000, doing a shoot from over Quesnoy. I climbed up above him and approached, with Odell in close tow, but he saw us and wheeled gradually eastwards.

Before beginning the dive after him, I took a careful look round for other Huns, and there they were, eight Albatri sitting on a cloud at about 8,000, just waiting for us. My booby trap all over again! Meanwhile, the L.V.G. kept level on his course trying not to look like bait. I loosed off fifty rounds at long range, then saw the Albatripe beginning their dive, so turned smartly west, and when safe from attack, circled slowly, waiting to see what came next.

But they didn't follow, and soon the two-seater came back to his shoot. Once more I went towards him, and fired 100 rounds at 300 yards' range, Odell doing the same. Amazingly, my gun didn't jam, and one of us must have winged him, even at this distance, because he suddenly started to go down in a steepish glide eastwards.

Then the Albatripe dropped into another dive, this time opening fire at long range, as we saw from the tracers, but they didn't hit us, and within seconds we were haring full speed westwards. They gave it up, turned away, and disappeared behind a vast cloud.

We stayed round the Comines–La Bassée area for another half-hour without seeing anything, then, as the set time was up, dived down to 500 feet and used up our ammo on the Boche trenches opposite Festubert. There was a lot of fighting in this area two years ago in the Battles of Neuve Chapelle and Loos, and the ground is still a wilderness, with not a building, not even a tree. The Huns let us have it hard in return for our effort, we could hear the bullets cracking past us, so we beetled off home, to find that we'd both been hit several times.

I then learned that our archie had watched our initial cut-and-run show, and phoned the squadron that we were badly outnumbered. The Major sent out three more planes to reinforce us, but we never saw them. Some time after we'd landed we watched the return—but only two of them. The missing one was Tonks. He hasn't come back yet, and there's been no message, and as it's now after dinner, it looks as though he's had it. This was his first trip over the Lines. The others, Barrager and Shadwell, said they met no Huns, so he must have lost contact, because he'd done no formation flying, become completely lost, and either landed or been caught by prowling Huns.

This is yet another example of how wicked it is to send pilots out here inadequately trained. Tonks following on Cameron and Mitchell is good proof of this. By the way, we've already heard that Cameron—he pooped off at the moon—is a prisoner. About Mitchell we've heard nothing yet.[1]

I had two other patrols during the day, the first providing an indecisive skirmish with Albatri, the second a decisive skirmish with a giant storm cloud, complete with lightning flashes and torrential rain, by which we were definitely driven down. We landed just in time to escape a two-hour downpour, which flooded out both the men's quarters and ours.

The new 'C' Flight commander has arrived, named Scott. He's from 54, and we're told he's pretty good. He's small and wiry with a decisive manner, as though he knows what he's doing. He'll do us fine, I'm sure, but I'm sorry Kay didn't get the job.

Friday, June 22nd

I would have had my first victory this morning but for my darned gun. Even the engine, which has been ailing, played up well, but the ammo let me down.

Kay led six of us on an O.P. at 6.0, drawn from all three flights, with Barrager as deputy. The weather wasn't too good, masses of soft cloud with medium visibility. After half an hour I spotted a formation of eight V-strutters to the south-east. Kay saw them too, and led us towards them. I began to tremble with excitement, all tensed up for the coming scrap. They were on our level, and almost within shooting distance, but instead of coming for us they began to wheel around each other. Kay made for them, and we closed, all our guns going. They scattered, and we broke up to attack.

A green one, with yellow stripes round the fuselage, came across my front, and I turned after him. The pilot didn't attempt to manœuvre, but turned off in a shallow dive. I banked steeply, got right behind

1. Lieutenant D. R. Cameron was driven down by Leutnant Benig, a member of Jasta 28. Second Lieutenant H. A. C. Tonks was shot down and killed by Hauptmann Hartmann, also of Jasta 28. Lieutenant A. P. Mitchell was driven down and made prisoner by Leutnant Oberländer of Jasta 30.

him, sights on, and pressed the trigger. Almost at the first three shots he jerked into a steepish dive.

I gave a hasty glance over my tail. It seemed too easy, too good to be true. But nobody was behind me. I was close behind him still, and I pressed the trigger again. The tracers seemed to go right into his back, I had him cold—then that maddening blankness—a jam! Cursing like a maniac, I followed him in the dive, hammering at the cocking handle. It wouldn't fall. He drew away, and there was no point in following further. I was practically apoplectic with rage.

Back on the tarmac, I learned that all the other Huns had fled without firing a shot, and had easily drawn away from the pursuing Pups. This isn't the usual Albatros attitude, and we assumed that they were a bunch of advanced flying trainees.

As soon as I landed, almost before I'd wiped away the whale grease, the C.O. sent me off to a Court of Inquiry sitting at La Gorgue on the mystery of the shot sergeant. I spent over an hour there with a captain, a lieutenant and a second-lieutenant. They all wore an ominous look, and eventually decided to inspect the scene of the crime tomorrow.

Shooting frogs is not our only activity in natural history. We also wash sparrows. At least, one sparrow. A group of us were standing talking on the tarmac yesterday, after patrol, when we noticed a sparrow flapping round a puddle of oil, unable to take off. The half burnt oil comes from our rotary Le Rhônes, which throw it out over the cowling and undercarriage, and when we land and the engine stops, the oil drips and drips and makes puddles. Hence the foolish sparrow giving himself a bath in what he thought was a pool of water.

However, Asher and I caught him, gently cleaned off the oil with a petrol rag, polished him up with our handkerchiefs until he was giving full revs, then Asher threw him off. He shot away eastwards, and we hoped that in return for our help he'd drive down a few Hun sparrows.

Asher, I've learned, was the cousin of the Lieutenant Giles who was killed in a B.E. crash at Filton. It was during the spell when pupils were doing flat spins to the right when taking off in B.E.s, simply because, during dual, the instructors never let us have control of the rudder, which was stiff and heavy compared with the Avro, and needed stronger pressure on the rudder bar. That's how Pechell was killed too, crashing on to a hangar. An hour later I did a flat spin myself in a B.E.2d, but was luckier.

Had a brief trip to St Omer the other day, in between jobs, on a tender going to fetch stores. In the town I ran across Bonar Law, and during lunch at the Hotel du Commerce he told me the latest news about mutual friends. Same old story—by now, a third of the ones we knew have gone west.

Saturday, June 23rd

Dawn patrol again today. It was one of those too-bright mornings that usually herald rain later. The air was sharp, there was the smell of dew on the grass, and the canal was shrouded in mist as we walked from our quick breakfast to the waiting tender.

It's a wonderful feeling to be flying when everything is still asleep, long before the sun has reached the horizon, though its rays were already flecking the high cirrus with gold, and we were climbing hard towards them. The grey mist clung to low-lying ground and winding streams, and wisps of smoke rose from where the world was waking up to another day—of war. Before long we entered into sunlight, and each machine became alight in its rays. But this is the snag of the dawn patrol, for you can't see clearly to the eastwards. The glare is right in your eyes, and it may hide a bunch of Huns intent on surprising you.

There were Courtneidge, Odell and me led by our new skipper, Scott, who took us up and down the Boche side of the front for no result, for we saw nothing. The weather, after starting so nicely, grew misty, and heavy banks of cloud came rolling from the west. After one and a half hours of this probing into Hunland at 9,000 there was suddenly a nerve-jerking break in the smooth purr of my engine, a sort of miss, then a spurt, then another miss. The rev counter flickered to and fro, showing less than half the required revs.

Within seconds I was nearly stalling trying to keep in formation. I couldn't even dive in front and switchback, so I turned off and away. It's always an odd sensation to leave a patrol. At one moment the four of you are all apparently stationary, tied together by invisible threads, but as you bank away, the others acquire movement, flash on, dwindle swiftly in size, and in seconds they're out of sight.

I had a jittery journey back, with the wind against me, and I only just made it, staggering over the trenches at 400 feet, and being shot at heartily from below. You can hear every shot and every crackle as the bullets whizz close by you. Very hair-raising! I managed a good forced landing, no damage, but my rigger later found seventeen bullet-holes. The trouble was broken ignition leads, and I was soon home.

At midday the Court of Inquiry arrived, and I scraped up Court-neidge and Kay to help entertain them with drinks, then lunch fol-lowed by coffee and cognac. But it was a waste of effort and money, for their integrity was unsullied, and after inspecting the pond they went off looking more ominous than ever.

Sunday, June 24th

We had a scrap this morning, led by Scott, who has soon shown him-self to be an aggressive type—against the Huns, I mean. It was an O.P. with Courtneidge and Odell, and we were at 10,000 over Lille when I spotted, away to the north, tiny specks flashing in the sun. I shot ahead and pointed. Scott saw, and began climbing towards them. They were seven Albatri, but they spotted us, climbed higher, and kept higher.

Scott wanted a scrap, but while they had the height we couldn't attack. He circled round slowly right below them, inviting them to dive on us, but they didn't. It was quite extraordinary, there we were trailing our coats with all the odds against us, and they wouldn't attack. So Scott, apparently giving up, led us south, climbing hard, and made a wide circuit into Hunland until the Albatri were almost out of sight, though we saw that they were also flying south. Scott then came back at them from the east, with an advantage of 500 feet. As we closed, they saw us, and began to outclimb us again, and Scott then began firing at 400 yards in a shallow dive, and we all followed suit.

I put my Aldis on to one of them in rear, yellow with patches of blue, and put 100 rounds into him. Then I realised that my tracers were converging with those of another Pup. The two others were also having a pot at this fellow, for his pals had left him and drawn away east. He was in difficulties, and as we closed, he dipped his nose into a dive. It was no good following, the Albatri are so much faster, especially in a dive.

I watched him going down steeply, then saw a thin red trickle licking along the fuselage below the engine. He was alight! A moment later a tongue of yellow-red flame leapt out and the machine burst into a mass of fire. All this took barely ten seconds. Then it went vertical, a diving furnace, leaving its column of greasy black smoke. He didn't jump, maybe he'd been hit. As usual, it made me quite queasy to watch. The flames and smoke petered out, and we couldn't see exactly where he'd fallen, but it was south-east of Loos, well on the other side.

Back at the office, we couldn't decide who'd got him. I was the first to fire at him, as he was on my side of the Hun formation, but then Scott had joined in (his were the converging tracers) and then the others. Scott got closest, so his were probably the vital shots, and though he said we could divide it as a flight show, and count a quarter each, the Major credited it to him, and so far as I was concerned, he was welcome, I'm just not keen on getting flamers.

We were baffled at the Hun's refusal to attack, but Scott reckoned there must have been another British formation higher up, which we didn't see, but which the Huns did, and they suspected a trap. The flamer was unlucky, a long-range bullet must have hit him from our first bursts.

We were rather braced today over the Major going up on a patrol led by Scott, with Dimmock, Ferrie, Hughes, and yet another new man, Captain Fortin, who arrived a couple of days ago. They saw no Huns, but it's the idea of him joining us on patrol that we like. There's supposed to be a rule that C.O.s of squadrons mustn't fly closer than five miles to the Lines, because the R.F.C. is so short of experienced officers, but if there is a rule he ignored it. He's far from being the only one, for in Comic Cuts one regularly reads of C.O.s of squadrons, such as 60 and 43, taking part in scraps or downing Huns.

Fortin is a cheerful, chubby, round-faced Canadian, and a great acquisition, for he's a top-notch pianist, and has quickly got going on the Mess piano. As I write, he's banging out some of the musical show melodies in London. He's just started on *Chu-Chin-Chow*, the Cobbler's Song—'I sit and cobble at slippers and shoon, from the rise of the sun to the set of moon'—wonderful song, that. Dimmock, who doesn't pretend to do any more than strum, will have to take a back seat in the world of music, I'm afraid.

This afternoon, while we were hanging round the squadron office on standby, we were given an interesting exhibition of gas-bag strafing. Suddenly we heard a quick succession of explosions, and there to the east, at about 6,000, was a group of white shrapnel bursts—our archie. As we watched, a balloon to the northwards lit up, and instantly became a vast blaze of yellow-red flame, which after what seemed quite a time, fell headlong, leaving behind a mass of billowing black smoke.

We saw two parachutes beneath, like white parasols, and through field glasses spotted the dark blobs below which were the observers, going down very slowly, and only narrowly escaping, as it seemed to us, having the blazing tackle drop on them. Before they were halfway down the next balloon in the line was alight, but the two balloonatics were already well on their way. As we gazed expectantly at the next we saw the two parachutes spring into existence and begin the downward journey. Several seconds later the gas-bag above them burst into flames.

By this time we'd spotted the Huns, four small specks racing for the next balloon to the south. This was already being hauled down—they have a quick-action lorry drill for the job—and the parachutes were nearing the ground. The sky all round was plastered with archie, and the barrage was obviously too hot to break through, for the Huns went off eastwards. Still, their bag of three without loss was pretty good.

I'd hate to be a balloonatic, dangling on a parachute with that enormous blazing mass just above me, though they seem to get away with it every time. As the parachutes work so well for balloonists, I can't see why they shouldn't do as much for aeroplane pilots and observers. It's not only that lives would be saved, many lives. To know you had a sporting chance of escape from a break-up or flamer would make you much braver in a scrap.

Fortin switched to *The Maid of the Mountains*—'What e'er befall, I still recall, that sunlit mountain side'. Golly, how hearing these tunes gives you that nostalgic feeling! Now he's going on to *A Bachelor Gay am I*—'At seventeen, he falls in love quite madly with eyes of tender blue'. Ah, me! What wouldn't I give to be going to Daly's tonight!

Monday, June 25th

I had twenty minutes of jolly good fun gambolling among the clouds today. Kay was leading Courtneidge, Wilcox and me, and once clear of the heat haze, we were among enormous banks of cumulus reaching up to 14,000 feet, and not all that room between them. Kay was cheerful and excited over being given 'B' Flight, and wanted a fight to celebrate his promotion. So he led us ten miles and more over, and for two hours we trailed all over Hunland without seeing a single Hun.

He now took us above the clouds to 15,000, where the sky was a deep blue dome, then dived on the snow-white mountains below, and started a follow-my-leader party around the alpine tops, a chain of us sliding steeply down the slopes and zooming nearly vertically up the other side, then sailing along winding valleys, diving into precipitous canyons and climbing out again, and banking round bulging cliffs, wings skimming the solid-looking bluffs. It would have been interesting to have run into a bunch of Huns playing the same game. I thoroughly enjoyed it. In some ways contour chasing over cloud is one up on doing it over the ground—no risk, no red-tabs to report you, and the most wonderful sensation of being as free as a bird.

Back at the office, I found that the Case of the Shot Sergeant had taken a turn for the worse, for the orderly-room sergeant told me that there is talk he might peg out, as his wound has gone septic. Holy smoke, I'll be for the high jump if that happens, murder or manslaughter or something.

Last night a Hun bomber paid us a visit, dropping a string of bombs across the aerodrome. One fell with a terrific crash just outside our hut, which seemed to bend over under the blast, while a shower of stones and chunks of earth rattled down on the roof. In seconds the whole squadron was out in the open, in pyjamas. More bombs fell, and flames leapt up in La Gorgue. As it all petered out, somebody shouted, 'How about a swim, chaps?', and as it was a very warm night, we grabbed towels, trooped down to the canal bank, and within

Marchant, Babington,
Dimmock, Luxmore

Williams, Joske, Barrager

After a bathe in the River Lys. *Left to right:* Joske, Courtneidge, the author,
Asher, Marchant (with Jock), McDonald, Kay

Sketches from 54 Squadron's Song Book

Hughes

Courtneidge

Manfred von Richtofen (in cockpit) and members of Jasta II in the spring of 1917.
His brother Lothar in front, seated

Wilcox

Odell (with Jock)

Sopwith Triplanes
of No 8 Naval

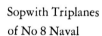

Sopwith Pups of No 46

Sopwith Camel

The author's Sutton's
Farm Pup, and his fitter
and rigger

R.F.C. mechanics escort a
salvaged Albatros fuselage

Third Battle of Ypres. A crashed D.F.W.

A Fokker D.R.I. Triplane of J.G.I. In rear, a Pfalz DIII

Izel, October 1917. *Left to right:* Dusgate, MacLeod, Hughes, Babington, Ferrie, Scott, Wilcox, the author, Odell, Thompson, Robeson, Joske

Izel, November 1917. *Left to right:* Thompson, Wilcox, Stevens, Babington, Cooper, Warwick, Atkinson, Allan, Robeson, Bulman

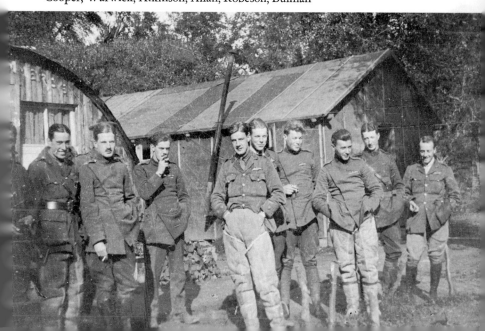

Battle of Cambrai. A D.F.W. shot down near Flesquières. 51st Division Highlanders examine it. The black crosses have been cut out of fin and fuselage

A Camel trench-strafing,
S.E.5 in rear
(Artist's impression)

minutes were all floating on the steely waters, hoping we wouldn't swim blindly into a dead cat or a bunch of stinging nettles. This morning we inspected the hole, thirty feet across, thirty yards from the hut. Near enough, thanks! Let's hope they won't do it again tonight, we're all set for a special do.

Tuesday, June 26th

Last night's binge was a send-off for Pratt (his second farewell party!) and to salute the two new flight-commanders, Scott and Kay. Marchant had already gone, and this latest binge made us realise what a mainstay he was in the Mess as a sort of cheer-you-up lunatic.

Normie Dimmock still reigns supreme at the piano, as Fortin prefers to be among the crowd doing the drinking and shouting. Dimmock's liquor needs are modest, in fact the piano gets more than he does. The sing-song was livelier than ever because Scott has brought with him a priceless book, properly bound and illustrated, of the songs sung by 54 Squadron. They had it done in Cambridge, and its title is *Cinquante-quatre*, which, so far as we're concerned, means 'Forty-six'.

Several ditties were new to us. Here for example is *The Song of Fifty-four*, sung to the tune of *We've Come Up from Somerset*. We sing it as *The Song of Forty-six*, and if it doesn't rhyme, who cares? The chorus goes:

> Oh, we've come up from Forty-six,
> We're the Sopwith Pups, you know,
> And wherever you beastly Huns may be,
> The Sopwith Pups will go.
> And if you want a proper scrap,
> Don't chase B.E.s any more,
> For we'll come up and do the job,
> Because we're Forty-six!

Another which we enjoyed, though it's a bit difficult when you're full of drink, is sung to the tune of *Sister Susie's Sewing Shirts for Soldiers*.

75

Heavy Handed Hans flies Halberstadters.
In handy Halberstadters for a Flight our Hans does Start.
His Oberst says, 'Oh, dash it!
For I fear that he will crash it.'
See how Heavy Handed Hans ham-handles handy Halberstadts.

The binge went on riotously until midnight, but I packed up at
11.0, because of the early job. I left the Mess to the tune of *Another
Little Drink Wouldn't do us any Harm*, and was asleep almost before I
could undress.

We had a good laugh at an article in one of today's newspapers
about the way the Huns paint their machines all the colours of the rainbow. They do it, wrote some 'expert', in order to give each other
confidence. What drivel! They don't need war-paint to give themselves confidence, they've got too much already, with their Albatros D-IIIs outclassing us on almost every count. The fact that nearly
all Huns are coloured, while we're chocolate-brown, is very useful
in dog-fights, when your shooting is in split-second bursts, because you
know instantly who is who. And their colourings sometimes help us
to know who we're scrapping with. For example, every Albatros in
the Richtofen Circus has some red paint on it, and the Baron himself
has an all-red machine. That's what the chaps say, and if it's true, we've
had several scraps with them.

Wednesday, June 27th

Another awkward episode with a dud engine today on a standby. My
companion was Scott, and we dashed off to La Bassée, where the Hun
was supposed to be, and searched among the clouds at 4,000, but he
wasn't there. For twenty minutes Scott hunted into Hunland at this
suicidal height, with archie continually at us, then he climbed northwards. Soon we saw, well to the east, some fifteen E.A. in a loose
group, and Scott climbed steeply towards them. We got closer and
closer, and I began to sweat, especially when I saw they were D-IIIs,
and especially when my engine began to run roughly. Suddenly there
was a horrible grinding falter in the beat of the engine, then a heart-
stopping clanking, and everything in front of me wobbled as if the

whole plane was going to break up. I switched off, and after a final hellish clatter the engine stopped with a lurch, and so did the propeller.

Meanwhile, Scott swept on unknowingly by himself. But there I was, nearly five miles over, with a dead engine and a stationary prop. I was facing east, but I soon rectified that. I glided west in complete silence, with not even the pluf-pluf-pluf of the turning prop, only the slight whistle of the bracing wires, in fact had I not been jittery over whether I'd get home or not, I'd have enjoyed a nice, soothing ride.

It was bad enough the other day, with just a dud engine, but then I at least had *some* revs, now I had nothing except height, 15,000 feet of it, though I was losing that fast. And, of course, I was a sitting duck for any Hun. Luckily, the wind wasn't against me. As I approached the Lines, archie started, and I had to lose a lot of height putting up my speed in a zigzag dive. Once clear, I made for La Gorgue, and arrived there at 800 feet, circled slowly and fired a red light. A whole platoon of men ran out to the centre track, and waited there for me to crash. They'd seen the dead prop. I pulled away for the run-in, lost height in a succession of S-turns, doing about 45 mph—any other machine but a Pup would drop out of your hand at that speed—and landed without trouble.

To cut a long story short, the big-end bearings had gone, and the inside of the engine was just a mess of chewed-up scrap metal. No wonder the poor old thing had felt a bit tired lately! The mechanics are on the job now, installing a new engine.

Scott landed not long after me, having mislaid his Huns. He had an encouraging word for my getting home without breaking anything. At the office he learned that his third pip had come through, which means another binge this evening. I think he'll make us a darned fine skipper, as he knows the ropes, coming from a squadron with longer experience of Pups than us—54 came out with them in December. Before that he had a spell as observer. He's something of a stunt artist too, and has started the chaps on it. Since my ticking off by Pratt, I haven't done much, nor has anybody else, but that's all changing.

This para is added after dinner. Bad news about Kay. He and McDonald went on a trip this evening to visit friends in 12 Squadron, at Wagonlieu, just west of Arras. When they took off on leaving, Kay stalled, fell into a spin, and crashed. He's badly injured. Poor old Kay, just as he won his captaincy. What damnable luck. The news snuffed out the binge, which had got under way before dinner.

Thursday, June 28th

News has just come that Kay is dead. Poor Kay. And poor me, too, another good friend gone west. It's bad enough when they go in a scrap, but to be killed through a slip while flying—what a waste! And he was such a topping fellow. It's odd that though we'd got friendly during the past week or so, I never knew his first name, and still don't, though I see from D.R.O.s that his initials were G. P.

The chaps seldom call each other by their Christian names, except when it's a nickname too, like Normie Dimmock. There are other nicknames, of course, such as Mac for McDonald, Chaps Marchant, Pic Williams, Taffy Hughes, Nobby Scott, but few people use them.

Friday, June 29th

An exciting show today on the 7 a.m. patrol, with six of us led by Scott. It was nice clear weather, with scattered masses of cumulus. We'd climbed gradually to 18,000 plus, and were well to the east of Arras when we saw eight Albatri 1,000 feet above, approaching from the east. You could scarcely see them, their wings seemed transparent in the early sunlight.

I had my usual fit of shaking with excitement as they began their dive, and just had time to touch wood as they closed, guns flashing, tracers smoking at us, then we'd scattered, they were among us, and six separate scraps were in progress. Everything was confusion. One, yellow and black stripes, swung on to my tail, but I saw him, kicked on right rudder even before I heard the rak-ak-ak, skidded off, nearly hit another Pup, zoomed sharply, machines whizzing all round me. More rak-ak-ak from behind, more tracer, I kick the rudder again, the Pup lurches out sideways, a Hun flashes above me on the tail of a Pup, tracers come from every direction, and I haven't fired a shot yet.

A blue-and-white Hun crosses in front, with leader's streamers— they're much longer than ours—I yank the Pup behind, squirt tracer, he banks steeply round to try to get on my tail, I out-turn him, keep firing short bursts, suddenly he rears up and goes over sideways, and I lose him.

More rak-ak-ak-ak and bullet-holes appear in the fairing just in front of me, one smashes along the Vickers. I kick the rudder hard and skid round most of 180 degrees, the Pup's nose dips in protest, a red-and-green Albatros is rising in front of me, fifty yards off, going my way, this is my chance, I press the trigger, twenty rounds, then rak-ak-ak behind me, another flat skid, the Hun, old yellow stripes, sweeps by in a climbing curve, below him I see the green chap diving away, I twist behind him, firing, but he's moving much too fast, and I level out.

Now I'm below the fight, and as I look up, a black-and-red Hun comes hurtling down in a spin, whizzes past me, barely twenty yards away, nearly corkscrews into me, my heart stops. I see the pilot's helmeted head bent forward against his gun-butts. It all happens in seconds, and I'm climbing up to the fight again. But before I can get there, first one machine, then another, pulls away, everyone scatters, the fight's over. I sit there panting, mouth open, gasping in air.

It couldn't have lasted more than three or four minutes, five at the most. Talk about one crowded hour of life, we live it in crowded seconds. But six of us had amazingly outfought eight Albatri. Once more it was the height that enabled us to do it, the D-III just can't turn as tightly as a Pup at 18,000.

As we re-formed on Scott, he fired a red light, the distress signal, and set off in a half-glide westwards. Back at the aerodrome, he said we'd sent three down out of control, of which he reckoned one was his—the one I'd seen fall with the pilot apparently out of action—but nobody knew who'd got the others, as we'd all put bursts into two or three of them. As nobody had been able to watch whether they crashed, it was all officially inconclusive. This is the hell of dog-fights, with every pilot shooting at every Hun, and the whole thing over in a couple of minutes. Just to see one drop out of the fight doesn't count for much. You may use all your ammo, your machine may be riddled, you may have escaped death by inches in a fierce little battle, yet you've nothing positive to report, and it's all written off in the records as—an indecisive encounter with E.A.

Scott left us because he'd shot away half his propeller. The Sopwith-

Kauper interrupter gear with which the Pup is fitted is complicated mechanically, and sometimes goes wrong, and then the bullets go through the prop. It's this gear which slows down the rate of fire of the Vickers. In the air, when you press the trigger, instead of getting the fast rattle of a ground gun, you have a frustrating pop! pop! pop! pop! The Huns have a much more efficient gear, for the Spandau fires very fast. In fact, when you hear the twin Spandaus of the Albatros opening up on your tail, they sound like some vast canvas being ripped by a giant. And your answer is pop! pop! pop!

Looking back on this scrap, I realise that however much you're scared before you start, once you're in it you don't feel excitement or fear, you fight in a sort of daze. When it's over, and you find you're still alive, you feel both exhausted and exhilarated. In fact, what with the sun shining, the blue sky above, and the white clouds below, and your engine running smoothly, and the Pup handling like the spirited thing she is, you *can* feel that you've enjoyed it. Like you enjoy a plunge in an icy-cold mountain pool—once you get out of it.

Saturday, June 30th

Rain since dawn, and no flying at all. We've all been down in the mouth because Kay's funeral was hanging over us. He was laid next to Gunnery and Stephen. To me it was a very depressing hour. It was bad enough with the other two, though one I never knew and the other only slightly, but Kay had become a friend.

June 30th (Diary)

Thank goodness, they were able to provide Kay with a coffin. I was dreading the job of having to handle his corpse in sackcloth.

Sunday, July 1st

I'm writing this in the Mess for a change, drawing inspiration from Fortin, who's banging away at the piano. You'd never believe it, but he's been playing hymns, because it's Sunday, I suppose. But he was playing them in ragtime. Now he's switched to *The Bing Boys*—'If you were the Only Girl in the World'. He's always playing these catchy tunes, with the result that since he arrived, everybody goes around humming and whistling them.

As a week had passed since the C. of I. came, and I'd not heard a word, and hadn't a notion of whether or not the sergeant had passed away, and was beginning to go grey with worry, I tackled the new R.O., Lieutenant McNeil. He rang up somebody, and learned that the sergeant was back on duty, and the whole thing had been washed out. Nobody had bothered to send word to the criminal on trial, but at least it's good to know that I won't spend the rest of the war in jail.

In the afternoon I was so bored I went up alone on the excuse of an engine test, but actually for an amble round the countryside. The rain had stopped, but the clouds were solid at 500 feet. I decided to have a close look at the Lines to the south-east, which at their nearest are only three and a half miles away. I flew to Armentières and beyond until I hit the trenches, then swung south and passed over Neuve Chapelle and other places that were battlefields in the big push of March 1915.

Everything was quiet as I slid smoothly along at 300 feet over our trenches. Not a single gun fired at me from the Boche trenches 100 yards or so distant, and nothing much moved in ours, except when troops looked up and waved. It was all so peaceful I was puzzled, especially when I noticed that along one lengthy stretch of no-man's-land, and the trench systems on either side, the earth was tinged with green.

I went down as far as the La Bassée canal, then turned back to have another look at the greenery. It was the portion of the Line opposite Laventie, and I soon realised that the reason the earth was not the usual raw pockmarked brown was because the grass was growing! They obviously don't do much shelling around here, I thought. From ruined cottages and shacks behind the support trenches troops came out to stare and wave as I circled over them as slowly as I dared. Suddenly I realised from their uniforms that they were Portuguese, and that explained everything. On this part of the front both sides sensibly agree to live and let live.

But what amazed me was when out of a cottage with the roof half gone and covered with tarpaulins, not more than 300 yards behind the front line, four women, all youngish, came out and waved with shawls. French farmers, all elderly, are wonderful the way they ignore the war and cultivate their fields within shelling range, but they don't venture as close as this. Anyway, these weren't old men but young women. Obviously, the Portuguese are sensible about sex too, and set up their brothels within easy reach of the front-line troops. And why not? Why should only the bases and depots enjoy such conveniences?

I think it's pretty good that the Portuguese joined in this war at all, but you'd hardly say they're tough troops. If the Boche were to attack this part of the Line in strength he'd come slap through, and probably reach our aerodrome in a few hours. A cheerful prospect. I only hope it doesn't happen while I'm here.

[This casually noted possibility was to be dramatically enacted nine months later, when on April 9th, 1918, the Germans, their main offensive towards Amiens having been halted, launched a secondary attack on a narrow front centred on Neuve Chapelle. Their seven divisions overwhelmed the single Portuguese division holding the Line, as well as adjacent British divisions. By evening, advanced German troops had reached La Gorgue aerodrome.]

After I'd landed, the Major sent for me and spoke with some asperity, saying, 'Here you go up on an engine test in bad weather, when not another machine's in the air, which should only take ten minutes, and you stay out for forty, so starting alarms that you'd crashed or lost yourself. Do try to behave with a little sense in future, Lee.'

Ah, well! I said scarcely a word, but that makes the fourth—or is it the fifth?—little chat I've had with the Major.

Tuesday, July 3rd

The most important news today is that I've got back the second pip that I had to give up when I came to the R.F.C. eighteen months ago. Of course, this means nothing so far as pay and appointment are concerned, but two do look better, and make you feel better, especially when you've been finding yourself junior in rank to youngsters who came direct to the R.F.C. practically from school.

Two jobs yesterday, both of which came to nothing, one led by

Courtneidge, the other by Joske, who took over 'B' Flight when Captain Plenty went home. Joske will be acting as C.O. when the Major goes on leave this evening. Today, two more uneventful patrols, but the other flights were luckier, and got two Huns down.

A Captain Long has arrived to take Kay's flight, and he's very much a star in our modest set-up, for he has the D.S.O. and M.C. He is short, round and red-faced, his nickname is Tubby, and we gather that he's extremely fed up with life because he was a squadron commander in England, but got annoyed with a too-officious A.P.M. in London, and punched him on the nose, which is a thing every self-respecting R.F.C. type would dearly like to do. Punishment: unstuck and sent to a flight in 46!

But his ribbons have brightened up the Mess quite a lot, as so far we've only had the Major's M.C. to gaze upon. The squadron still hasn't won a decoration, and we can't fathom why, as apart from Pratt, both Joske and McDonald have well deserved them. It's not so good for morale when chaps in other squadrons get them right and left.

Apart from Captain Long, we have other newcomers, Bird, who is also chubby and cheerful, Thompson, a Scot who's had a crash that has scarred his face, and Armitage, who's just another pink-cheeked Warbabe. It's amazing how young they come, and all now in R.F.C. maternity jackets and split-ass caps. Maybe that's why we older types hang on to our regimental uniforms.

I see from the papers that the Germans raided Harwich yesterday with a dozen bombers, killing twelve and wounding thirty-six. I wouldn't be surprised if they had a go at London soon.

P.S. I'd finished this letter and sealed it for the post, but have opened it to add news that has just come in, at 10 p.m. The squadron has to move to Bruay, a town thirty miles south of here. So it's goodbye to La Gorgue and our wonderful, dirty old canal—and to the wonderful croaking old frogs, too!

Friday, July 6th

We duly moved this morning, all the squadron equipment being packed and ready by six. A squadron of eighteen machines has a tremendous amount of bulky maintenance gear, and it all has to be manœuvred into a set number of transport vehicles, but they were well on the road by the time we took off at 7.30. Joske led the three flights to the new aerodrome, which is good level grass, very different from La Gorgue, though not pleasant for flying as it is so close to the town. We share it with 40 Squadron, and are using their Mess until ours is ready. There are several chaps in 40 whom I know, among them the Field of Agincourt Barlow who was in the ferrying fiasco to Candas.

We spent the morning settling in to our snug little separate cubicles. Immediately after lunch, Courtneidge, Odell, Eberlin and I went on attachment to No 8 Naval Squadron at Mont St Eloi, just this side of Vimy Ridge, scene of much savage fighting during the Battle of Arras in April. No 8 have Sopwith Triplanes, the only British scouts the Huns avoid. The squadron is under canvas, and the landing area is continuously lined by spectators, namely troops, mostly Canadian, in rest from the front.

We visitors are on standby duty, and within ten minutes Courtneidge and I went up to chase an artillery two-seater. Later we were told that as we approached his beat our listening station heard him signal his unit that he 'was forced to descend as two enemy scouts are preparing to attack'. He certainly beat the gun, as when we spotted him he was already off eastwards, nose down.

We continued the patrol along the Scarpe valley towards Douai, and here we ran into a scrap, four F.E.s doing their usual defensive circle while four D-IIIs tried to break in. We crept up close, hoping to catch one unawares, but as soon as we opened fire at 100 yards' range they pulled away eastwards.

We stayed throughout the day at St Eloi, and did several chases more, but without once getting within effective range. The Hun two-seaters here are very on the alert, probably because they have no chance at all if they let themselves be caught by Tripes. When evening came we had drinks in the Nautical's Mess, in a marquee, followed by a good dinner.

What we Pup merchants didn't find terribly laughable was that the reason we are working with No 8 is that half their pilots are away collecting new machines, and we're helping out until they get them.

They once had Pups like us (though a *year* before us!), but gave them up as obsolescent in April last, the month that 46 was equipped with them, and replaced them with Triplanes. Now they reckon the Tripe is out of date too, and they're getting the new two-gun Camel. The 40 Squadron boys feel even more sore about this than we do, for their Nieuports are older than our Pups.

[The R.N.A.S. were at this time converting their fighter squadrons from Triplanes to Bentley-engined Camels because their pilots had found that the latest mark of Albatros, the D-V, was slightly superior to the Triplane. This favoured treatment, so baffling to indignant R.F.C. pilots flying obsolete and obsolescent aeroplanes, was one of the consequences of years of maladministration by the higher echelons of the R.F.C. and R.N.A.S. The background to this far from creditable history is examined in Appendix A, *The Failure in High Command.*]

Saturday, July 7th

Up early again this morning, this time on an O.P. of four led by McDonald. It was a beautiful clear morning. We left the ground at 7.15, and Mac took us up to 20,000, well into Hunland. The Huns were still abed, so we just floated along, high above some hefty icebergs. But for some reason it wasn't nearly so cold as it usually is at this height.

Every time I go up to the 20,000 level I get that strange feeling of having ceased to be an ordinary human being. I'm sitting there in a tight cockpit, the whirling prop ahead, with wings reaching out to either side, miraculously sustaining me, motionless in the sky among other motionless winged machines, the roar of the engine unnoticed.

I'm four miles up. I look down, and the earth is a vast bowl, with the horizon curving up to my level. The ground below is an immense patchwork of little shapes, green, brown, grey, with a network of veins which are the roads and rivers, and snaking across it all, the Lines, the long brown battlefield where millions of men are fighting each other in dank holes, like rats in sewers. But up here one feels part of the sky and the clouds, remote from the shambles beneath.

Dreaming away like this, I suddenly came to when Mac rocked his wings and dropped at once into a steep dive eastwards. So there we were, the four of us, at one moment motionless, the next plunging towards earth, the wind screaming in the wires. I soon spotted the target, four D-IIIs about 5,000 feet below, and going our way. It was a madly exhilarating feeling, swooping down on them out of the sky, the nearest thing to a cavalry charge I can imagine.

They hadn't a notion we were coming. I touched wood, glued my eye to the Aldis, took aim on the Hun at the right rear of the formation. At about eighty yards Mac's tracers went away, and we all fired. The Albatri immediately scattered, and we swerved after them. My Hun, blue and green, zoomed up and swung over in a half-roll, and I followed him under the impetus of my dive, got well above, banked steeply, dived at him again, fired twenty rounds, the tracers splashing all round the pilot. But at this height he had the advantage. He turned sharply, climbed steeper than I could, came back at me firing, but went underneath me. By the time I'd banked to find him, he'd vanished below.

He was an experienced pilot, and would probably have got me eventually, at the height we fought, 15,000, but was put off by the other Pups. I can't think why I didn't hit him in the first dive, my shooting must be very bad, or my sight is not accurately aligned. When we landed, Mac claimed his Hun, having closed to within twenty yards of it, where he couldn't miss, and it went down vertically, clearly out of control. Courtneidge and Eberlin also had brief scraps, but, like mine, indecisive. But we all enjoyed that glorious plummeting down through space to the attack, it was really thrilling.

Sunday, July 8th

I hardly know how to begin. Such wonderful news! It is 5 a.m., and we're all up, dressed, waiting, ready to fly to England!

Yes, the squadron is coming to England. Today!

Just after midnight we were roused out of bed and told to report quickly to the C.O.'s hut. There, Joske announced, with enforced calm, that he'd had orders from Advanced H.Q. that we were to fly to England at eight o'clock. At first we thought it was a spoof, that

Joske had been out on a secret binge, but when we realised it was true our yells must have wakened all Bruay.

My kit is packed and I'm all set. In three hours' time we'll be leaving for Calais and good old England. But surely it's all a dream? Soon Watt will awake me with 'Fine morning, sir, four o'clock, you're on patrol in half an hour'.

I could be with you even before you get this letter, but I'll send it all the same, just before I take off. One never knows!

Hell! Hell! Hell! It is six, and it has just started to rain!!! Nasty drizzling stuff from low clouds that look as though they could last until midday. We're just off to have breakfast in 40 Squadron's Mess. And are they all green with jealousy!

I can't bear it any more. Eight p.m. (*p.m.*) and it has rained all day without pause. This is positively agonising. We have sat around hour after hour, feverishly biting our nails until now we've none left to bite. The men went at 8 a.m. to Boulogne with light transport and our kit, and we should be safe if they get over the Channel before the high-ups change their minds, a catastrophe we've been expecting every minute.

It's past eleven and we're still here. As our kit and Mess servants have gone, we're having to stay the night at a hotel in Bruay. Thirteen of us had a madly boisterous dinner (13!). We sang everything we knew, then came to bed praying for fine weather. But in spite of the intake of liquor I can't sleep, and shall finish this off before hitting the pillow.

It's a terrific feeling to know that tomorrow, at the first break in the clouds and rain, we shall be heading for home. Apparently we have to thank the Hun for it. The Gothas made another raid on London yesterday, killing many people and causing a public outcry for proper air defence. And 46 is going to try to stop them doing it again.

Monday, July 9th

We've been pottering around the Bessoneau hangars all the morning, looking up every other minute at the low clouds in search of that snatch of blue that would signal a break, but the rain just goes on and on and on. It really is torture waiting from hour to hour like this.

It seems true that 46 is being called to England to prevent any more day raiders reaching London, at any rate for a couple of weeks or so, until the defences are organised. We shall be stationed somewhere near London, we hear, which is an extra lump of sugar.

We've just had lunch, and most of us are going into Bruay, where there's an Army Canteen concert party. I expect we shall stay the night at the hotel again. There won't be much to write about, so I'll get this letter off now.

No 1 A.D., St Omer,
Tuesday, July 10th

I'm scribbling this note to help pass away what would otherwise be a trying wait, and to put down what has happened while it is fresh in my mind. We (there are three of us here at the Depot, the others are at Calais) were up at dawn, and had pre-flying tea and biscuits, but the weather is against us once more. I'm writing this in the ante-room while we wait until breakfast proper starts, about seven.

The whole squadron (except me!) landed here last evening, but Joske and Thompson had engine trouble, and had to stay behind when the rest continued on to Calais. We are very worried in case we can't catch up the squadron before it sets out to cross the Channel.

But I'd better start at the beginning, to explain why I'm here, and especially why I came by road. I mentioned that we drove into Bruay, and after tea went to a concert party. The first few turns were good, and we were looking forward to being well cheered up, when in the middle of a comic song a corporal appeared, who came to us with loud whisperings, upon which we all (the first two rows of the stalls) got up and excitedly trooped out of the place. I felt sorry for the chap on the stage—we should have sent him an apology.

Outside, we found that the rain had stopped and the clouds were lifting. Crossley cars waited, and we rushed up to the aerodrome to find the Pups all lined up ready. We climbed blissfully into them, ran up the engines, and began taking off in succession by flights, 'C' Flight being last, and me second to Courtneidge to move off. (I forgot to mention that Scott is on leave, as well as the Major and Dimmock.) We had to borrow two pilots from 40 Squadron, the C.O., Major Keen, who was to lead us, and another chap to take Scott's machine.

I was on the left of the line of 'C' Flight, and some thirty yards to my left were the Bessoneau canvas hangars running alongside my take-off course, but there was plenty of room, with an open aerodrome ahead. As Courtneidge shot away, I opened up and moved off, but then, out of the corner of my eye (fortunately, my goggles were up, or I wouldn't have seen him), spotted that a machine on my right had moved off out of turn. As my tail came up for the take-off, I sensed him coming towards me. He'd swerved across the other 'C' Flight Pups, and was charging broadside into me. Instinctively, I banked violently to the left, and went slap into the side of a hangar.

I was doing 70 mph when I hit, and the prop and engine cowling went through the canvas, but it held the wings. I wasn't hurt, except that I cracked my face against the gun-butt. I suppose I shall have a black eye tomorrow.

By the time I'd scrambled from my badly bent A6202, all the others, including the fellow who caused the crash, were in the air and on the way to Calais. Imagine my feelings! I swore and swore until the 40 Squadron mechanics looked at me with a certain respect. They told me the villain of the piece was the 40 Squadron pilot, whom they thought had never flown a Pup before. He had swung badly taking off, and but for my panic swerve, there would have been a nasty double crash.

So there was I, sole member of 46, as miserable as hell. I saw myself remaining there, without even my shaving kit, for all the two weeks while the machine was repaired, and was wondering whether suicide wasn't the best way out when an orderly came sprinting from the squadron office—an officer of 46 was wanted on the phone. I ran across, very puzzled.

A voice said, 'Are you an officer of 46 Squadron?', and when I said 'Yes', went on: 'The General Officer Commanding wishes to speak you.' Just like that! For a second I couldn't think who he meant, then there was a click, and a deep, gruff voice asked, 'Have all the squadron got off safely?'

That deep, gruff voice. I'd heard it before. Boom! It was General Trenchard!

Can you imagine me having to reply, 'Everybody but me, sir.' 'And why haven't you gone too?' he asked. I felt about two feet high having to say, 'I had to crash into a hangar to avoid being hit by another machine.'

I expected him to snort 'You clumsy oaf!', or some worse tick-off. Instead he asked, 'Are you hurt?' And when I said 'No, sir', he went on: 'Go immediately to No 1 Aircraft Depot and collect a new machine. Tell the O.C. Depot that this is on my personal authority. Then join the squadron without delay.' I mumbled, 'Very good, sir', there was another click, and he was gone.

I stood there in a daze for quite a time. Then something exploded. I grew up to ten feet. Then I rushed out feeling as though I'd been promoted colonel. It was amazing what it did just to say, quite casually, 'General Trenchard's personal orders'. He'd said I had to go to St Omer immediately—I was on the road in a Crossley in five minutes. He'd said I'd to hurry. The driver went like the wind. And at the Depot, when I saw the C.O., the mention of the magic words set the whole place spinning in small circles. I was practically invited to go and choose the best Pup they had.

And I did! Within half an hour I'd taken over a beauty, a new one, B1777, with along the fuselage a label, BRITISH GUIANA. It was one of the aeroplanes provided from their contribution towards the cost of the war. I was panting to test it, but the weather had turned too dud again.

Soon after, I found that Joske and Thompson were there. What none of us could understand was why General Trenchard should take so much interest in 46 getting away safely, even to making a personal enquiry, when he has hordes of staff blokes to do all that. There must be something very top-level in all this.[1]

We all three went down to St Omer and dined at the Hôtel de Commerce, then came back, scrounged some blankets, and slept in our clothes, hoping for a decent morning. But it isn't.

From noises coming from the dining-room it sounds as if breakfast

1. The reasons that caused General Trenchard to show personal interest in the move of 46 Squadron are made clear in Part Five, *The Air Defence of London*.

is nearly ready, so I'll finish off this note. I suppose it's hardly worth while posting it, I could be in England before lunch. But you never know. If luck still goes against us, we could be here another week!

Calais 8 a.m.

I never got that breakfast, nor even had time to get this letter off. The clouds suddenly lifted, Joske started yelling, and we rushed out to our machines. Five minutes later we were in the air. It took half an hour to get to Calais, with a strong bumpy wind. My new machine is lovely to fly, and has a first-class engine. The whole squadron is taking off in ten minutes' time. We hope! But I'm taking no more chances, I'm posting this in the Mess now!

Part Five

Air Defence of London

[During the time the squadron was in England, I wrote no letters, for the simple reason that my wife was with me.]

Not until 10.30 did sixteen of us take off from Calais aerodrome and nose out to sea in a loose three-flight formation, which climbed to 8,000 feet to cross the Channel. A vast blanket of cloud, stretching to the western horizon, hid England from view.

In an empty sky, the squadron flew steadily on until, when halfway across, Courtneidge, leading 'C' Flight, suddenly fired a green Very light, the signal of distress, began a downwards glide and eventually disappeared as a minute speck through the level bank of cloud far below. Led now by me, the rest of the flight pressed on until, as the squadron gradually lost height and dropped beneath the cloud, the welcoming line of white cliffs showed ahead.

We landed our craft safely at Lympne, near Folkestone, and from there sent off telegrams to wives, sweethearts, relations, friends. No one could find out what had happened to Courtneidge, and not until next day did we learn that he had ditched near a patrol boat, and been picked up, little the worse for his adventure. From Lympne we resumed the journey over Kent to Sutton's Farm aerodrome, by Hornchurch in Essex.

We were met by Major Babington, with Scott and Dimmock summarily recalled from leave, and by the other ranks who had left Bruay with baggage and light equipment on the Sunday morning. We all settled at once into our new home, four wooden hangars and an encampment of huts and tents sited close by the farmhouse, at the edge of an immense aerodrome of smooth grassland.

The squadron was immediately placed on a stand-by basis from dawn to dusk, and nobody was permitted to leave the camp. Within the hour, the Major held a practice alarm, to the alerting screech of a raucous triple-horn klaxon. All ranks were instructed in what they had to do, and during the next few days further practice alarms quickly brought the squadron to satisfactory competence, not only in speedy taking the air, but in the manœuvrings of the three flights in squadron formation.

To every pilot the sudden transfer from the strains of offensive patrols to this carefree readiness for the one purpose of chasing Gothas was almost as good as being on leave. The other ranks shared in this happy condition, and because nobody expected to be in England for more than a fortnight, no time was lost in making hay while the sun shone. Relations sped to Hornchurch from all over the kingdom, and soon there was not a spare lodging to be had in the district.

On a sudden inspiration I had, within an hour of my arrival, gained the Major's consent to take a room for my wife and myself in the only place where I could 'live out' of camp and yet be virtually in it, Sutton's Farm itself, right alongside the Officers' Mess hutments.

As the farmer's wife, Mrs Crawford, could offer only a bedroom, I won permission to erect a small marquee between her garden and the Mess, and here my wife, aided by batman Watt, provided most of our meals during our stay at Sutton's. As the weather was usually fine, she was able to enjoy the use of the farm's gardens and to play tennis on the lawn.

Naturally, she became known to all the pilots, and joined in the displays and other special occasions, ranging from air demonstrations to cricket matches, with which Major Babington sought to relieve the tedium, which affected all ranks, of waiting hour after hour for air-raid alarms.

The first days sped swiftly with relations and friends, who were allowed to enter the camp at set times. As for the evenings, London was within easy reach, and despite the gloom of lighting restrictions, London meant theatres, restaurants, night-clubs, dancing, and for the bachelors, girls. None of us paused to consider what lay behind our good fortune, other than to thank the Gothas for it. We would not have been profoundly interested even could we have known of all that lay behind our unexpected withdrawal from the fighting line.

For reasons that reached back a decade, Britain entered the war without the means to resist air attack. During 1916 an unco-ordinated assortment of naval and military aeroplanes, mostly obsolescent, was able to dispose of the menace of the Zeppelins, but when the Germans turned to day raids by fast well-armed Gotha formations the planes that rose to meet them, some from training units and acceptance parks, were hopelessly outmatched by the concentrated fire of the Gothas' guns, three to each machine.

The first raids, which caused casualties at Folkestone in May and Sheerness in early June, evoked little reaction, but when on June 13th fourteen Gothas reached London and circled around dropping bombs at their pleasure, causing a casualty list of 162 killed and 432 injured, people and government woke up. Lloyd George and his War Cabinet hastily decided to double the size of the R.F.C., a futile gesture when even existing demands for aircraft and engines could not be met.

But they also sent to France for Field Marshal Haig and General Trenchard, who as G.O.C. of the Flying Corps in the Field was the Commander-in-Chief's voice and hand in all matters of the air. Trenchard declared that no bombers were available to attack the Gotha bases, but as a temporary measure, while an efficient Home Defence organisation was built up, he could provide two front-line fighter squadrons to patrol on either side of the Channel, but only on condition that they should return to France by July 5th, to take part in the coming offensive.

The Cabinet accepted this proposal, and on June 21st Trenchard sent No 56 Squadron, with S.E.s, to Bekesbourne, near Canterbury, and No 66 Squadron, with Pups, to Calais. During the fortnight that followed, no raids took place, but the respite was not long enough to build up a Home Defence system. Nevertheless, on July 5th and 6th, on the order of the C.I.G.S., Sir William Robertson, the two squadrons returned to their normal front-line duties. By an oversight the Cabinet were not informed of this move.

On the next day, Saturday, June 7th, the Gothas came again, twenty-one of them releasing their bombs on the capital without interference, and causing 250 casualties. Only one was shot down, although seventy-eight pilots of the R.F.C. went up, and seventeen of the R.N.A.S., but as an outraged Cabinet now learned, not the pilots of Nos 56 and 66 Squadrons. Aghast at the renewed outburst of anger and censure from public, parliament and the national press, the Cabinet held an immediate meeting in an atmosphere bordering on panic. The C.I.G.S. wrote to Haig: '. . . much excitement was shown. One would have thought the world was coming to an end. I could not get in a word edgeways.'

Following this meeting, Robertson telegraphed Haig: 'The Cabinet have decided at a special meeting this afternoon that Home Defence Forces must be strengthened at once by two first-class fighting squadrons, and have ordered me to direct you to despatch two squadrons tomorrow to England.' He added that the Cabinet wanted a retaliatory bombing attack on Mannheim.

'Two good fighting squadrons will proceed to England tomorrow,' Haig telegraphed, and Trenchard selected No 46 and another squadron. As already related, his orders reached No 46 at midnight. But Haig added a warning: 'Fight for air supremacy preparatory to forthcoming operations commenced by us this morning. . . . Withdrawal of two squadrons will certainly delay favourable decision in the air and render our victory more difficult and more costly in aeroplanes and pilots. If the raid on Mannheim is undertaken in addition, the operations may have to be abandoned.'

Forced to think again, the Cabinet decided on the 9th to make do with one squadron and to drop the Mannheim project. Both squadrons would already have been in England, as Haig had promised, but for the bad weather. The second squadron's orders were cancelled on the 9th, but now arose the possibility that while No 46 was held up by rain, the Gothas might be better favoured. At R.F.C. Headquarters, anxiety mounted as rain persisted through the 9th. Then in the evening came the break—but it was an opportunity for the Gothas as well as for 46. There could be no excuse if the squadron failed to get away, to reach England before the raiders paid another visit. It is understandable that General Trenchard wished personally to be sure that 46 was on its way, and that there would not again be an incensed Cabinet to placate.

Oblivious of these hidden happenings, the pilots of 46 prepared light-heartedly to meet the Gothas. We had two main tasks to tackle, the first to get off the ground as quickly as possible after the alarm had come from the Home Defence Group, the second to develop tactics for a concentrated squadron attack on a powerfully armed bomber formation.

With every alarm, practice or in earnest, the squadron became more and more adept at speeding up the take-off. As soon as the warning *Readiness* came on the phone to the squadron office, and the klaxon shrilled, the whole camp leapt to action. Every man dropped whatever he was doing and ran to the hangars, the mechanics to haul the Pups to the tarmac and start them, the pilots to throw on their flying kit and clamber into their planes.

Within ninety seconds the eighteen pilots could be seated in their cockpits, taxi-ing out by flights to predetermined positions on the aerodrome. If the order to patrol had already come, flights took off at once and assembled in the air. Barely two minutes would have elapsed since the klaxon blared out its summons. If the order were held, the pilots waited, blipping their engines ready for instant take-off. Then as the call to patrol reached the office, a white Very light shot into the air, and immediately came the impressive roar of the three flights leaving the ground together. They settled swiftly into a steep climb, in vic formation, with Babington in command, flying on a flank.

The appointed patrol height reached, 15,000 feet, the squadron flew up and down its beat, which ran from Hainault Farm aerodrome, some twenty miles to the north-west, to Joyce Green aerodrome, near Dartford. Orders forbade the squadron to leave this beat except to tackle approaching bombers.

With almost daily practice, the squadron quickly reached expert standards in formation flying. Major Babington evolved a system of air drill, the three flights responding to his signals, given by arm waving and Very lights from his independent machine. The three flights wheeled to right or left, or turned about, as a squadron or by flights. They flew in line abreast of flights, in line astern, or in echelon, or at different height levels, or in line abreast of all eighteen planes. Steep dives at the hangars, taking the role of an enemy formation, were practised in both squadron and flight formation.

It was 'C' Flight commander, Scott, who set the pace in these screaming, near-vertical descents, sometimes so fast as to give us all uneasy moments with thoughts of wings folding back, and similar possibilities. An alternative finale was for the six of us to spin down in formation from around 6,000 feet to 500, then level out, re-form, and land sedately as a well-drilled flight.

These exercises gave pilots immense confidence in each other's exactness of flying. The flight of six would close up very tightly, the leader's echelon men edging their wing-tips to within three feet of his fuselage, spaced halfway between his main planes and tail. Then the next pair would edge in similarly, then the sixth man, until all were set in as tight a bunch as was humanly possible. On a slow glide, pilots could even conduct a shouted cross-talk. All impractical from the angle of air fighting, but a satisfying demonstration of piloting skill.

These various exhibitions set a new standard in formation flying, for nothing so expert had yet been attempted by a whole squadron. Developments in later years in formation aerobatics by aeroplanes with much more powerful engines may well have outshone these efforts, but in 1917 they were unique. From these manœuvres evolved a further distinction, for 46 Squadron was the first to develop a tactical plan for staging a concerted three-flight attack on an enemy bomber formation, with the design of first breaking it up and then, taking every advantage of the Gotha's known blind spots, of moving in on individual machines by flights and half-flights.

It was a great disappointment to the squadron that no chance came to try out this well-rehearsed plan, for we were convinced that we had the measure of even the largest formation. But although we took the air for alarms on July 22nd, August 8th, 12th, 14th, 18th (during a rainstorm) and 22nd, the raiders were content to attack coastal targets and never approached the squadron's set beat.

The one raid when there might have been a fight was that on August 12th, when ten Gothas appeared off Felixstowe. The squadron was in the air within two minutes of the alarm reaching Sutton's Farm, and it was unfortunate that it was not at once released from its normal line, for it could almost certainly have intercepted the enemy bombers as they flew south-westwards towards Southend.

As it was, edged as far to the east as Babington could risk without breaking orders, the pilots watched the bursts of archie over Southend and the tiny specks that were the enemy. The German commander may well have seen, in addition to the locally based defence aeroplanes climbing up to his level, the distant, disciplined formation waiting between him and London, for his raiders dropped their bombs in the Southend area and turned seawards for home. This raid, and that on Kent coastal resorts on August 22nd, were the last to be made by day.

Among the many senior army officers and other distinguished people who visited Sutton's Farm to witness the quick take-off and the formation drill was Field Marshal Sir John French, C.-in-C. Home Forces, but his visit was unfortunately marred by the squadron's only fatal accident in England. During the final formation spin of the air demonstration, Eberlin of 'C' Flight failed to pull out early enough and dived into the ground. The only other crash was a spectacular effort by the Canadian, Captain Fortin, who while skimming low across the aerodrome gave too much attention to a girl in the road alongside. His wheels touched the ground, and the plane somer-saulted for 200 yards, disintegrating as it went, but amazingly the pilot's only serious injury was a broken ankle.

Apart from real and practice alarms, and air drill, the only flying that we could enjoy was firing practice against a ground target, and brief 'engine tests', which meant joy-riding around the locality, never far from the aerodrome, and usually at very low altitudes. The popu-lace, much impressed by the formation flying, and convinced that the squadron was keeping the Gothas away, were cheerfully tolerant of roaming Pups skimming over their chimney pots and brushing the tops of the trees in their gardens.

Through the hot dog–days of August, confined to the camp, we all had too much time on our hands. We tried to fill it in a variety of ways—cricket, tennis on the extemporised court, badminton in a hangar, gardening around the Mess huts, throwing each other in the ornamental pond, or working up six-a-side water fights, with fire buckets, basins, jugs and chamber pots. Sometimes we were reduced to betting on how many goldfish could be grabbed from the pond in a minute. The pond was also useful to sit in half naked when the sun was high, and especially to give 'Guns', now messing officer, a ducking whenever the food failed to satisfy.

Under such conditions we grew to know each other more closely than had been the habit in France, and formed friendships deeper than were possible before, as was evidenced in part by the general use of first names and nicknames.

A sideline activity was the christening of the Pups, for everyone had the label of his fancy painted along the fuselage. In 'C' Flight, Scott's machine was *Wonga!*, Odell's *Otazel*, Hughes' *Brandy*, Courtneidge's *Will-o'-the-Wisp*, and my own *Chin-Chow*.

Occasionally, when the weather was unquestionably unfit for flying, Babington obtained permission from Headquarters for an early wash-out, which meant a long evening in London, the chief limitations being the cost and the need to catch the last train back from Fenchurch Street. This journey could hold its thrills, for it was Tubby Long's hobby to drive the train, which he contrived to arrange quite often. You could always tell when he was on the footplate by the jerky way the train drew up at Barking! But Long was soon to leave the squadron, having regained his rank of major on posting to command a squadron in Palestine.

Sometimes on these visits to Town those with business at Charing Cross Station would see a succession of ambulance trains bringing badly wounded troops by the thousand. They were some of the casualties from the desperate fighting that had developed in the Flanders advance, later to be known by the sinister name of Passchendaele. Ugly rumours spread that we were suffering far heavier casualties than authority admitted.

Reports came too that the air fighting was more savage than ever before. Richtofen was there with his enlarged 'Circus', the three-Jasta, Jagdgeschwader I, spearhead of the German attempt to gain mastery of the air over the battlefield, and casualties were heavy, as they were on the ground. The pilots of 46 Squadron began to feel a guilty unease over their prolonged absence from the Front. Surely we were needed more urgently there than on undemanding defensive duties in England?

But the Government did not hold this view, for Home Defence had taken priority over the Expeditionary Force. The continued retention of 'a first-class fighting squadron for a vital period' was not the only diversion from the field army, for despite the protests of Haig and Trenchard, Sopwith Camels earmarked for the replacement of obsolete machines in France were allotted to Home Defence squadrons.

But much more important consequences than these were to flow from the public reaction to the appearance over London of a couple of formations of Gothas. The resultant casualties were fewer than those normally incurred in thirty seconds of a sizable infantry attack, but because they proved that Britain was no longer inviolable, they swiftly brought about a revolution in British defence strategy.

Ever since the war began the air services had been cursed by the feudings and intrigues that arose from the competition between the War Office and the Admiralty over the provision of aircraft for the R.F.C. and the R.N.A.S.[1] These preposterous rivalries, which led to tragic inadequacies of equipment in the R.F.C. in the field, worked almost to stalemate in an area of divided responsibilities such as Home Defence.

Procrastinating government, afraid to grasp the nettle, had tried to co-ordinate these conflicting interests by appointing a succession of Committees and Boards, but these, including the current Air Board, had failed because they were given no executive authority. But the raids of June 13th and July 7th at last triggered off resolute action. On July 11th, Lloyd George appointed Lieutenant-General Jan Christian Smuts to examine not only the deficiencies of Home Defence but the organisation and operational direction of the air services in general.

Smuts had little difficulty in disposing of the muddle of Home Defence. His first report, accepted at once by the Cabinet, resulted in the strengthening of the Air Defence forces and their unification under the executive command of a senior R.F.C. officer, General E. B. Ashmore. Three fighter squadrons were formed, and a circuit of anti-aircraft stations to provide barrage fire. Both aeroplanes and guns were largely diverted from the Western Front.

In his second report Smuts went to the heart of the problem, for he saw that there was only one solution to the incessant private war between the War Office and the Admiralty, and this was to form an independent Air Force with its own Ministry. His recommendation, with its far-reaching potentialities, was also accepted without argument, at least in the Cabinet, and on August 24th an Air Organisation

1. See Appendix A.

Committee was set up, over which he presided. The outcome was the formation of the Royal Air Force in April 1918.

Thus it was that although during the six weeks that 46 Squadron spent in England, it never once came within shooting distance of the enemy, and achieved nothing except skill in air drill and tactics, and the possibility of having helped deter the Germans from further day raids, yet it had been privileged to touch British history in the making. Though its role was that of a pawn, it was a key pawn at the centre of the moves that resulted in the creation of the first autonomous Air Force in the world.

But of the significance of all this not even the first glimmer reached us in 46. We were content to live each hour as it came, knowing well that the palmy days would not last much longer. And at length, towards the end of August, the new Air Defence organisation was ready to take over the squadron's duties.

Orders arrived on the late afternoon of the 27th, and there followed a day of hasty packings, farewells, bills from panic-stricken local tradesmen, and final parties in Town. Then next morning came bad weather, the departure of the transport, no flying all day, more farewell parties in London. But on August 30th the skies were clear. At nine in the morning we said our final good-byes, climbed into our cockpits, waved so-long to Sutton's Farm, and two minutes later nineteen Pups lifted into the air in their practised squadron formation, and set out for France.

[I was not to see Sutton's Farm again until eighteen years afterwards, when I returned as Wing Commander to control three fighter squadrons, Nos 54, 65 and 74.]

Part Six

The Third Battle of Ypres

A brief note to say we arrived here this evening after a sticky journey. The aerodrome lies west of Ypres and south of Cassel, and is already occupied by two other squadrons, Nos 20 and 45, but it is fairly large, and we should be able to squeeze in without overcrowding the air.

I'm writing this uncomfortably on scrounged notepaper in a bell tent that I'm sharing temporarily with its rightful occupant, a 45 Squadron pilot, but he will spend the night in his comfy camp-bed, while I shall be on the ground. None of our equipment has arrived, and there is no accommodation for us, so we and the men and the machines are distributed around the Nissen huts and tents and Bessoneaus of the two other squadrons.

I hope to borrow some coats and blankets, and also a groundsheet, as the tent has no floorboards, and it has been raining most of the day. If I survive the night, which is hardly possible, I'll write more fully tomorrow about our trip here. One way and another, today hasn't been exactly a beanfeast.

Friday, August 31st

It wasn't until I began to write this letter and put down the date that I remembered this is my birthday. Twenty-three! I certainly feel it this morning, unshaven, unwashed, and creaking nicely after a non-cushy night. In fact I feel much older than twenty-three, but I suppose that's because this war ripens people pretty quickly.

Each of the squadron's three flights is the guest for meals of a flight mess of 45 Squadron, ours being that of Captain Harris, the senior flight-commander, who tells me that he was the first C.O. of where we've just come from, in fact he opened Sutton's as an aerodrome. Until a week or so ago, 45 had aged Sopwith two-seaters, but they're re-equipping with Camels, and absolutely rave about them. They say they can now make the Albatros look foolish, and have already shot down a few. A nice change after being seen off in droves in the 1½-strutters, like the formation written off in the Messines show by Richtofen's squadron.

The Camel is a stubby-looking machine, shorter fore-and-aft than a Pup, with a slight hump between engine and cockpit where the two guns are set. Hence the name Camel. Instead of both wings sloping up from the fuselage (dihedral), like the Pup, the top ones are horizontal, which makes top and bottom wings seem to curve towards each other, especially in the air. I sat in one—it's a little roomier than a Pup. And to see those *two* Vickers in front of me made my mouth water.

We've spent half the day erecting the marquees and tents, which arrived from the depot mid-morning. We've pitched our camp next door to 20 Squadron, who have F.E.2ds, and for some strange reason don't seem to mind them, though they're only a fattened-up version of the Maurice Farman Rumpety I learned to fly on.

We had a jolly time putting up the big Mess marquee, as nobody knew how to do it, and the experts among the N.C.O.s and men were too busy putting up *their* marquees. Ours collapsed twice, burying some of us underneath, but eventually we persuaded it to stand up. As a Mess, it's hardly thrilling, an empty, cold, damp, smelly, cheerless cavern that nobody enters except at mealtimes. By comparison, La Gorgue and Sutton's seem like dreams of paradise.

Since writing the above, our personal kit has arrived, and I can at least shave and sleep on a camp-bed. I'm sharing a bell tent with Charles Courtneidge. Everything is clammy, including our blankets and sleeping bags. The tents have no floorboards, which means they'll quickly get muddy if this rainy weather goes on much longer. I know the P.B.I. in the trenches have it a thousand times worse than this, but we're not hardened to it. Thank goodness there's always whisky toddy before we turn in.

Actually, it's come rather as a jolt to drop into this makeshift set-up after starting out so full of beans from Sutton's Farm. We kept in good formation across Kent, and landed at Lympne to refuel, and to put on cork lifebelts (we forgot this when we flew the other way!) which made a pretty tight fit in our narrow cockpits. We had a good Channel crossing, with nobody dropping into the water, but the French coast was covered with high, dark clouds.

After making the round of Calais we went on to St Omer, forced lower and lower by the clouds, which gave us a bumpy ride, but we circled the aerodrome in our usual tight formations. Nobby Scott nosed down smartly with 'C' Flight and landed us first, in formation, of course, then we hurriedly taxied to the hangars and watched the others. A strongish wind was blowing, with the cloud base below 1,000, and the air seemed crowded with machines intent on colliding, but nothing happened apart from a show by Thompson, who came in too low over a Bessoneau, and was thrust down by a gust of wind, so that his wheels sank well into the canvas top. Instead of somersaulting, he just bounced off and made a second landing on the ground. Somehow, it looked perfectly normal.

We resumed the journey after lunch, when the drizzle had turned to light rain. We'd learned that our destination was St Marie-Cappel, and by the time we arrived there the clouds were down to 500 feet, but once more 'C' Flight were first down, and once more we taxied to the hangars and jumped from our Pups to see the fun. Everybody else on the aerodrome was watching too. To have three flights of scouts arrive together at 500 feet, in the rain, skimming just over the hangars, was a unique spectacle, with every prospect of a crash or two. They were not disappointed.

'B' Flight came in next, and landed in formation, but Shadwell stalled his engine, and he and his machine stayed put in the middle of the aerodrome while the rest taxied clear. 'A' Flight were already gliding down in tight formation, and one of them, Bird, his eyes glued on his neighbour, made straight for the stationary plane. Shadwell leapt out and sprinted to one side, and three seconds later Bird landed neatly on top of the stranded Pup. Both machines were write-offs, but Bird wasn't even scratched.

Today, low clouds and rain have stopped all flying, but it looks as though things might improve in the evening, which will give us a chance to inspect the district. Compared with La Gorgue, we are quite a distance from the Front, about twenty miles due west of the Messines ridge. We're now back in the 11th Wing, the same as at La Gorgue.

The fellows in 20 and 45 are very intrigued by the fancy names painted along the fuselages of our Pups. They aren't allowed to decorate their buses at all, and say that we'll soon be told to cover up our advertisements.

Saturday, September 1st

We were supposed to start patrols today, but last night's orders were washed out early this morning, as the squadron isn't yet ready to operate, part of our technical equipment having gone astray somewhere.

Last evening around seven the weather cleared enough for flying, and we all took the air, independently, to get the aerodrome locality sized up, and to have a look at the Front. The 'drome is easy to find, as it lies just south of two hills that stand abruptly out of the plain, with Cassel perched on the top of one of them.

I flew along the Poperinghe road towards Ypres, taking a quick look at Dickebusch Lake, now well behind the fighting line, and then went on to see the new front east of Ypres. The army has been battering the area with every sort of artillery during the past month, and what they've done makes an incredible sight. I couldn't recognise much—the villages to the east of Ypres have been wiped out. Stretching away to the east and north-east of the town is one continuous sea of shell-craters, touching each other or overlapping, and all filled with water from the heavy rains of the past few weeks.

I flew fairly low, below 1,000, but couldn't distinguish any sort of trench line, in fact I couldn't work out where British territory ended or German began. I couldn't even see the troops until they looked up at me, and I spotted the little groups of white blobs which were their faces, and then I realised they were in sandbagged defences of sorts. I suppose their uniforms are so smothered in mud that they've become part of the landscape. It's just not conceivable how human beings can exist in such a swamp, let alone fight in it.

From the Ypres front I went south along the Lines to Armentières, then back to Bailleul and Hazebrouck, hedge-hopping most of the way in Sutton's Farm style. It's a bad habit, but one does get a thrill out of it.

Coming down to land, with the air over the aerodrome thick with machines from all three squadrons, I edged my way in very carefully, watching every plane around me, when suddenly I felt rather than saw a shadow come from behind and fall over the cockpit. I jerked up my head, and there, about three feet above, were the wheels of a Pup, also coming in to land. We'd come in on the same vertical line without spotting each other—almost like Bird's mishap, but in the air. I dived clear, then saw it was Nobby Scott of all people. The types on the ground saw us closing together and expected a spectacular crash.

Although this incident showed that flying can be tricky at times with so many planes on one aerodrome, it is rather fun to have several Messes to drop into, and so many fellows to chat with. As usual, I knew quite a few, from flying-training days. They tell us we've been lucky to be on holiday in England during the past six weeks, we've missed some of the hottest air fighting of the war. The ground offensive, which began on the last day of July, at first made good progress, but was held up by the rains. Apparently it's been the wettest August for thirty years in these parts, and the battle areas are so waterlogged, as I saw for myself, that the P.B.I. have come to a standstill.

But the air offensive goes on regardless of what's happening on the ground, and there has been some tough fighting, as the Hun fighters are numerous and, so the fellows say, obviously experienced. They're led by Baron Richtofen's Circus, though it's not a slaughter of the innocents as in April, but stiff scrapping, because now we have Camels, S.E.5s and Bristol Fighters, as well as the last of the Naval Tripes, all of which can handle an Albatros, and that includes the latest version, the D-V. Let's hope the Pups won't do so badly either, we're all pretty expert fliers now, after six weeks of practice, and in spite of the rain and the mud, our tails are well up!

Sunday, September 2nd

As it was raining hard this morning, with no prospect of flying for hours, I grabbed a place on a Crossley going to St Omer, where

McDonald, Courtneidge, Wilcox, Barrager, Asher and I had a cheerful lunch together, preceded by a long drinks session, Mac being in expansive form on getting command of 'A' Flight in place of Tubby Long. Wilcox, we learned, has a brother[1] in the R.F.C., serving with 15 Squadron, with B.E.s, poor devil.

About six o'clock the weather cleared, and yesterday's performance was repeated, everybody leaping into the air for a joy ride round the front line. Once more I spent some time flying low over the ugly quagmire of a battlefield, pitted with untold thousands of shell-craters, lip to lip, and all brimming over with dirty green water. This time, I distinguished churned-up tracks among them, the remains of metalled roads, I suppose, and thin duckboard paths. I also spotted, on this side of the bog, lines of troops in linked craters, which weren't quite so full of water as the rest. How they put up with such an existence, standing in a foot of mud for twenty-four hours a day, I can't think. And when the order to advance comes, how do they get across the miles of flooded craters?

[The advance was resumed when the craters dried up in the middle of September. Later, there was more rain, but the High Command persisted in the assault, in the resolve to gain the Passchendaele ridge. After three terrible months of hopeless struggle in a sea of mud, the offensive ended in November, with a gain of four and a half miles and a casualty list of 300,000, of whom a third were killed.]

Probably the Boche has a similar watery waste on his side of the quagmire, but I couldn't see far into the misty obscurity of Hunland, and didn't venture into it at the height I was at, the idea of being shot down into that slimy mess didn't appeal at all, especially as the gunners had started their evening hate. I saw stabbing flashes from the Boche guns, and explosions on both sides, bursts of flame suddenly appearing and becoming little swelling clouds of smoke, like blobs of dirty cotton wool, which stayed put for a while, as there was no wind. Looking into the dank and mushy gloom eastwards, it all seemed like an eerie nightmare.

1. Herbert Wilcox, afterwards the well-known film producer.

More and more I realise how lucky I am to be out of all that shambles. It's bad enough to have the risk of being killed or wounded, but to be made to face it in such miserable conditions must be hell. We flyers face our risks too, but at least we do it in reasonable comfort, which counts a lot in helping us to keep our tails up.

Monday, September 3rd

I've just come back from my first patrol, and am writing this to fill in the time before my next, at 3.30. The news is not good. The squadron has take a hammering. McDonald, Barrager, Bird, Asher and Williams are all missing. Everyone is feeling pretty bad about it.

The first patrol ran quickly into trouble, five of 'A' Flight, led by Mac, who met Richtofen's Circus and had a hectic scrap. The Pups were completely outclassed by the D-Vs, and most of their share of the fighting consisted of trying to avoid being riddled. Mac and Bird were seen to go down in Hunland. Asher might have reached the Lines. The two chaps who got away, badly shot about, said that one of the Huns was flying a triplane, coloured red. It must be a captured naval Tripe, I suppose.

[This was not so. The first two of the new Fokker Triplanes, the Dreidecker I (Dr I) had arrived at the Front a few days earlier, and were flown by Werner Voss and Manfred von Richtofen. The latter claimed his first victim on September 2nd, when he shot down an R.E.8, whose unsuspecting observer, as Richtofen recorded, made no attempt to fire at what he assumed to be a Sopwith Triplane closing in behind him. On the 3rd, again flying the Fokker, he and five members of his Jasta 11 attacked 'A' Flight over Menin. Lieutenant A. F. Bird was thus his second victim on the Fokker—his sixty-first all told—and in his memoirs he paid tribute to a skilled and plucky opponent, whom he abstained from killing, and made prisoner.]

The next patrol, 'B' Flight, at nine o'clock, fared little better. Joske led Dimmock, Barrager, Williams and Ferrie, and after half an hour's patrol they saw four Fees of 20 Squadron being beaten up by twelve Albatroses, and went to their aid. Four Bristol Fighters joined in too.

There was a devil of a fight, and it went on for quite a time. The Fees bagged a flamer, and the Bristols one out of control, and eventually Joske nipped in and shot down a D-V which a 20 Squadron observer saw crash. But when the affair fizzled out, and Joske led the way home, Williams and Barrager weren't with him.

At 11.15 it was the turn of 'C' Flight, and the knowledge of what had hit the other patrols wasn't awfully inspiring. But one thing we learned from the survivors—that our swanky, tight Sutton's Farm formations were absolutely useless when it came to fighting, and we reverted to the old loose formation that allowed room for each man to manoeuvre on his own.

We climbed up steeply eastwards, wondering what was in store— at least, I did. There were Nobby Scott, Charles Courtneidge, Taffy Hughes, Odell and me. As we approached the Lines I saw the sky ahead spotted with aeroplanes, fifty or sixty of them, milling around at different levels, like flocks of starlings assembling. We drew closer, and I began to get that tingle of excitement I'd not known for nearly two months, especially when I saw a machine fall out of the swarm in flames and tumble down, leaving its long black trail of smoke in the sky.

We were still climbing hard, making for a scrap right ahead, some 500 feet above us, between Camels and Albatroses, swirling round each other, their tracers making a sort of geometric design. It was the first time I'd seen Camels in action. They turn in almost their own length, which must absolutely stagger the old Hun. It staggered me too.

As we watched, I saw a V-strutter drop below the others, with a long tail of white vapour streaming behind him. It was petrol—he'd been hit in the tank. He was right in front of us, about 100 yards away. Suddenly there was a flash of flame below the pilot, and the whole machine burst into a ball of fire. It went hurtling down, and seemed to melt away a couple of thousand feet down, leaving the trail of smoke hanging behind. We passed right through it. I shall never forget the smell of it.

We couldn't reach the Camel scrap, and Nobby led us into the next level of the main scrum. But strangely, although there were enemy planes of several formations all around us, they were too scattered for us, as a formation, to attack. And nobody attacked us. But Nobby kept climbing, and a few minutes later, at 14,000, we saw a group of seven V-strutters coming from the east, about 1,000 feet below. They were D-Vs, as I could see from the rounded fuselage—the D-III is flat-sided. Nobby waggled his wings and dived steeply. We swooped down with him, me touching wood as usual, but they'd seen us, and before we could open fire they'd opened out and started swerving.

In seconds we were among them, and the circlings began, between pairs, with their two extra men trying to nose in on somebody's tail. After two tight turns inside my opponent, mauve wings, blue fuselage, and not very experienced, I'd say, because I got on his tail so quickly, I opened fire and saw the tracers apparently hitting the pilot, and then—tracers flashing past me, and rak-ak-ak-ak. One of them had nipped in behind. Through sheer lack of practice—I'd not been in a scrap since Bruay—my reactions weren't quick enough, and I was lucky not to be hit when another burst of tracer whizzed just over my head, and my right rear centre section strut shot out a little cloud of splinters.

That made me come to, and as I was already on the turn I half-rolled on to my back. He sped under me, a grey and green, this one. I was about to complete the roll and dive after him when there was a horrible cough and splutter, and my engine conked right out. That ghastly blankness, the sudden stopping of the engine's roar, it hits you like a brick. In the silence I heard instead the roar of other people's engines all round me, and the sharp crackle of their guns.

And there was I, upside down, in the middle of a stiff fight, and I could do nothing except dive vertically out of it, and hope that no Hun would follow. Fortunately, none did. When I was safely 2,000 feet below, I levelled out and looked up, and then I realised why I'd made so easy a getaway. A patrol of Camels had joined in, and the Huns were very busy. I gave no more attention to them, I had my own worries, as Hun No 2 had obviously hit me in the engine some-where, and there was a strong smell of petrol that I didn't like at all. It was squirting on to my flying boot, and I could feel the chill of it coming through the sheepskin. I switched off and glided west, with a wary eye on the split strut.

I was on our side of Lille at 10,000, and decided to make for the nearest aerodrome I knew, La Gorgue. At first I had visions of a nasty end in no-man's-land, but I was fortunate, the wind was westerly as usual, but not strong, and my next headache was the chance of being picked up by a Hun patrol. But the only planes I saw were two B.E.s clinging together, and somehow looking quite pathetic—imagine these crocks having to risk meeting the Baron's crowd!

I was duly archied, but dodged it by some cunning swerving, crossed the Lines at 3,000, and arrived with ample height to fire a red light, circle round, as I did once before, and land right into the arms of a squad of expectant mechanics—expectant for a crash, as I realised when I found they were used to Armstrong-Whitworth two-seaters—35 Squadron, who found and repaired a broken petrol pipe.

Back home, I learned that Nobby had seen me dive vertically after being shot at, and had reported me as downed, but ten minutes later 35 Squadron phoned to say I was with them. 'C' Flight had no luck in our scrap, nobody could claim even an out-of-control. These D-Vs are much too good for us. But at least we all got back whole, which was something.

I shall have to stop writing now, as Joske, who leads my next patrol, in half an hour's time, wants to have a conference about tactics, which I much approve of, we all need a little guidance in the business of trying to make our Pups do the work of a mature mastiff.

I'm continuing this in the evening, after dinner, sitting in the bell tent. First, good news about Barrager. He was wounded in the leg, and landed at 23 Squadron at La Lovie, near Poperinghe. He has a brother in a field hospital nearby. Good old Barrage, a blighty for him, maybe even to Canada.

My second patrol wasn't too thrilling for me—or perhaps I should say it *was* too thrilling. There were five of us led by Joske, and after an hour we had an indecisive brush with eight Huns. In the middle of it my engine cut out again, and once more I had the risky business of gliding home. I had ample height this time, but was savagely archied. Approaching the Lines, there was suddenly a terrific explosion just beneath me, the Pup jerked up and fell over sideways, and I was engulfed in black smoke, whose fumes made me gasp. I dived away steeply, clear of the next salvos. Archie bursts have several times come pretty close, but this was the first time that one almost got me—and when I had no engine to make a quick get-away.

Gliding west and feeling quite naked, I spotted three machines making for me, and thought, now I've had it! But they were Pups from 66 Squadron, and when they nosed up close, and I pointed to my engine, their leader waved reassuringly, and they escorted me across the Lines, which I thought was very decent of them.

My trouble was a broken petrol pipe again, and I'm becoming very bored with it. This was not the one brazed by 35 Squadron but a new one installed by my fitter. There's obviously some vibration causing them to fracture, but when I got back home nothing abnormal could be found.

News has just come that Asher's all right. Apparently he came down in our front-line trenches, and isn't even injured. He'll be back to-morrow, I suppose. It's odd how my two patrols met with no excitement to speak of, while all the others have had too much. Asher's is not the only narrow squeak. Thompson, for example, was badly shot about on both his jobs, one bullet grazing his temple. These were his first scraps too, as he arrived only just before we left Bruay.

There's still no news about Bird, Williams and McDonald.[1] What bad luck Mac being downed just when he'd got his flight. But the squadron did manage to destroy one E.A. and send down two out of control. 45 Squadron did better, destroying five, but they lost four. Like a game of draughts. Captain Harris[2] got a flamer, the second one I saw this morning, I think. Like everyone else in 45 Squadron, Harris is enthusiastic about Camels.

'Lights Out' signal has just gone—bombers are on the way, and I'll have to finish this letter by flashlight. We were bombed last night, though we scarcely noticed it, as the bombs fell two fields away. But Hazebrouck had a bad pasting.

Orders have just come in for tomorrow. I have two jobs, including an early one, which means getting up at five. There's a Hun overhead,

1. Lieutenant K. W. McDonald died of wounds inflicted by Lieutenant Mohicke, of Jasta 11. Lieutenant S. W. Williams was shot down and made prisoner by Oberleutnant von Boenigk of Jasta 4. Both Jastas were units of J.G.1 —Circus.

2. Later Marshal of the R.A.F. Sir Arthur Harris, G.C.B.

and our archie is getting agitated. I hope his shrapnel drops clear of our tents. Must stop now.

Tuesday, September 4th

I've got a Hun at last! And all on my own. *And* confirmed. An Albatros V-strutter, a D-III. But I'll start at the beginning. First of all, the weather's turned fine, and there's been lots of work for everybody, three patrols for me, one at 6.15, another at 12.0, and the third at 3.30, which was the important one, and which I'll describe first.

It was a North Offensive Patrol, with Charles Courtneidge leading me, Wilcox, Thompson and Asher, who got back about midnight, apparently little the worse for his adventures. But he had engine failure just after take-off, and forced-landed on the aerodrome. There wasn't much air activity as the four of us approached the Front, and we made for a large cluster of dark specks well east of Ypres, which turned out to be Camels scrapping Albatri. As we drew closer we saw a Hun going down vertically, with a Camel on his tail, squirting short bursts, then the Hun broke up and went down in three pieces, the pilot falling clear. He could easily have got away with it if he'd had a parachute. When we tried to join in, the Huns decided they'd had enough, and broke east, with the Camels after them.

We climbed to 16,000, spent an hour there without seeing anything, so came down to 8,000, and at once found a D.F.W. We all dived and fired, closing to under 100 yards' range. He fell into a spin, and we watched him flicking down for what seemed five minutes until he crashed into the middle of the marsh of shell-holes south of Polygon Wood. I suppose we all shared in this, though Charles was nearest, and it ought to be his. Then we continued the patrol until 5.30, seeing nothing more, and Charles gave the washout when we were over Comines at 6,000.

Coming back, the formation split up and we made our separate ways. It was a lovely evening, very clear, with a pale blue sky, and I thought it was too nice to go straight back, I'd have another look at that incredible morass east of Ypres. I was half gliding down, northwards, just this side of the Hun balloon lines—for once, archie couldn't be bothered with just one aeroplane—when I saw an R.E.8 approaching on my left front, about 500 feet below. And tracers were spitting out from the observer's gun.

It was then that I realised that he was being followed and attacked by an Albatros V-strutter from about 150 yards' range, also firing short bursts. Before I could react, the Hun ceased firing, and turned east. I assumed he'd broken off because he'd spotted me. The R.E. whizzed past below, the observer waved, and the Albatros continued on a level course eastwards.

Suddenly I woke up and dropped into a wide sweeping curve that brought me dead behind the Hun, and 200 feet above him. He was still flying level, due east, but not going flat out. It seemed incredible that he hadn't seen me when he turned aside from the R.E. It looked so easy I suspected a trap, and searched carefully around, but there was no other machine in sight.

I came down closer and closer, holding my fire. My heart was pounding, and I was trembling uncontrollably, but my mind was calm and collected. I closed to ten yards, edged out of his slip-stream, drew nearer still until I saw that if I wasn't careful I'd hit his rudder. His machine was green and grey, and looked very spick and span. He had a dark brown flying helmet, with a white goggles-strap round the back of his head.

I aimed carefully through the Aldis between his shoulders just below where they showed above the fairing. It was impossible to miss. I gently pressed the trigger, and at the very first shots his head jerked back, and immediately the plane reared up vertically. He must have clutched the joy-stick right back as he was hit. I followed upwards, still firing, until in two or three seconds he stalled and fell over to the left, and I had to slew sharply aside to avoid being hit. He didn't spin, but dropped into a near-vertical engine-on dive.

I went after him, throttle wide open, firing in long bursts, but he gradually left me behind. I followed, still firing through the Aldis, until he was 300 yards distant, then I stopped, there was no point in pumping any more lead into him. But I stayed in the dive and saw that he didn't pull out.

I was peering intently down, watching as he fell towards the east of Polygon Wood, when rak-ak-ak-ak! So other Huns *were* around! I kicked my right rudder and skidded off, still in a dive, then pulled up in a sharp turn. Two D-IIIs shot past me. I turned steeply west, and by the time they'd swung round I was a quarter of a mile to the west of them. They fired, but after some five or six bursts, which I heard quite nicely, though they didn't hit me, they gave it up.

Soon after I'd returned to the aerodrome, our archie rang up to confirm. They'd seen him diving down, with me after him, and said he never pulled out after I stopped firing. They couldn't see where he crashed, owing to rising ground, but reckoned somewhere north-east of Polygon Wood, which was what I reckoned too.

I fired about 150 rounds, but it was the first two or three that counted. I think they must have killed or mortally wounded him, probably went to the heart. He wouldn't have known anything about it, which is much the best way to be written off.

I suppose I ought to say that when I saw him go down, quite certain that I'd got him, I was filled with a wild sensation of triumph, and all that sort of thing, but in fact I was so busy concentrating on what I was doing that I forgot to be excited. In the Mess, afterwards, celebrating, I did feel pretty thrilled, but not at the time.

After all this, my other patrols were ordinary, though I did have a scrap in one. We went up at 6.30 a.m., with Joske leading Dimmock, Shadwell, Ferrie and me. We went straight into Hunland, and at 13,000 found several formations in sight, of both sides. Joske made for a group of six D-Vs which wasn't in action. There were Camels, Spads and S.E.s occupying other Huns.

After a lengthy sparring match, with both formations circling, jockeying for position, the Hun leader suddenly fired a white light, and they came at us, all firing. We broke up, and the usual duels started. My opponent had yellow and black stripes, like a wasp, and as we began to circle another Hun took an angle shot at me, tracers flashed between the centre-section struts, I pulled up sharply and half-rolled, and was in the thick of it again. A D-V went down in front of me in a spin, with a Pup on its tail, firing bursts, and as I swung clear there was the wasp again, coming straight at me, guns blazing. Up I went again, another half-roll, then some rough rudder work to escape yet another Hun shooting from behind. Then quite suddenly every-body scattered, and as I levelled out I saw five Camels dropping plumb out of the sky. The Albatri, taken completely by surprise, just bolted.

It was at this moment that my engine decided to pack up, and I assumed I'd been hit and gave the distress signal. Then as I started gliding westwards I smelt petrol—another fractured pipe! I was lucky once more and met no Huns, and because there was an easterly wind for once was able to make St Marie-Cappel. By now I was completely fed up with broken petrol pipes, they were using up too much of my luck. My fitter and the flight-sergeant are almost out of their minds about it, so I sent for the technical sergeant-major and had a few hot words with him, whereupon he promised to thoroughly examine my machine himself.

It was Joske whom I saw on the tail of the Hun spinner, which I reported as a pretty certain goner, but he was credited only with a 'driven down'—indecisive combat. It was certainly indecisive for the Pups, for though we achieved nothing definite, we were all holed. I had seven in the cowling and top planes.

The third patrol was an extra. Some of us, the experienced ones, are going up voluntarily to increase the size of our formations. We'd sooner do four or five jobs a day than have a repeat of yesterday's mauling. But it so happened that this patrol, led by Nobby Scott, didn't see a single Hun in two and a half hours. Of course, patrolling when there is so much potential trouble around—and the Huns are far more active now than in the pre-Messines period—is a big strain even when you don't have a scrap. You're on edge for two hours, searching the skies continuously, for you know that at one moment they may seem empty, and then, thirty or forty seconds later, you may be bounced out of the sun or from behind a cloud. Just the tension of never relaxing for over two hours, of waiting for it to happen from minute to minute, can be pretty punishing.

Wednesday, September 5th

Only one show for me today, at 8 a.m., the second, in the evening, being washed out because of rain. Scott led Charles C., Taffy Hughes, Armitage and me, but we were joined by three volunteers from 'A' Flight. We first went for two D.F.W.s and shot them up at longish range, then Taffy chased after them, and sent one down out of control. The other got away.

A few minutes later, at 7,000, Scott dived on a group of five D-Vs about 1,000 feet below, and the eight of us might have knocked them into a cocked hat but for one small thing. Fourteen—yes, 14!—more Abatri rushed along and joined in. We learned the number afterwards from Armitage, whose engine cut out in the dive, and who watched them swooping on us as he glided westwards.

When we dived, I picked out a red-and-grey Hun, and followed him round as he took avoiding action, but kept above him while waiting my chance for a burst. It was a free-for-all as usual, with planes whirling around in every direction, tracer flashing like fireworks, and I was concentrating on getting a bead on my Hun while in a very tight vertical turn, and had just sent in one burst, which went in half-way up his fuselage, when—rak-ak-ak-ak! Tracers spitting past my head. Joystick right back, full right rudder, a twist of a spin, dive and zoom, and suddenly I realised that the sky above was crowded with aeroplanes, all Albatroses, all thirsting for our blood.

I had a maniacal two minutes, skidding to left, to right, diving, zooming, and generally throwing the poor old Pup around like a drunk on skates. I must admit I began to quake, as we didn't seem to have a hope in hell, but I managed to find a spare second to touch wood, and I also put in a snatch burst whenever a Hun whizzed past my nose. We Pups all lost height quickly, with D-Vs buzzing over and among us like a swarm of wasps, to the tune of a continuous rattle of guns, with tracer criss-crossing all over the sky.

It was incredible that we escaped, and the main reason was that there were so many of them they got in each other's way, but somehow it all ended and we weren't even badly shot about, thanks to the Pups' amazing manœuvrability. Two of the 'A' Flight types were driven down to 300 feet, and had to slither westwards to safety among the tree-tops. Scott and I were also lucky to get away, as he had a gun jam, and my engine started to miss and vibrate badly. I managed to stagger to Bailleul, where I found Armitage with *his* dud engine. My trouble was two broken plug leads, which had wound themselves round the shaft.

There was another exciting show in the early afternoon, Scott leading 'C' Flight again, but with Odell instead of me. They were patrolling north-east of Ypres when Odell, who had seen a triplane coming down from behind, but taken no notice, thinking it was a

Nautical, was amazed to find it firing at him. He turned, assuming the R.N.A.S. pilot had gone off his rocker, then saw the black crosses. The others turned too, and a brisk little scrap followed, the Hun being joined by a D-V. The triplane, which was painted red, had a stupendous performance, and when he decided he'd had enough he lifted up above everybody like a rocket. He was a pretty hot pilot, for he holed most of the Pups, but nobody could get a bead on him.[1]

This triplane was working with only one other Hun, though it seems that they now operate in large formations, like the crowd that jumped us this morning. Apparently Richtofen has three squadrons in his Circus, and they usually go around in big swarms. It all shows that we shall have to go in for big formations too, in fact, we're doing so already. But as we've all found, large formations don't mix it like small ones. Instead of short close-up dog-fights, with in-fighting and duels and quick results, we're having long-drawn-out skirmishings between massed groups taking nibbles at each other.

Tactics are not the only thing to change. The squadron too, with four fellows gone, three new pilots already here, and Mac's flight taken over by Captain Robeson, a quiet but incisive chap in his middle twenties, I'd say.

At last we've found why I've had so much trouble with fractured petrol pipes. The tank was loose, as we thought, but it only moved when the machine was upside down or diving steeply in a dog-fight. So I hope I won't have that trouble again.

General Trenchard visited us today, but I don't imagine he found much to be pleased about. He spoke to nobody except the Major, and didn't stay long.

September 5th (Diary)

I had a good roasting last evening from Joske, who seems to have become the Major's right-hand man. Some of us were holding forth in the Mess before dinner about the way we've run into trouble, and, of course, I opened my big mouth too wide as usual, this time about our being condemned to fight D-Vs on machines the R.N.A.S. gave up as obsolete a year ago. Somebody must have ratted, for Joske said

1. He was Manfred von Richtofen, again flying the new Fokker.

the Major took a poor view of such talk, especially in the hearing of the new boys. Bad for morale, and all that, and I'd better stop it. I suppose he's right, but if somebody doesn't speak up sometimes, how are the high-ups ever to know how we feel? But it was rather a surprise, because a ticking-off wasn't exactly what I expected after getting my first Hun!

Thursday, September 6th

We ran into the new Hun triplane this morning. Scott led Hughes, Shadwell, Armitage and me, and we were well on the other side of the Lines by six o'clock. It was a nice clear morning except for the sun's glare from the east, and with a promise of real summer weather at last. After an hour at 13,000 without seeing much except a strong formation of D.H.4s making east on a bombing raid, and of course the inevitable artillery spotters apparently standing still far below, we were bounced out of the sun by nine D-Vs.

Fortunately I had been keeping a very keen look-out, and so had Scott, and we saw them coming soon enough to give the signal, and so we were ready, split up, circling. They came in among us, and were beginning to shoot us up most unpleasantly, in spite of our tight turns, when to our surprise and delight, we found that the number of Pups had suddenly doubled.

Another patrol, 'B' Flight, had set out half an hour after us, and had fortunately come into our area just in time to see the Huns come down on us. They rushed up and joined in, and the Albatri, thinking no doubt that it was all a trap, began to pull clear. It was then that I had a brief contact with the triplane, which stood out not only because it was a tripe but because of its performance. It was an astonishing sight to watch it soaring up over the other Huns in a steep effortless climb. It's very like a Sopwith Triplane, rotary engined, but the middle and top wings are longer than the bottom, and when it approaches, the wing-tips seem on the slope.

I can't think why the Huns didn't resume their attack, they were nine to our ten, but they could have bested us, especially having the triplane. Instead, the two formations spent several minutes confronting each other, about 300 yards apart, in loose groups, with everybody circling, climbing and generally sparring for advantage but not taking it. There were individual dashes forward, with bursts of fire, then quick withdrawals, for nobody on either side seemed inclined to do an Albert Ball solo charge into the middle of the enemy.

Then the triplane, becoming bored, started a little war on his own. He climbed up well above his pack and dived alone at whichever Pup happened to be handy, fired a burst, then zoomed up and away back to the others. I happened to be one of the handy Pups at a moment when I was in a steep turn after firing fifty rounds at a Hun dappled like a snake. I heard the rattle of guns, saw tracer flash by my right shoulder, jerked the machine into a split-ass turn towards him, but he zoomed as I fired, half-rolled and slid back to his own team. Afterwards, I found he'd put twelve rounds in a neat group through my right upper wing, a foot from the centre section strut. I sincerely hope my brief burst holed him too.

He was all-red, even to the underside, so he could have been Richtofen himself.[1] If so, I'm lucky to be writing this letter. Anyway, after four or five of these dive-and-zoom efforts with no results, he climbed away and made south, with two D-Vs hanging on their props trying to reach him. The other Huns wheeled round and followed, and so an encounter which ought to have been a slap-up fight, in which we should have come off worst, just petered out. Maybe Richtofen was still getting the feel of his new plane, and didn't want to risk it in the chancy business of a free-for-all dog-fight.

Thursday, September 6th (second letter)

I've already sent off a letter this afternoon, but am posting this in the evening with news that I suppose we should regard as good, though most of us take it with mixed feelings. The squadron is being moved from this front, as it is too hot for us. We can't hold our own against the newest Huns, especially now that they have triplanes which can literally make rings even round Pups. It's too much like pitting pigeons against hawks.

1. The pilot could have been Richtofen, though later in the day he set out on delayed convalescent leave, following on a spell in hospital after being wounded in the head in July.

Of course, we'd prefer to stay here where the war is, but only if we had Camels or S.E.s. We know too well that at the low heights where all the air fighting now takes place, the Pups haven't a hope. During the time we've been in England the Germans have produced the D-V, the Triplane and another good scout which one of our patrols has met, the Pfalz, and so, relatively, our Pups are far more outdated than even in July.

There's also the point that the lack of daily fighting and patrolling for nearly two months has put us older pilots out of practice, and we have five inexperienced chaps, including the two who joined us at Bruay—the third, Bird, has already gone. Another thing that doesn't help is to find that our cracked-up formation flying is useless. The fine offensive spirit that we brought back to France is getting thin. All this and our first-day losses have shaken us, I suppose.

We're sorry not to take part in this Ypres war, but glad to get out of it while the going's good. How the two other Pup squadrons, 54 and 66, which as far as we know are to stay up on this front, will get on I can't imagine, but they'll be badly hit before long, I'm afraid.

So tomorrow we pack early and fly to Izel le Hameau, west of Arras, which is now a quiet part of the Line. Apparently there is a good aerodrome, and it's a pleasant place to live.

September 6th (Diary)
I wonder if one of the reasons we are to move is that my outburst in the Mess did percolate via the Major to General Trenchard when he came here yesterday?

Part Seven

The Arras Front

We are in our new home, and a very pleasant spot it is too, a vast aerodrome in open countryside, with accommodation for three squadrons, though we're the only occupants at present. Our quarters are most civilised, as we have a pleasant Mess, Nissen huts for officers and N.C.O.s, a hard tennis court of sorts, and a badminton court in an empty hangar next door. And all this sited in a large orchard full of luscious fruit trees, which most of us have already raided.

We made the trip from St Marie-Cappel at 500 feet and I was first to land with a smooth three-pointer close by 60 Squadron hangars. I taxied up in style to the tarmac, but it was wasted on the pilots waiting by their machines, whose glum faces told how little they relished leaving this cushy station for tents at Marie-Cappel. Soon afterwards they took off, their S.E.5s decorated with jerries and other indelicate articles attached to the undercarriage struts.

The orchard is part of Filescamp Farm, a fine old place like a château. Even the midden doesn't worry us. This is where Albert Ball was stationed last year, flying a Nieuport. Bishop was here too with 60 Squadron, but he went on leave to Canada last month, complete with V.C., two D.S.O.s and the M.C.—and he arrived in France only a couple of months before I did! He's shot down about forty-five planes. How do people do it?

We've spent the day settling in. I have a cubicle of my own, a quarter of a Nissen, which Watt and I, by dint of some quick scrounging on his part from the other huts, have made into quite a comfy den. A few of the other Nissens aren't divided, and the half a dozen or so chaps in each one prefer the dormitory atmosphere.

Saturday, September 8th

There was heavy ground mist and low cloud all day, but by six o'clock the clouds broke, the sun appeared and the whole squadron set out to inspect our new front, which extends from Arras to St Quentin, where the British army joins up with the French.

Nobby Scott, who was an observer around here before becoming a pilot and going to 54, led 'C' Flight on a special Cook's Tour. As we saw in July when flying from St Eloi, the chalky trenches look very different from those in Flanders, and south-east of Arras the present line merges into the trench systems of the fighting in April.

Going further south-east we flew low along the Hindenburg Line to which the Boche retreated in March and April. The first lines of trenches are clearly marked by the very deep belt of barbed wire on this side of them. The wire hasn't been there long enough to rust, and from 300 feet it glimmered in the sunlight like a bluish-grey veil.

Scott quickly got down to applying the tactical ideas worked out at Sutton's Farm. He held a flight conference and explained how he wants us to work, as a disciplined flight and not as a flock of soloists, especially when attacking two-seaters, which he reckons will be our main job down here. His scheme is for the attack to be made by the leader and his deputy (and by No 3 in a patrol of six) and for their tails to be covered by the others. The same thing when we meet a flight of Hun fighters—no break-up into duels, unless forced to it, but the leaders doing the shooting while the others keep guard.

We had a further discussion about whether to use sights in a dog-fight or to hose with tracers. Hosing is supposed to be inaccurate, especially in angle shots, but in a confused scrummage you don't have time to aim carefully, and anyway to have your eyes glued to the Aldis means you can't keep them skinned for Huns attacking *you*. Even goggles cut down the scope of vision, and Nobby admitted he often pulls his up. The answer was to get really close, then tracer should be accurate enough. All very instructive, and I wish Nobby had been around to start this sort of talk when I arrived. It's good for us, but even better for new pilots. And we have several of these now.

In addition to the three who came to Marie-Cappel—Paddle, Small-man and Dusgate—we have another Canadian, MacLeod, and Robinson and Bulman.

The system we're to work to here in the 13th Wing is for the early patrol to be detailed the night before, and the others to be on a stand-by rota, similar to La Gorgue, but here we're called by the klaxon at the squadron office, which is barely 100 yards from the Mess. We've already had a trial run. The klaxon screeches the alarm, then sounds in Morse the letter of the flight required, the four pilots having been previously detailed. Thus you can be lying on your bed or playing poker in the Mess up to the sounding of the alarm. You take a minute to run up the slope of the orchard to the hangars, and you're in the air in 3–4 minutes, not much longer than at Sutton's.

Sunday, September 9th

I was very braced yesterday to see my name mentioned for the first time in Comic Cuts, when I was credited with the Albatros which I sent down last Tuesday. It's taken me a long time to get there, but I think I'd have done it sooner if I'd been flying a Triplane or a Camel or a S.E.5!

The klaxon is going. 'C' Flight. Must stop!

Back again after two hours, and all we saw was a solitary D.F.W. south of the Scarpe, which fled in a panic eastwards as soon as we dived from 8,000, his back gun going continuously until he was almost out of sight. We felt somehow that we were rather cads frightening him so much.

But this happened to be the wrong place to go below 4,000, as we were in the Hun balloon lines, where they keep every sort of hate to fling up at you. So we were met not only with bursts of shrapnel and high explosive but also flaming onions, a string of greenish phos-phorous fire-balls, linked together. You see them coming up at you, turning and twisting like a live thing, moving quite slowly and seemingly chasing you, determined to get you, whichever way you turn to avoid them. In fact, they seldom do hit anybody, but they are rather menacing.

It is not easy to get your bearings on this front, because you're confused by large areas of devastation west of the Lines, not only the Arras battlefield but the regions further south ruthlessly laid waste by the Boche when he withdrew to the Hindenburg Line. What swines they were to blow up every town and village and house in an area until then relatively unspoiled. Now it's a desert—they even poisoned the wells and cut down the fruit trees.

Arras is a good landmark, with a citadel like Ypres. Further south there are the straight chalky-white roads radiating from Bapaume to Arras, Albert, Peronne, Cambrai. Though they're all but obliterated where they cross the Lines, you can still judge your position from them, as they faintly persist through the maze of trenches and shell-holes, like a forgotten Roman road submerged in the English countryside.

Tuesday, September 11th

We tried out our new flight tactics this morning, and they worked well. Net result, one two-seater L.V.G. shot down out of control, shared between Scott and me.

We were a patrol of four, and after half an hour, when five miles across, south of the Scarpe at 9,000, I spotted a dark speck slide across the sunlit cloud well below. He looked like a Hun, and I signalled Nobby, who thought so too, and at once dropped into a dive with me, as No 2, well out on his flank, and a little in rear, and Hughes and Armitage astern to watch our tails. The dive was very steep, with wings throbbing and wires howling, yet after a few seconds Nobby and I, descending almost side by side, seemed suspended in space, while the patchy green Hun magically rushed up to us.

The observer's gun was firing, first at Nobby, then at me, and as the tracer came I felt the kick of a couple of shots hitting my machine. Instead of diving away, the pilot turned under us, which forced us to steepen our dives in order to keep him in our sights. The result was that after firing fifty rounds Nobby all but collided with him, sliding a couple of yards behind his tail. By jove, that observer must have had a fright! Nobby too! I fired thirty rounds, also at close range, and suddenly he jerked into a steep twisting dive to the eastwards with no

125

shooting from the observer. He went on diving until I could no longer see him.

Nobby, already below, went on after him, followed by Hughes, but I stayed put, as I'd seen two Albatros D-IIIs swing on them from the north. I swerved behind them and fired through the Aldis at 200 yards at the nearest, fifty rounds, upon which he suddenly pulled away eastwards, followed by his companion. I also followed, but my gun jammed. Obviously they never saw me, and thought it was a trap. I then joined Nobby and Taffy below, where Armitage also soon appeared.

Today's is the first bad gun-jam I've had for some time. It looks as though the makers are not turning out so much faulty ammunition now. Also, the routine that many of us usually follow of checking the ammo personally as it's placed in the belts has produced results.

We christened the new bar in the ante-room last evening, and the binge that developed went rather rough, with lots of horse-play, wrestling matches, debagging, chair-smashing and so on. Also a shocking loss of bar stock. While I was standing near the bar, holding a drink, Nobby made a sudden rush at me with the idea of bowling me over, and quite without thinking I bent down as he reached me, then jerked upright as he sprawled over my back. Under the impetus of his rush, he went flying over the bar and knocked the barman for six, with a crash of breaking glasses and bottles.

I didn't do it deliberately, I wouldn't have known how, but everybody thought I did, and they steered clear of me in the later rough-housing. Damn funny, the idea of inoffensive me as a Hackenschmidt! Poor old Nobby has an assortment of cuts and bruises, but nothing that counts. I wouldn't have hurt him for the world, but he did ask for it, and, anyway, bears me no ill-will.

This crash quietened things down, and we turned to a sing-song, with Normie at the piano, giving our usual repertoire plus a few from the London shows, such as *Hello My Dearie*, *I'm Lonesome for You* and *Some Girl has Got to Darn His Socks*. The 54 Squadron song-book was also in use again, *Sister Susie*, *Hush a-Bye Baby*, *Haven't Got a Hope*, and another which I don't think I've written out before, *The Only, Only Way*, from *Tonight's the Night*. It runs as follows:

If by some delightful chance,
When you're flying out in France,
Some old Boche machine you meet,
Very slow and obsolete,
Don't turn round to watch your tail,
Tricks like that are getting stale;
Just put down your bally nose,
And murmur, 'Chaps, here goes!'

Chorus   It's the only, only way,
It's the only trick to play;
He's the only Hun, you're the only Pup,
And he's only getting the wind right up;
So go on and do not stop
Till his tail's damn near your prop.
If he only crashes this side in flames,
Well, you'll only know they'll believe your claims.
    So keep him right
    In the Aldis sight.
It's the o-o-o-only way!

Friday, September 14th

No war flying during the past two days, but several engine tests, as my new one is temperamental. In one of these I went with Charles Courtneidge on a joy-ride to Bellevue aerodrome, ten miles south of here, to see one of the 11 Squadron chaps we knew. They have Bristol Fighters, and are doing very well on them, mainly owing to a Canadian, McKeever. He told me that he handles his machine as if it were a scout, fighting with his front gun while the gunner protects their tail. Between them they've shot down several Albatri.

Our patrol this evening was uneventful but pleasant. Charles Courtneidge led, and as the patrol height was 15,000 our faces were properly greased, something we've not done for some time. Charles took us up to 20,000 for half an hour. It's quite a time since I flew at this height, and I noticed it, my heart began to thump and I was breathing in long gasps, open-mouthed.

But I enjoyed it, there was a lovely sunset in a clear sky, and even from this part of the front, well south of Arras, I could see, away to the north-west, the Channel glittering like a belt of gold, and, above it, apparently suspended in the sky at my own level, a faint grey line that was England. I could follow the coast right along to the Isle of Wight. The sun went down somewhere behind Land's End, but its rays still glinted into the sky like the beams of searchlights. As I flew along, gazing at them, they faded away, the horizon became dark, the Channel changed to silver. I think Charles must have been watching it all too, for we overstayed our time, and it was practically dark when we landed.

The real happening today is that our Sutton's Farm pet names have all been painted out, and so we're green-brown once more. Our flight wheels, too. Even the flight numbers have gone and been replaced by letters, so that I'm now X, which too resembles an Iron Cross for my liking. At least they've allowed us to keep the red, white and blue roundels!

Saturday, September 15th

As soon as I began to write, the alarm sounded. It's rather fun so long as you're not next for duty. The klaxon sounds first, de-dah, de-dah, de-dah. Then after a pause the letter of the flight required, A, B or C. Just now 'A' Flight was called, and everybody else came tumbling out of the Mess or the cubicles yelling, '"A"' Flight, '"A"' Flight! Buck up, you slackers! Run for it, you brave lads!' and so on, whilst the 'A' Flight pilots, replying rudely, scurried to the hangars, fastening flying kit as they went.

'C' Flight's call came at lunch-time—we'd taken the precaution to have our meal at midday. Two and a half hours at 15,000, twelve miles over, down south beyond St Quentin, and we found not a single Hun. The sky was steely blue, very clear, we could see for many miles into forbidden Hunland, and it was all rather boring. With the other three machines static around you, the ground too distant even to look at, you feel almost disembodied, infinitely remote from war.

In spite of the need to keep a constant look-out, your mind begins to wander. Of course, I chiefly ponder on leave, when it comes, and all the things I'll do in London, the shows and the shiny restaurants.

But sometimes I dwell on less worldly things. I reflect on how amazing it is that I'm here at all, sailing along nearly three miles up in a flimsy contraption made of wood and quivering fabric, suspended on air, sustained only by the wind rushing under the wings. I think how not long ago the aeroplane didn't exist at all, no man had ever flown into the skies, and now there are thousands of us sharing in a marvellous adventure, but half of us out to kill the other half.

But all these airy-fairy notions vanish when you come down to 1,000 feet and lower, and then turn west, as Charles did for the last part of our patrol. First you fly over the countryside turned systematically into a shambles by the retreating Boche, and then on to the old Somme battlefield, gashed with networks of crumbling trenches and smudged with the remains of towns and villages. You see smashed aeroplanes still lying there, on their backs, where they've been rotting for months. Other things are rotting there too. We passed over parties of pioneers digging out the remains of corpses, and shovelling them on to horse-drawn carts for collection into mass graves. All this makes you realise that whether you like it or not, you've got to be in this war as long as your nerve and luck last out.

September 15th (Diary)

In my letter today I touched on the things one thinks of during a boring patrol. Today I found myself thinking what a stupid thing war is, especially when you don't really know what it's all about, yet I couldn't have stayed out of it. Now I'm stuck in it, with no thought for the future. If I don't get done in, what follows? To begin with, everyone thought the war would be over by that famous first Christmas, but now we can't imagine life without war. I suppose older people can, but most of us have never tasted anything else since we left school or university. And what's so strange is how easily all of us accept this existence of killing or being killed as absolutely the normal.

Sunday, September 16th

Early this morning I was awakened by strange snorting noises, to which I listened for some time, half asleep. Then I came to with a start to find a cow's head five feet away from mine. She was stuck in my doorway, and I jumped up to find, behind her rump, Charles and Armitage puffing and blowing, and doing their damnedest to push her right into my cubicle.

For one priceless moment we all stared at each other, then I seized my water jug and soused the three of them. This was all tit-for-tat for Odell and I throwing half a dozen chickens into *their* cubicles a few mornings back when *we* were on early patrol. That's why Charles and Armie were around so early, but their show was washed out through dud weather.

Later, things improved, and 'B' Flight went out to chase away a two-seater. Soon after, the local shortage of Hun scouts ended, for down by St Quentin they ran into seven Albatros D-IIIs and in a brisk scrap Joske and Ferrie each sent one down in a spin, and Normie Dimmock got one out of control. Shadwell was seen to go down in a spin, but the others were too busy scrapping to watch what happened to him afterwards.

I was up at the hangars when they landed, and waited half an hour with them in the hope of seeing Shadwell come in. It's a very uneasy feeling, standing there waiting for somebody overdue, and thinking that every distant speck must be him. That's hours ago, and he's still overdue, but maybe he's reached our side in some remote spot. Ferrie managed to do so, although his controls were shot away and he had to crash-land. He's a nice fellow, Ferrie, short, quiet, but as pugnacious as hell.

There are rumours that leave is about to open at any time. Charles is due to go first, then me, and we're both practically starting to pack.

Tuesday, September 18th

I thought I'd come to an understanding with my latest engine, but I was too previous, for it ran very bad-temperedly yesterday, and this morning, after an hour's test, I landed with two cylinders missing. However, it was ready for another combined sweep this afternoon, 'C' and 'A' Flights and five Bristols of 11 Squadron. In a trip that went nearly fifteen miles over at 14,000, a long way behind Douai and Cambrai, I had a wonderful time waiting for the engine to die on me, but it didn't. The only group of E.A. that we saw, eight of them well beyond Douai, vanished towards Valenciennes. Probably trainees.

We landed at Bellevue after the show, and found everyone very braced at McKeever getting the M.C. for attacking a formation of D-IIIs on his own. He is an amazingly stout chap.[1] We noted several M.C.s around in No 11, and our not having a single one in 46 makes you wonder. Aren't we brave or clever enough? Or is it that our Pups aren't good enough to get results?

There was a gusty wind blowing, and Nobby crashed taking off, and badly too, though he escaped with bruises. Smallman wasn't so lucky, he crashed badly on landing and has gone to hospital.

No news yet of poor old Shadwell. It looks as though he came down on the other side.[2]

Wednesday, September 19th

'C' Flight was called out at eight this morning to chase a two-seater whose direction was indicated by a large white arrow set out by the A.A. battery at Feuchy, east of Arras. This is a routine now on the standby system, and it enables us to make straight for the E.A. without wasting time scouting around. We found him at once, a striped brown L.V.G. over the Scarpe, and carried out our new tactical attack. But a stout-hearted observer, with double guns, kept Nobby and me at a distance by quickly swinging from one to the other. He shouldn't have lasted long except that his shooting was good and ours wasn't.

Suddenly there was a terrific clang! and the joystick jerked out of my hand and hit me in the stomach. Instantly, the Pup's nose tipped up and she began to rise. For an alarmed instant I was dumbstruck, then I realised that a bullet had hit the metal joystick between my legs. The only damage—my hand and fingers bruised and tingling for several minutes.

This had taken but a few seconds, but it put me behind the others,

1. Captain Andrew McKeever, D.S.O., M.C. and bar, and his observer Sergeant L. F. Powell, D.C.M., one of the outstanding two-seater teams of the war, shot down thirty E.A. on Bristols in 11 Squadron.

2. Lieutenant L. M. Shadwell was shot down and made prisoner by Leutnant Joerfe of Jasta 12.

and when I reached them they were circling round angrily, for the Hun had dived away and escaped. Coming back, we were heavily and accurately archied by the battery at Quéant, which has a reputation, the 11 Squadron chaps say, for being much too accurate. I had a chunk through a wing, which made a six-inch gash.

There are disturbing rumours going round that peace negotiations are afoot. I do hope they won't interfere with our leave!

The klaxon's hooting—good, it's 'A' Flight. 'B' are already up. Damn! It's calling 'C' too. Must stop.

Friday, September 21st

I have very sad news—we lost Warbabe today. An 'A' Flight formation, Robeson leading, ran into seven D-IIIs this side of Douai, and a stiff fight followed. Wilcox shot down one, which was seen to crash, and Robeson and Bulman each got one out of control. But Asher met trouble, and was seen to come down in Jigsaw Wood, about a mile behind the Boche front line, east of Arras. He was apparently under control, but an Albatros was circling round him.[1]

'C' Flight also had some excitement, and got another L.V.G., shared by Scott and me. We were on the 8 a.m. job and found a two-seater about three miles over, south of the Scarpe. Using the new tactics, Nobby and I fired 100 rounds each, then Taffy Hughes, whose Celtic blood doesn't take easily to the duty of guarding other people's tails, joined in with fifty rounds or so, but the L.V.G. was already starting a twisting dive down, obviously out of control.

We then awoke to the unpleasant fact that five D-IIIs were diving down on us. Two went at once for Odell, who was higher than the rest, and two got on my tail and started shooting me up. Nobby came dashing in and drew one of them off, and I began a circling duel with the other. After a minute of this, with both of us firing short bursts off-target, he pulled away and climbed clear. I then saw that the other Huns were drawing off too, and quickly discovered why—a couple of Bristols were coming up.

In your last letter you ask why I touch wood just before a scrap

1. Lieutenant R. S. Asher was shot down and killed by Leutnant Redel of Jasta 12.

when I could pray. But why should God grant me any special favour? The Hun I'm fighting may be calling on Him too. It isn't as though I have any great faith in religion, but even if I had, would it divert a bullet? Anyway, how can anybody who has to fight believe in God, with all the mass killings, and with British, French and German priests all shouting that God is on their side? How can I call on God to help me shoot down a man in flames?

But you do need something to stiffen you. Maybe some fellows do appeal to God. Others are just superstitious, have charms or cross their fingers, or, like me, touch wood. That's different. You're asking chance not to lay the odds too much against you. It's a kind of talisman to ward off evil.

You never hear anybody talking religion, whether in the Mess or privately. We do have padres, and they occasionally hold services, but mostly they organise cinema shows and bury people. They can't even do much for anyone whose nerve is beginning to crack, the doctors come in on that.

Saturday, September 22nd

We ran the flag up on 'C' Flight hangar today. We bagged four Huns! Naturally we are slightly brimming over. It was a very similar patrol to yesterday afternoon's, four Pups at 12,000 with four Bristols at 8,000. We went out at 9.30 and within half an hour found a two-seater Albatros at 6,000, which Nobby, Charles and I attacked in a steep dive on converging lines as I forgot all about guarding tails. The observer stopped firing and collapsed. The machine at once went down in a dive over the vertical.

We climbed up and half an hour later engaged five Albatri on our level. Exactly like yesterday, I met trouble straight away, as two got behind me and I couldn't shake them off. The other Pups were also fully engaged. I was twisting and skidding violently, as my two took it in turns to fire at me. I saw them both, one a pale blue, the other green-grey, in between bursts of rak-ak-ak and tracer flashing past my nose. For once I really had the gust up, I couldn't think how I could get away from them. And I couldn't get even one burst at either of them.

Evading fire from the green-grey, I nearly collided with the blue one when I did a half-roll and found him just beneath me going on the same course. I was upside down and could see right into his cockpit. For one petrifying second I thought the two machines would close into each other. The pilot was looking up—he wasn't wearing goggles. He had a small moustache, like me. In fact, I might have been looking at myself! We were so close I could almost have reached down and shaken hands. Fatuous thing to flash into one's mind in a fight, but it did, and the mind works fast. Then he'd pushed his nose down violently, and vanished. I'm sure he had as big a shock as me!

I levelled out, sweating with sheer funk. It's odd how the risk of collision frightens you more than the risk of bullets. I had to lift my goggles which had misted from the sweat on my forehead and as I did so, rak-ak-ak-ak! Two more on my tail. But this time, thank goodness, Nobby saw and came to my aid, and drove one of them down. Then Charles joined in and tackled the second one, and drove that down too. Meanwhile, a Bristol had climbed up and joined in the party. As I swirled around, I saw a D-III try to get behind and below him, but I slid behind *him*, drew close, fired thirty rounds. He jerked up behind the Brisfit, fell over and span down. I watched him for about 4,000 feet, and with safety, because by now all the Bristols had joined us, and the two remaining D-IIIs wisely fled.

Result: One scout to Nobby (the blue one), one to Charles, both confirmed by our A.A. One scout to me, out of control, confirmed by the Bristol and Charles, who was close to it as it span down, and watched it continuing the spin for several thousand feet. Plus one two-seater shared between Nobby, Charles and me. Odell had no luck, his gun jammed after 100 rounds or so.

September 22nd (Diary)

It was an odd feeling today to look at that D-III pilot from my upside-down position and see practically my double. Later on, I thought about it. It made me realise that the Hun pilots and observers are just the same types as we are in the R.F.C., all young, keen on flying, volunteers for the job. We'd probably get along together like a house on fire, yet all we're here for is to slay each other. It's daft when you think of it. And for whose benefit, when we're all done in, and the war's over?

Sunday, September 23rd

Another D.O.P. this afternoon, 'B' and 'C' Flights, plus four Brisfits. One two-seater driven down—nothing to do with me! Otherwise completely a waste of time and petrol again. I can't see the point of these big distant sweeps, they merely frighten small formations away, and there aren't enough Hun fighters on this front to produce equally big shows—they're too busy up north. What's the point of parading round empty skies miles over Hunland at the constant risk of losing machines through dud engines?

In yesterday's scrapping I had a bullet pass between my left **arm** and my chest. It tore a hole in my flying coat and tunic, but I didn't notice it, and knew nothing of it until this morning when Armie asked me about the hole in my tunic sleeve. I then checked up the leather coat, and there the hole was too.

We've had definite news at last about the casualties of September 3rd. McDonald died of wounds, but Bird and Williams are prisoners. We get this information through Huns flying over our side periodically with a streamered message bag containing the list of R.F.C. and R.N.A.S. casualties. We do the same for them, and even more. For instance, when Boelcke, then their top scorer, was killed last October the R.F.C. not only dropped a message but also a wreath because the chaps thought him a brave and chivalrous opponent.

This mutual consideration is one of the few decent things in this mutual-killing business. In the trenches anything like it would be looked upon officially as fraternisation, which shows that us flyers on both sides have our own code in this nasty war. Although we often get to very close quarters in our dog-fights, our scrapping is impersonal. We don't hate each other. In fact, we probably hate strikers at home, stabbing us in the back, far more than the Huns we have to fight, who are risking their skins for their country just as we are—only they happen to have been born in Germany.

Wednesday, September 26th

No flying today, clouds at 300, but we hear that there's much air activity up north, and, according to Comic Cuts, we've had some bad knocks—thirty-nine machines missing last week. On the other hand, we shot down Werner Voss, second German ace to Richtofen. He fell to 56 Squadron, which is doing very well on its S.E.5s. A fellow called McCudden seems to be their star turn.

The Major, who took over the Wing for a time while the Colonel was away, has returned with the glad news that leave will not reopen until the squadron has been back in France for three months. *Three months!* They must be off their heads. Most of us will be prisoners or dead by then. Charles and I are sadly unpacking.

Thursday, September 27th

This evening I took up my first passengers. While on patrol, in formation at 10,000 in a clear sunlit sky, with the customary illusion of sitting motionless in space, my eye was caught by a glitter behind one of the flying wires, just alongside the cockpit. Then I saw, trailing out horizontally in the slip-stream, half a dozen spiders' webs, a couple of feet long. Further down, around the strut bracket, a network of webs bulged in the wind, marvellously not breaking. They were the very fine kind that float in the air and catch your face when you're walking alongside a hedge. Incredibly, they stayed put at ninety miles an hour. I pictured their owners cowering in corners, and when I got down, found some of them, tiny red creatures, apparently none the worse for their adventure.

We didn't see a single Hun in the two hours, and the patrol became a bore. These uneventful patrols can be more fatiguing than having a scrap. Even in a cloudless blue sky you can never relax, you must constantly search every quarter for those distant specks which can so quickly materialise into Huns with flashing guns. And as I've mentioned before, twisting round every half-minute or so to make sure there's nobody coming up on your tail gives you a stiff neck. But it has to be done, and I've been particularly careful to do it ever since my first Hun up at Polygon Wood, as I've not forgotten how easily I slid up behind him in a clear sky.

Nobby kindly livened things up when the patrol ended and took us down low by St Quentin and led us at 100 feet on a round tour, westwards, to the Somme and Ancre battlefields, mile after mile of ruined, deserted country, with thousands of shell-holes, mostly filled with water. Heaps of bricks and rubble mark where villages and farms once stood. Patches of splintered tree-stumps were once woods and coppices. We again saw pioneers on the ghastly job of digging out what is left of the thousands of corpses and transferring them to mass graves.

Further north are signs of life. Smoke rises from makeshift shelters. There are occasional hopeful patches of cultivation where trenches and shell-holes have been levelled and ploughed. The French farmer just won't be beaten. In one stretch a light railway engine was steaming along the middle of the old no-man's-land. Further north-eastwards still, below Arras, are scores of large army camps and depots, horse lines, even a tank depot, which we circled. Cumbersome beasts they looked too. Heaven preserve me from ever going to war in one of those!

Saturday, September 29th

At long last the squadron has won a decoration! News has just arrived that Joske has the M.C. This is the very first in the eleven months (less one and a half months at Sutton's Farm) that the squadron has been in France. He well deserves it, he's been a thrusting flight-commander, and has sent down seven Huns. The inevitable binge is to be held tomorrow evening, as today's bar stock isn't large enough for a real occasion.

Patrols today and yesterday were spoiled by bad weather. This afternoon we filled in the time by hunting rats instead of Huns. Although it's most pleasant to live in an orchard, alongside a large farm and its outbuildings, there are snags, particularly wasps, millions of them (worse than the mosquitoes at La Gorgue) and, of course, rats. We see them around our quarters too often, and they're rather large and Hunnish-looking, and so today we organised a hunt. We mobilised all the squadron mongrels, armed ourselves with clubs and Very pistols, and beat up all the likely spots. The procedure is simple, you fire a Very cartridge down a hole and wait. We bagged fifteen rats, plus two dogs and one officer with our flailing bludgeons.

Old Jock, the Officers' Mess special dog who declined to show any interest in the rat-hunt, favoured me with a visit. He wanted to be scratched. He has some skin trouble which makes him scratch himself all day, but sometimes he gets tired doing it, and comes and asks you to help, with a comb for preference. Dusgate, one of the new pilots in 'B' Flight, who says he knows something about animals, is going to try and cure him.

There are three other newcomers around, Allen, Atkinson and Cooper, the last an amusing Scot, an Argyll and Sutherlander, whose pet exclamation is Hootsmon, and who in consequence now has it as a nickname. The same with Bulman, who addresses everybody of every level (except the Major) as George, and so is called Georgie, though his real first name is Paul.

Sunday, September 30th

Quite an exciting patrol this afternoon, three Huns down for 'C' Flight, and maybe a fourth. Scott led Odell, Armitage and me, and while we were at 10,000, south-west of Douai, we found two two-seater D.F.W.s well below. Nobby gave the signal and was about to lead us into a dive when five D-Vs came roaring down on us from out of the sun. We had let ourselves fall into a trap.

We were instantly in a mad dog-fight, and while we were still whizzing round each other, two Bristols and a D.H.5 rushed up and joined in. I'd already paired off with a green-yellow (I think green is becoming my favourite colour on Albatroses!) and tried a couple of bursts at him as we turned in a tight circle, but I at once realised he was a practised pilot, as I had to work hard to keep inside his turn. By yanking my stick right back I got behind him, and put in a good burst of twenty rounds at about fifty yards. The tracer was hosing him fine, but he must have been wearing an iron suit, for nothing happened.

Then tracer started flashing by me from behind, and as I skidded off to the left, my attacker shot by on the right, himself being shot up—and by Nobby, who had seen me in difficulties again. I glimpsed the

Hun push his nose down and dive away with Nobby just behind, pumping lead. He afterwards claimed it, down out of control.

Then, as I turned into the scrap again, a Brisfit barged right in front of me, front gun firing. I was so close I had to yank the Pup up vertically, and she fell over into a spin. As I was pulling out of the resultant dive, well below the scrap, I saw below me the D.F.W.s we'd originally spotted. They were passing slowly beneath us, about 2,000 feet down. The opportunity was too good to miss, and I pushed the nose into a vertical dive.

The two E.A. were in line about 300 yards apart, and I made for the one in rear, a dark brown and dirty yellow. The observer began to fire as I came down, but I dived behind and below him, then zoomed up under the impetus of the dive. From underneath, before the pilot could jink, I got in a long burst along the underbelly. The machine reared up, fell over sideways on to its back, and dived slantingly, turning on to its back twice more before I lost it. The observer wasn't firing as I followed it down to 3,000, still giving occasional bursts. As I watched, a piece of what seemed to be the cowling came away, and I expected the thing to break up, but it didn't. I think it came down east of Jigsaw Wood, where Asher fell.

I was now over 3,000 feet below the others, and as I climbed up, a D-V came spinning down past me, with a Pup on its tail. It was Nobby, who levelled off alongside me, and we watched it until it too was lost to sight.

When we'd climbed up to the others, the remaining Huns and the D.H.5 had gone. The Bristols stayed with us for a while, as Nobby continued the patrol, then they too pushed off. Within minutes we found two more D.F.W. two-seaters. The first at once turned east, and, forgetting Nobby's new tactics, we all dived on the second. As it dived steeply away, the observer fired at me and Armitage, who were nearest, but after about twenty shots I ran out of ammo. As I was pulling level, I saw Armitage, on my flank, also pulling out. He then gave the distress signal and started for home. He went down in a half-glide, and I thought his engine had gone dud, and kept alongside him.

I was the first to land, then Nobby who had caught us up, and then Armitage, who made a bumpy landing. When he joined us at the hangar we found he'd been wounded in the leg. It was painful, as the bullet was still there, but nothing very serious, though good enough for a blighty. He was sent off at once to 19 C.C.S. at Agnez, halfway between here and Arras, furious at missing tonight's binge for Joske's M.C.

My rigger counted twelve bullet-holes in my machine, mostly in the fuselage, with a compression strut splintered, so one of my dog-fight opponents did some goodish shooting.

My two-seater was confirmed by the Bristols—one of their observers watched it go down. Neither 'A' nor 'B' Flights came across a single Hun in their patrols today.

11.30 p.m.

Am just off to sleep after a very rowdy binge. All the usual sing-song. They're not finished yet—in fact, they're starting all over again with *Haven't Got a Hope in the Morning*. But I'm on early patrol and felt I'd had enough drink, so I left them to it. Now they've switched, they're yelling *Some Girl Has Got to Darn His Socks!* If I'm not careful, I'll be getting up and going back to the party.

Monday, October 1st

Nobby is very fed up over Armie's wounding, for we were the only flight still with the same pilots as at Sutton's Farm. He has always looked after us in scraps, as I well know, for he has pulled Huns off my tail two or three times. But Armie's hit was something that could happen at any time—a plucky observer shooting straight. Armie's replacement, called Warwick, has arrived and the batmen are putting his things in the cubicle behind mine, previously occupied by Ferrie, who has just moved to another hut because we other three in the Nissen groused about the noise he made in nightmares—dreaming his machine was in flames or breaking up, and so on.

Today's first job was an ordinary chase patrol, but instead of a two-seater we ran into three D-Vs, and had a running fight for ten minutes without getting to grips. The second job, this afternoon, was the largest combined show I've yet seen in France, eight Pups, eight Bristols and four D.H.5s. It seemed a very impressive set-up, but was, of course, only the same as our squadron formations at Sutton's. We flew in three layers, the D.H.5s lowest (they're no good high up) at 5,000, then the Bristols at 10,000 then us at 15,000.

After a two hours' coat-trailing tour around Hunland, during which we saw not a single Hun, we came back, having been archied to hell. We were all winged, Ferrie having a narrow squeak with a footboard smashed. I still can't think in what way such futile mass D.O.P.s help to win the war!

Tuesday, October 2nd

Early patrol this morning, Nobby leading, dived on two D.F.W.s, fired 100, they fled, later had a brush with three D-IIIs, they too retreated when we closed. All very frustrating.

In the afternoon several of us drove over to see Armitage. He'd had an operation, but seemed comfortable, and very cheerful at the prospect of being soon back in England. That's more than could be said for the man in the next bed, an infantryman, shot through the stomach. I couldn't bear his expression of utter misery. He must have known he hadn't a hope of living, and he was in great pain. Armie whispered that if he wasn't stuffed with morphine every hour or two, his moaning was too awful to listen to. The other men in the ward, all P.B.I., seemed pretty serious cases, too. It shook us quite a lot.

Thursday, October 4th

There's been no serious flying for two days, and this afternoon 'C' Flight took the opportunity to go and see Armie again, and take him some chocs and apples, but were surprised to find him looking so ill. The nurse would only allow Nobby and me to see him, and then only for two minutes. She said he'd had another operation and the gas upsets him. The poor devil in the next bed died during the night.

We're all running around bursting with enthusiasm over good news just arrived which (risking Mr Censor) is that we're shortly to be re-equipped with Camels. It will be agony waiting for them, but we'll endure it for the prospect of shooting with two fast-firing Vickers instead of our single pop-pop-pop gun. They're wonderful machines, too, for stunting, a good pilot can do anything with them. No 8 Naval's C.O., Commander Draper, flies here occasionally, and gives us a pretty hot demonstration. He has one stunt we'd not seen before which he calls an upwards spin. He told us how to do it (you can't manage it on a Pup) and we're all panting to try. *And* to try out those two guns!

There was another binge last night, this time on the strength of Nobby Scott and Normie Dimmock being recommended for Home Establishment. I shall be sorry to see them go. Normie is a most cheerful and likable chap, and so is Nobby, as well as a darned fine flight-commander. I do hope he gets a decoration before he goes, he's earned an M.C. ten times over. With Normie going, we lose our sing-song king, but fortunately one or two of the newcomers know how to handle a piano.

Friday, October 5th

Early this morning came the shocking news that Armie died last night of gangrene poisoning. We can't believe it. Although he looked pale yesterday, he seemed cheerful enough, braced at the expectation of soon being sent to England. What on earth could have caused a simple wound like his, under treatment by hospital staff within an hour of it happening, to go wrong so quickly? It has made us all very gloomy, as Armie was very popular. We could have taken it better if he'd been killed in a scrap.

This seems to be a day for bad news. We have the rumour that Asher was shot dead by Boche soldiery when he came down in their lines. And I hear that Captain Bonar Law was recently shot down and killed up north, also Barlow of 40 Squadron, of Field of Agincourt fame, also reports that 66 Squadron had a mauling, two Pups shot down the other side, two this side, and the remaining two badly shot about and lucky to escape. But what can you expect with Pups? Compare this with 56, with S.E.s, who've just shot down their 200th Hun! And they only came to France in April! Their pilots can't be all that more brave or skilled than the chaps in 66 or 46. They just have the right tools for the job. Well, we'll see what happens when we get Camels.

October 5th (Diary)

Today's list of killed makes one wonder why such good chaps are the ones to die. Bonar Law, who'd probably have been a big public man like his father, or Armie and Warbabe, who'd scarcely started life. You ask yourself, what are fellows like these, and hundreds of thousands more, giving their lives for? I hope it's not just to make England safe for bolt-holers, profiteers, strikers, fake conchies, ponces and all the rest of the indispensables.

Saturday, October 6th

It is pouring with rain, and miserably cold, as if we were in December. I've spent a couple of hours writing to various friends at home, but the snag is that I can't remember their addresses. My memory, which was always pretty good, just won't function. They say this sort of thing happens when you've had a few months of war flying, also you get restless, fidgety, irritable, absent-minded and start muttering to yourself! So I'm keeping a sharp eye on my behaviour!

We went to a cinema show at Bellevue last evening, arranged by our padre, a very good chap with the M.C., which he won in the infantry. Afterwards we had dinner with 11 Squadron. As a two-seater squadron, theirs is a large Mess and I much prefer our small, comfortable and more friendly set-up. There are always people in the ante-room, and one is never lonely.

This all helps to create a tight squadron spirit. We pilots live in a world of our own, and except in long spells of dud weather, like now, are so wrapped up in our daily routine of patrols, and the excitements of scraps, that we're not interested in what goes on outside. Even with other squadrons near us, like No 11, we're not much involved. As for what the Army and Navy are doing, or the politicians at home, we're not interested at all. We're just a close-knit community of fliers drawn from every level, from all over the Empire, a miniature democracy. The men in it change frequently, but the community lives on as a cut-off little world.

That's not all. Each one of us lives in his own individual little world, too. We seldom talk to each other about our private affairs. You

143

seldom get to know much about a fellow's background. His accent, education, bank account, don't matter, nor who his people are. You never ask. You don't even want to know. The only thing that counts is whether a chap has guts and can shoot straight. You share the same risks every day. Some get shot down the other side, and that's the last you hear of them. Some go home, and probably that's the last you hear of them, too. Yet here, in France, we're a sort of brotherhood. It's a rum life.

Tuesday, October 9th

Posting orders for Nobby and Normie have arrived and they leave for England this afternoon. No time even for another binge. But what a disappointment that Nobby hasn't been awarded his M.C. He's the best flight-commander the squadron's had since I've been in it, setting the pace for everything, looking after his flight in scraps, and shooting down seven or eight Huns. I don't understand it.

Charles is getting 'C' Flight, and so he should, he's led many patrols, and has long experience, having been an observer before he came to 46. With Normie going, Joske, Charles and I will be the longest-serving pilots in the squadron. I wonder what my chances are for a flight? I must say, I'd love to finish my time out here with three pips—but I'd better touch wood on this!

This afternoon a party of us took a propeller cross made by the squadron carpenter to the cemetery at the pretty little village of Izel, where Armie is buried, on the other side of the aerodrome. We erected it over his grave. Unlucky Armie.

Wednesday, October 10th

When the clouds lifted this afternoon, Charles took us on his first patrol as flight-commander. The cold was so intense at 15,000 that I forgot all about the war, and gave my whole attention to keeping alive. The trouble with Pups is that there's no room to move, except to clap your hands and slap your knees. The best way to keep the circulation going is to yell out songs at the top of your voice, and during the patrol I got through all the Mess songs and London shows, and even went through several operas on a tra-la-la basis. Eventually, even Charles couldn't endure it any longer, and we came down to 5,000 feet, almost hoping that a few D-IIIs would appear, because there's nothing so warming as tracer whizzing around. As usual, archie did his best instead, but this time I wasn't hit once.

Thursday, October 11th

I shot down another Hun today, a D-V shared with Joske. It was during another of these big combined D.O.P. sweeps, this time of thirty-five machines, eleven from 46 and the rest from 11 and 41 Squadrons, in layers as before. The Pups, under Joske, led the whole crowd, and we went over about twelve miles, not expecting to see any Huns as usual, when six D-Vs showed up and made faces at us. They put up a very good show, and we ought to have slaughtered them, but there were so many of us, all milling around at the same level, with no proper system of attack, that we got in each other's way, in fact one spent half the time dodging Bristols and D.H.5s. A D.H.5 all but collided with me head on, and we had both to loop. It all showed how essential it is in big sweeps of this kind for pilots to be trained to work in flights and squadrons, as at Sutton's Farm.

The Pups were highest to begin with, but as soon as a mêlée started below, Joske got three of us together by waving his arms, and led us down in a dive. The Hun he attacked span down a short way, then climbed up again. Meanwhile, we dived on another Hun, who also span. One of the Pups, flown by a newcomer, Allen, of 'A' Flight, didn't pull out early enough during one of our dives, was caught by a D-V, and went spinning down through the middle of their formation. There was nothing we could do about it, unless a whole flight had gone to the rescue, but as I say, there was no cohesion at all among our people. Allen hasn't returned at the time I write this, and I'm afraid he's down on the other side.[1] Bad luck, he only joined us a couple of weeks back—I'd scarcely spoken to him.

Eventually I joined Joske in a quick dive on a D-V which had drawn a little apart from the others. We both got in close and fired fifty

1. Lieutenant A. A. Allen was shot down and killed by Vizefeldwebel Donhauser of Jasta 26.

rounds each. He immediately jerked up, fell over, a chunk of something flew off him, and he went spinning down quickly until we could no longer see him. If he'd not been hit, he would have climbed up and joined the others, so we claimed him as sent down damaged and out of control.

We've just had the good news that Nobby has been awarded the M.C. after all. What a pity it didn't arrive when he was here—we'd have had a hot celebration. Lucky chap—captaincy, Military Cross and H.E. Just what *I* would like—but what a hope in Heaven!

Monday, October 15th

This is the first time in four days that I've had anything of interest to write about, as bad weather cut down patrols and made them uneventful. Today, our dawn patrol was ruined by ground mist, and the second by heavy rain. For the third, we went up immediately after a big storm, just before sunset, and as we climbed up among the irregular masses of wispy cumulus it left behind, we ran into some extraordinary cloud formations and colourings, mostly vivid red in the sun's last rays, but changing and unfolding and merging continuously into flame, violet, yellow, gold, blue, like a kaleidoscope. Fascinating to watch.

Flitting among the larger clouds were scores of miniature rainbows, some upside down, and some apparently so close I felt I could have reached out and stroked them. There was also an immense one, spreading right across our front. Happiness lies at the end of the rainbow, the saying goes, but although I plainly saw the end of this one, I couldn't land there because it rested in the Scarpe valley in Hunland, and what's more, the closer we approached, the further it retreated towards Douai. Another Hun trap for the unwary, maybe.

A new squadron, No 64, with D.H.5s, commanded by Major Smythies, has just arrived from England, and is going into the accommodation next door to us, in the same orchard. At the moment, the officers have taken possession of our Mess, while their own is put into shape.

I have another Pup. My old bus, B1777, the *Chin-Chow* of Sutton's Farm, which I've flown continuously since, was crashed hopelessly by one of the new pilots to whom I lent it for a patrol. He's our prize

Pup-murderer at the moment. He's done four patrols so far, and has lost himself and crashed each time. As Charles has taken over Nobby's machine, I now have his old *Will-o'-the-Wisp*, B1802, and am very pleased with it, but I'm still letter X, and that I don't like!

Wednesday, October 17th

Spent most of this morning censoring a pile of letters as high as my knee. Phew! Not only our own, but those of 64 Squadron—they haven't got their routine going yet. Being fresh from England, most of their epistles were of intimidating thickness. I can't think how I managed to let myself in for this.

'C' Flight had no patrols to do all day, so in the afternoon we paid a visit to the local A.A. unit, 'K' Battery, stationed at Feuchy, close behind the Lines due east of Arras. Most interesting, too, especially as we picked up quite a number of tips on how to make things difficult for Hun archie. Why similar visits haven't been laid on months before, I just don't know.

Friday, October 19th

Today, no serious flying. Yesterday a very strong gusty wind sprang up while we were on patrol with the result that there were four landing crashes, including a bad one by Ferrie. And I, I regret to say, broke an axle. A gust of wind jerked me up just as I was doing my three-pointer, and I bumped heavily. Apart from my Dickebusch landing, and my Bessoneau mishap at Bruay, this is the first time I've broken anything on a Pup since I arrived in France. As everybody else has crashed three or four times, I've not done too badly.

The only important event today was the washing of Jock, for Dusgate decided that all that was wrong with him was sheer dirt, in fact he'd become so smelly that none of the other dogs would have anything to do with him. Even we had begun to notice it lately, and concluded he'd been rolling in the midden. The bath gave him a terrible shock. I thought he was going to faint. Nothing like that had ever happened to him before, and I'm pretty sure that as soon as it was over he dashed straight to the midden.

News has just come in that leave has reopened! Charles goes off tonight, and it's my turn next, though as I'll be taking over 'C' Flight, I may have to wait until he comes back. Charles is shouting for me to celebrate in the Mess, so off I go. He'll post this letter in England.

Saturday, October 20th

I led my first patrol this morning as acting flight-commander. It was good to see two streamers flying from my struts, and to know they meant not just *leading* but *commanding*. I had Taffy, Odell and Hurst with me, and was keen to find some Huns, but it was uncertain weather, big masses of cumulus, with high cirrus streaked against the blue—though good for ambush if there'd been anything to ambush.

During the first half of the patrol we saw three D.F.W.s all told, and dived on each one, using Nobby's tactics, but each time they dived steeply eastwards as soon as I opened fire. Later I spotted four V-strutters near Cambrai, and made for them, but they were not out for a fight, and went behind a cloud. I chased after them, and we fired at long range, but they faded out of sight.

I have another job this afternoon, a D.O.P. of eight, to be led by Joske. I hope he doesn't go too far over. Although my engine seems all right, you never know, and now that leave's so near I'm getting rather restive over the possibility of coming down on the other side. It's the sort of thing that does sometimes happen.

October 20th (Diary)

We hear news today of another mauling up north for Pups, this time 54 Squadron. A patrol of six ran into the Circus, and only two came back, both shot to pieces. Let's hope we get Camels quickly, or the same sort of thing may happen to us. The day before my leave, probably!

Sunday, October 21st

I reckon that I'm working myself to death as a flight-commander. Apart from the office paper work, rolls, demands, strength returns, etc. (actually, all I do is to sign them, the flight-sergeant writes them out!), I've had six flights already today, one a patrol, and I've got another patrol in an hour's time.

Three of my flips were engine tests, and the fourth a trip along the Lines for a newcomer, Sergeant Leigh, whom I wanted to show the front, before taking him on patrol this afternoon. We were out for an hour, and went down nearly to St Quentin.

My patrol this morning had its exciting moments. I had three combats, and everybody else had one. First we dived on two D.F.W.s from 12,000, but we were too far off, they saw us coming, and though we fired from 150 yards they dived away under full control. Soon after we found two more D.F.W.s, but they were protected by five D-V.s some 3,000 feet above. I climbed up to their level and made for them.

It was one of the most confusing fights I've ever had. They were good pilots, and as Hurst was inexperienced I had to keep an eye on him while trying to get a bead on a Hun, and meantime dodging other Huns shooting at me from behind. While we were mixing it up without anything much happening, two Bristols suddenly appeared, and went after the D.F.W.s, upon which the D-V.s tried to withdraw from us—their job was protection.

This gave us our chance, and we sorted out our opponents. I found myself sparring with a blue and grey, and we started the usual business of circling round each other. Very soon, by tight, vertically banked turns, I got behind and fired twenty rounds from no further than thirty yards, but he must have been another of these types wearing iron suits, for he just went on turning. Then suddenly his nose dropped, and he dived away, but I saw him level out and start climbing up to his pals.

The fight went on for a good ten minutes. I had two more scraps, repetitions of the first, but I just couldn't hit a thing. My shooting must have been terrible. I realise more than ever that the only way to get your Hun in a dog-fight is to be really close before you fire. The difficulty, of course, is to get there before he, or somebody else, shoots *you* down.

Meanwhile, the fight had spread over a wide area. The D.F.W.s had gone and the Bristols with them. The Huns began pulling away— and there were still five of them! I was relieved to see my three Pups still around, but soon Hurst gave the distress signal, and we escorted him across the Lines. He came down at an advanced landing ground near Bapaume, his engine having been hit.

We were all winged, I had eleven bullet holes, including one through an interplane strut. Although we'd all given as good as we'd taken, none of us could claim a thing, yet each of us had enough to say to put in his own combat report. All very disappointing. But one thing I have learnt—to be a good flight-commander like Nobby, to look after your pilots in a dog-fight as well as yourself—quite apart from shooting down the Hun—is not so simple a job as I thought!

I wonder if we shall get the same sort of thing this afternoon. We have a combined D.O.P. of eight Pups of 'A' and 'C' Flights, and eight D.H.5s and the amusing thing is that I shall be leading the lot. Robeson is acting C.O. while Major Babington is on leave, and I'm the senior pilot of both flights. As the Pups have to lead the combined sweep, I, a mere lieutenant, shall lead sixteen planes, two of them flown by captain flight-commanders in another squadron. Just as well they don't know!

11.30 p.m.

I'm writing this in the Mess at half past eleven, just a brief extra paragraph to my letter, which I'll pop into the letter-box, though I'll be in England long before it. For I'm sitting here, all dressed up, waiting for a tender to take me to St Pol to catch the leave train.

I duly led my combined sweep this afternoon, and we went at least twelve miles into Hunland, ranged in height from 10,000 to 15,000, rode through repeated and vicious archie, and never saw a single enemy plane. So my hopes of a glorious battle and much kudos faded away, but I did bring the sixteen machines safely back to this side. Then I fired the washout signal and came home.

I landed with never a thought in my head except maybe of making some thick slices of toast in front of the Mess fire, but as I switched off, unloaded the Vickers, and leisurely unfastened my belt, Taffy came up and shouted excitedly, 'Better get a move on, Lee, you're going on leave tonight!'

Robeson heard that an extra seat had turned up on the leave train, and nabbed it for us—for me! And Odell is to take over 'C' Flight until Charles returns. Good old Robey! What a stroke of luck. I'm even spared the 'I-may-be-shot-down-on-the-last-day' quivers.

And that's why I'm all packed and ready, waiting for the midnight tender to St Pol.

Part Eight

The Battle of Cambrai

Wednesday, November 7th

I arrived at Izel at five o'clock this evening, full of gloom after a cold and uncomfortable journey. Charles Courtneidge is back on the job, even more full of gloom than me. The Major is away somewhere and Robeson is acting C.O. Joske has been posted to Home Establishment, and a new flight-commander is on the way out from England. What price my chances of a flight now? Ugh!

The really important thing is that the Camels are coming! In fact the first is here, having arrived this afternoon, but only Robeson and Thompson have flown it. The weather has been dud all through my absence, but cleared up today.

The fellows are very braced with the ping-pong balls and the assortment of gramophone records that I brought back for the Mess. I can hear them blaring away as I write after dinner in my cubicle. They're playing *Three Hundred and Sixty-Five Days*—it transports me back to our last evening of leave at the Gaiety.

Thursday, November 8th

I've done five flights today, including two short ones on the Camel. First impressions—more room in the cockpit, so you can take a deep breath without feeling you're going to burst the fuselage at the seams. (But why on earth didn't they fit it with a parachute?) Second, the exciting pull of the 130 h.p. Clerget, and the surge of power at full throttle. Third, her amazing lightness on the controls, lighter even than a Pup, which is gentle-sensitive, while the Camel is fierce, razor sharp. She turns with lightning quickness to the right. You have to be

152

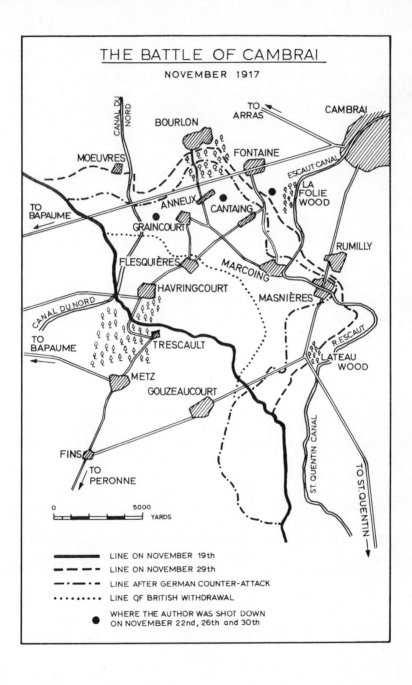

THE BATTLE OF CAMBRAI

NOVEMBER 1917

CANAL DU NORD

TO
ARRAS

CAMBRAI

BOURLON

MOEUVRES

FONTAINE

ESCAUT CANAL

LA
FOLIE
WOOD

TO
BAPAUME

ANNEUX

CANTAING

GRAINCOURT

RUMILLY

FLESQUIÈRES

MARCOING

HAVRINGCOURT

MASNIÈRES

CANAL DU NORD

TO
BAPAUME

TRESCAULT

R. ESCAUT

LATEAU
WOOD

METZ

GOUZEAUCOURT

ST. QUENTIN CANAL

FINS

TO
PERONNE

TO ST. QUENTIN

0   5000
                        YARDS

LINE ON NOVEMBER 19th
- - - - LINE ON NOVEMBER 29th
- · - · - LINE AFTER GERMAN COUNTER-ATTACK
· · · · · · · · LINE QF BRITISH WITHDRAWAL
● WHERE THE AUTHOR WAS SHOT DOWN
ON NOVEMBER 22nd, 26th and 30th

careful taking off, as the engine torque veers her to the left, and you have to apply full right rudder, but it's easy enough once you get the knack. I've not fired the guns yet, that's a pleasure to come.

Our one Camel has been taking off and landing all day as a succession of pilots tried their hand. Marvellously, nobody has broken it.

Of my other flights, two were tests, the fifth a D.O.P. of eight led by Charles. We met four D-Vs, and had a short scrap over Cambrai. MacLeod got one down out of control. I fired fifty rounds at another from 100 yards, but he seemed to thrive on it. We couldn't get any closer, as they kept withdrawing, and eventually they dived away.

Friday, November 9th

Another O.P. of four this morning and we saw no E.A., but were very badly archied by Quéant. I had a chunk of shrapnel nearly as big as a coconut through my starboard lower wing. I saw it flash past, and had a sharp dose of wind-up, expecting the wing to collapse, but it didn't. I flew home very gently. Incredibly, no internal damage to speak of.

My other flying was a low cross-country, and bomb-dropping practice. We were actually ordered to do the low-level flight, which normally is officially frowned on. Our machines have been fitted with racks under the fuselage to carry four 20 lb bombs and a target has been laid out on the aerodrome, on which we release our dummy bombs. I wonder what's afoot?

I've had the pip rather today. Looking back on leave, I have a mood of depression and disillusionment. I enjoyed every minute of it, yet now I'm back here among the chaps, I see things more clearly. I see all those lousy types in London, in fact all over the country, for whom the war is the big chance to make money and enjoy life. They don't want it to finish. You see all those fit men in bolt-holes, many of them in uniform, and you know that not one of them has any conception of what the people out here who do the fighting go through, especially the P.B.I.

They talk glibly about danger and bravery and so on, but these are just words, they don't mean a thing. They ask you how many Fritzes you've shot down, old bean, as though it's a cricket score. They just

don't realise that a machine destroyed means a life ended, some unfortunate devil, British or German, smashed to pulp, or burned alive.
Somehow, the air smells cleaner out here.

All the way on the journey back to Izel from London I had the
feeling that I didn't want to come, that I was forced to do so because
I was in the grip of a vast machine, like hundreds of thousands of other
young men, helpless, with no wills of our own, compelled to come
back to danger, maybe death. Yet as soon as I entered the Mess and
was greeted by the chaps, I had a sensation of coming home. The
familiar cheerful faces, the smiling Mess servants, my batman, even
Jock—and later the N.C.O.s and the men in the flight—they all made
me feel I belonged here, and not to the selfish mob in London.

It was then that I realised that what made me so often restless during
leave was that I was missing the squadron—and the war. Yes, the war.
Sounds darned silly, but that's what it was, the excitement, the un-
spoken friendliness, the feeling of doing something real. I hate the
war, of course, yet I was drawn back to it, I had a queer urge to get
back to where I belonged, even if it *was* dangerous.

I'm sorry to be full of the mopes like this. On second thoughts,
perhaps I'd better not post this letter, but stick it in my diary. It would
probably be too depressing.

Saturday, November 10th

Two more Camels have arrived, and everybody is having short
practice trips. I did twenty minutes, which brought me up to 300
hours solo. I tried a few stunts. She loops practically automatically, as
she is tail heavy, so much so that in level flying you have to press
against the joystick the whole time. Result, if you don't press, she just
goes up and over. But you have to watch your rudder. She does a very
fast flick-roll—on the Pup this calls for a certain knack, but the Camel
goes round effortlessly and instantly. I've not tried the upward spin
yet—I'll wait for that until I've got the feel of the machine.

Crash! Somebody's come a cropper!

I've just come back. While I was sitting writing this in my cubicle,
there came a terrific crash. I rushed out, as did everyone else, and we

ran through 64 Squadron's lines to the field immediately beyond. There we found the remains of a Pup—and the body of its pilot. He was Ballantyne, our newest arrival, who only joined the squadron the day I returned from leave. Several people saw it. While practising diving, he went vertical, then over the vertical on to his back, then into the ground. He must have fallen on his joystick. Poor devil, he hasn't lasted long. Four days!

Sunday, November 11th

Another crash today, and, strangely, in the same field as yesterday's. This afternoon we walked over to this same long stretch of grassland, nearly as big as our aerodrome, to watch a gymkhana held by the 51st Highland Division, who are in billets around here. Three or four of us had previously done ten minutes' stunting in Pups for them, rolls, loops and so on, before going to watch the racing and lay a bet or two. Soon some Bristols arrived from 11 Squadron, and they also stunted and did dives and zooms at the crowd of several thousand kilties lining the course.

One Brisfit shallow-dived directly towards a group of us from 46, me, Ferrie, Robinson, Thompson and a few others, and as we watched him level out there was a loud crack!—his right wing crumpled back, then the left, and the whole mass twisted downwards, throwing out the pilot and passenger as it dived into the ground. The two men came whirling towards us spreadeagled, and hit the ground barely twenty yards away. It was a grisly sight, they were so close, and the thud of them hitting the ground was horrible to us flyers. We looked at the bodies—we knew them both, had been on sweeps with them, had drinks with them in their Mess at Bellevue.

It was a miracle that nobody among the thousands of troops was hit, but both the plane and the bodies seemed to choose areas clear of people and horses. The engine was buried below the level of the ground, and you could have put the rest of the wreckage on a wheel-barrow. Fantastic that it should fall not eighty yards from Ballantyne's Pup.

It was the nastiest crash I have ever witnessed, and will take me a long time to forget. I suppose a main spar must have had a bullet through it in a scrap, which wasn't afterwards spotted. To see chaps killed in this way hits us much more than to see them shot down in a fight (except flamers), so it wasn't long before we all returned to the Mess, very subdued. Of course, the Scotties didn't see the thing in the same light, and continued their races.

In the morning we buried Ballantyne beside Armitage in Izel cemetery.

[The letters from November 12th to 16th describe uneventful routine patrols on Pups, mostly in bad weather, and the swift re-equipment of the squadron with Camels. Low-bombing practices continued on the aerodrome, and firing practice began on the range at Warloy aerodrome, west of Albert. More new pilots arrived. A feeling of suppressed excitement, not unmixed with foreboding, developed among the pilots as signs of a coming offensive built up, in which their role was clearly to carry out low bombing attacks on enemy troops.]

Saturday, November 17th

There are no more Pups in 'C' Flight! I took the last, my old 'X', to Candas yesterday, and received a Camel in exchange. She is to be my own, and is a beauty, B2501, made by Sopwiths, and the smartest in the Squadron. She has a handsome silver-finish cowling, with dark brown struts and woodwork. I'm longing to test the guns properly before the dirty work starts.

The new flight commander didn't last very long. He came up with us in 'C' Flight a couple of days ago, in cold unpleasant weather, and at the end of the patrol Charles led us in a steep dive against our pet aversion, the archie battery at Quéant, which received our spare ammo. When we landed, the new captain at once reported sick, as he'd almost fainted in the dive, and recovered only just in time. So he's been carted off to hospital.

Over the past few days we've been hard at it practising bomb-dropping. You dive at the target until you're at about 100 feet, mean-while judging the exact moment to release the bomb with the control on the joystick. Pretending you're on the real job, you then flatten out and swerve quickly aside to get clear of the upward burst of the explosion. Dropping dummies at the aerodrome target, with no bullets to bother me, I found it surprisingly easy to get close results, in fact mine were much the best in the squadron. My proudest four, dropped one at a time, were all within a yard or two of the target, compared with other people's 100 yards, and one man's 170 yards. I hope this unexpected skill doesn't land me into any awkward jobs!

Today Charles took 'C' Flight to 3 Squadron's aerodrome at Warloy, where there is a firing range. They have just re-equipped with Camels after having decrepit Morane Parasols and are naturally delighted except that they too are to do low bombing. It was a thrilling experience to shoot with two guns for the first time— the whole machine shudders with the rapid rate of fire and the double explosions. It has the new Constantinesco interruptor gear.

November 17th (Diary)

Something unpleasant is certainly brewing. We all feel it. First 3 and 46 both getting Camels in such a hurry. Then this intensive practice in low bombing, and low cross-country flying, which our neighbours 64 were doing even in England. Another squadron, 84, with S.E.5a's, under Major Douglas, has arrived at the other end of the aerodrome, and other squadrons have come to this area. Every village in the forward zone is crowded with troops (like the 51st) including artillery, and masses of cavalry with horse-lines everywhere. And there are hundreds of tanks around, too, from the air you see their tracks sprawling across the countryside. They move at night, but you can see them in daytime, hiding under camouflage in the woods beyond Bapaume. Obviously, a big push is coming any time now.

Sunday, November 18th

This afternoon, Charles, Hanafy and I set off to practice low flying in Camels, which after three days' practice we're supposed to be proficient at. Charles asked me to lead, as his compass hadn't been swung. Although we didn't know it, neither had mine.

We ran into mist and low cloud as soon as we took off. I set out on a bearing to take us to Bapaume, and as we were flying at fifty feet was much too occupied in keeping the compass steady to check our route on the map, but I wasn't worried. Bapaume, with its four straight radiating roads, couldn't be missed, even though the country around about looks like a battlefield.

Suddenly there was a tremendous racket of rifle and machine-gun fire from below, and bullets cracked past our ears. My faulty compass had led us bang across the Lines at Bullecourt. We slithered hastily around, and fled westwards, but Charles's engine had been hit, and he had to glide down and land, but turned over on his back in the muddy, shell-pocked ground. Hanafy and I circled low, watched him clamber out and wave as troops ran towards him, and, after pin-pointing his position, made for home. But it was almost dark when we landed, with the result that Hanafy crashed coming in too fast. He wasn't hurt, but it was an expensive jaunt, all told.

What's worse is that Charles may not be back in time for this coming show, and I shall have to lead 'C' Flight in it, which I've no wish at all to do.

Monday, November 19th

I led my first Camel patrol this morning, with Hanafy of 'C' and Dusgate and MacLeod of 'B'. We first checked up on Charles, who was standing by his still overturned machine, and waved to us. We learned later that he'd spent a restless night in a dugout infested with rats and lice.

The clouds were too low for comfort, and I made southwards, where things looked more promising, and soon the cloud did lift, and we reached 2,000, and, further south still, 6,000. By now we were beyond St Quentin, towards La Fère, over the French Army front, and I was making a wide turnabout over the River Oise when, in a feeble shaft of sunlight to the east, I spotted a bunch of black specks, well below us. I made for them, and found they were coming towards us, and also that they were being chased by another group, and that tracers were flashing between them.

These I recognised as V-strutters, but I couldn't identify the nearer ones, two-seaters. Then, as they passed underneath, I saw the roundel. They were an escadrille of five French Bréguets. The Huns, four Albatri, now spotted us, and turned back east, but we had 2,000 feet advantage in height, and I led the patrol into a 70-degree dive after them.

It was the first time I'd really dived the Camel, and the shrieking wires gave me a thrill, at 140 mph she cuts through the air like a knife, in fact our downward swoop put me in mind of hawks dropping on their prey. But the Albatros dives fast too, and we couldn't catch them up. We opened fire at long range, 400 yards, but nothing happened, and suddenly I realised we'd come down to 1,000 and were miles over. I turned back and climbed west by compass (adjusted this time!) until I regained my bearings, and made for home.

I find the Camel tiring to fly in formation for a long patrol. She's so sensitive you can't relax for a second, and you have the constant pressure on the joystick, which in two hours' flying makes your right arm ache. But she's such a marvellous plane these handicaps are unimportant.

But imagine after waiting all those months for Camels, striving not to be shot down on Pups, and looking forward to toppling Huns two at a time with my two Vickers, to find myself switched to ground strafing!

On landing, Hanafy crashed again. He's a keen and pleasant youngster, with a ready smile, but he just can't master the Camel, and every Camel knows it. But he's not the only one. So many Camels are being damaged in bad landings that the mechanics are working into the night, getting them serviceable for the coming push, which everyone feels is imminent. I do wish Charles would get back, this is not the time to be an acting stop-gap flight-commander.

After midnight

I'm adding this brief note before going to bed. The show is tomorrow —or I should say, now, today. Orders arrived during dinner. Thank goodness Charles returned in time. We were all up until midnight absorbing our very detailed instructions and special target maps, and also putting in a spell with the men up at the hangars, making sure our machines were ready. There'll be no time for that after we wake up, which will be before five, as we have to be in the air by dawn.

[With the capture of Passchendaele on November 6th, the Third Battle of Ypres virtually came to an end. Action now switched to the Cambrai area, where plans had been laid to stage an assault of the supposedly impregnable Hindenburg Line by tanks, without the normal preliminary artillery bombardment. The plan was to succeed beyond all expectations, and had reserves existed to exploit the break-through, the war might perhaps have been speedily concluded. But all reserves had been consumed in the futile struggle for Passchendaele.]

Wednesday, November 21st

At last I've found time, between tea and dinner, to write at some length. The weather has been completely dud all day, with no flying at all—except by me! I'll explain in the course of my letter, in which I want to describe an extremely exciting time. Like everybody else in the squadron, I've taken part in this wonderful break-through by the tanks, which you'll read about in the newspapers. I have lots to tell but the best of it I'll keep to the end.

Late in the evening of the 19th we learned that we were to support a surprise attack by tanks, without artillery bombardment beforehand, a new tactical idea which it was hoped might lead to the longed-for break-through. From all the preparations we'd seen in the past week, tanks, troops, cavalry, guns, we expected something pretty hot, and we were not disappointed.

There were four jobs for the squadron, three to bomb aerodromes just south of Cambrai, and the fourth, for 'C' Flight, to bomb batteries of 5·9 guns in Lateau Wood, also south of Cambrai, immediately in rear of the Hindenburg Line, and on the right flank of the main tank attack. We were all up and breakfasted before six, while it was still dark. It was a ghastly morning—low cloud, mist, occasional rain. The C.O. went up in the half-light, and hit the cloud base at fifty feet, but as Izel is 100 feet above sea level, we hoped conditions might be better in lower ground towards the Lines.

It was 6.30 before we could see to take off in formation, when we were immediately in the clouds, but Charles held us just below them as he swung gradually round to the south-east. How he found the way, I don't know, nearly forty miles across country in mist and rain, and never more than 100 feet from the ground. We followed blindly, our attention fully taken in keeping formation. He went to Bapaume, then south-east over the wide empty Canal du Nord to Gouzeaucourt, then along the straight road eastwards to our objective, a wood at the junction of three roads. We passed over a succession of unoccupied camps and horse lines, then, as we approached the Lines, saw large assemblies of cavalry waiting, and reserves of infantry moving up in scattered columns.

There were four of us, the other two being Dusgate and Hanafy, but at this point Dusgate's engine conked, and he turned away and crashed in what had been our front line less than an hour previously. A few seconds later we passed over the deep wide trenches of the dreaded Hindenburg Line, with its vast belts of barbed wire, through which the first waves of tanks had crushed hundreds of lanes.

From then on the mist was made denser by the smoke-screens laid in front of the advancing tanks from zero-hour onwards, which still hung around. We pass over the rear wave of the advance, reserve and supply tanks, field artillery, support troops and so on, then quickly catch up the first wave. Everything flashes by like a dream, and as we rush forward at over ninety miles an hour, twenty feet up, I get split-second glimpses that remain vividly in the memory.

I see the ragged line of grey diamond-shaped monsters, thirty to fifty yards apart, stretching into the mist on either flank, rolling un-evenly forwards, their tracks churning round, their exhausts throwing out blue-grey smoke. I see, behind each tank, a trudging group of infantry, casually smoking, looking up at us. Other knots of infantry stroll along a little in rear, between the tanks. To a flank, I see a dis-abled tank, flames leaping up, the troops standing helplessly around. A chance enemy shell bursts between two tanks, knocks down a small bunch of soldiery like ninepins.

The ground slopes upwards, trapping us under the clouds, so that our wheels almost touch the grass. I have to rise to clear a tank ahead, skim over it, dip down in front. It seems to be standing still. Then we've passed them, we're ahead of the advance and approaching the Boche. Smoke-shells burst ahead, a flash of red flame and masses of belching cloud, which we speed through—nauseous-smelling stuff that stings the eyes. In patches, where smoke merges with mist and cloud, we fly blind.

Now we reach the rear of the Hindenburg defence system, two lots of trenches, with troops in field grey waiting in them, their forward view blocked by the pall of smoke. We issue out of the screen so low and so fast that they have no time to fire and as we skim just over their heads, I see them staring up at us in incredulous amazement. Then they're behind. More smoke-shells burst ahead, and suddenly, unexpectedly, we're at the wood, at the Y-junction of our road and the two others.

All this time we've managed to keep in loose formation, but now we break up and climb, in order to dive and bomb. At once, we're in the clouds, and have to drop. The 5·9s below are firing, producing more smoke. Charles and Hanafy have vanished, engulfed in cloud and smoke, and so there we are, the three of us, whirling blindly around at 50–100 feet, all but colliding, being shot at from below, and trying to place bombs accurately. Even at this frantic moment, my mind switches to my beautifully dead-on practice bombing on our bullet-free smoke-free aerodrome, but I don't have the time to laugh.

The night before, Charles had indicated which of the seven groups of guns each of us was to tackle, but in this blind confusion there wasn't a hope of picking and choosing. The main thing was to get rid of the darned bombs before a bullet hit them. In a sharp turn I saw a bunch of guns right in line for attack, so dived at 45 degrees and released all four bombs. As I swung aside I saw them burst, a group of white-grey puffs centred with red flames. One fell between two guns, the rest a few yards away.

Splinters suddenly splash in my face—a bullet through a centre-section strut. This makes me go hot, and I dive at another group of guns, giving them 100 rounds, see a machine-gun blazing at me, swing on to that, one short burst and he stops firing.

As I climb up, a Camel whizzes past me out of the mist, missing me by a yard. It makes me sweat with fright. This is too dangerous, and I lift into the cloud to 300 feet, stay there half a minute, come down.

Lateau Wood is behind me. There isn't much room below, I nearly hit a high tree, swerve violently, skim through tree-tops with the mist clinging to the branches, then suddenly no trees, an open road. I fly along it, trying to get my breath. My heart is racing, and it isn't through being at 20,000!

A long column of artillery limbers—just what I need to recover my balance. I zoom, then switchback along the column, spraying short bursts in each little dive. I glance back—it is a shambles, half of them in the ditches. I'm sorry for the horses, though.

I'd no idea where I was, nor which way I was going. The compass was spinning madly. Suddenly the clouds lifted a little, I rose to 300 odd, and could see 300–400 yards. I didn't recognise the ground. There were no trenches, but ahead were encampments and military set-ups. The tents looked odd. And the soldiery—field-greys! Then suddenly— rak-ak-ak-ak! And tracer! I swung the Camel violently round. Two V-strutters were coming up behind me, guns flashing, a third behind them. Then beyond I saw a line of canvas hangars, a large field. A Hun aerodrome!

[This was Estourmel, five miles south-east of Cambrai, the home of Jasta 5, with Albatros D-IIIs, which had been bombed a quarter of an hour earlier by three Camels of No 3 Squadron. At dawn the weather was so bad, with clouds almost to the ground, that the Jasta's C.O., although aware of a British attack, refused to risk his pilots' lives by sending them up, even when ordered to do so by his Army H.Q. He obeyed only when the Camels arrived. Hurriedly taking off, the German pilots shot down one Camel, the other two crashing into trees. All three pilots were killed. I arrived when the German pilots were still angrily buzzing around their bombed aerodrome.]

I was in no frame of mind for heroic air combat at 300 feet, but to save my skin, swung sharply round again, put a burst into the first Hun as he whizzed past me, did another tight turn, put another burst at the second Hun—then my guns jammed.

There was only one thing to do and I did it—climb up into the clouds. I'd never flown a Camel for any length of time in cloud, and

I found it tricky. The tail-heavy feeling, the need for constant pressure on the stick, the tendency to swing left and to spin. My instruments showed speed 90, height 600, the compass was wobbling uncertainly. I flew as steadily as I could until the compass settled, wheeled gently until it showed 270 degrees and set off for home. I had to think of my petrol. I worked out that I should be safely across the Lines in a quarter of an hour. The compass kept straying because the engine torque was edging me always to the left, but I kept bringing it back to 270 degrees —as I thought! Meanwhile I cleared the guns.

The fifteen minutes up, I dropped down, came clear of the clouds at 200 feet, and circled round. Again I could recognise nothing. There was a large field immediately below, with men and women working, and I landed alongside, and waved them to approach. They hesitated, but before I could say anything I heard the crackle of bullets.

I looked round. Horsemen, a score of them, were galloping towards me from the further side of the field. I thought, these are our cavalry— we'd been warned to keep an eye open for them, and not to attack in error. But they were firing at me with their carbines. Bloody fools! I shouted, but there was no sense in being shot by our own side, so I took off towards them. Then I realised they were Huns, Uhlans or some sort of cavalry.

I swung over, dived, and let them have it. Some horses and men tumbled, the rest scattered. I went on to the sunken road they'd come from. It was full of horsed traffic. I dived on them and let them have it too, and saw men falling off stampeding horses. My dive carried me on to another road, with a column of marching troops. As I fired they bumped into one another, then broke into the side fields. Scores rushed into a thicket. I flew at it level at twenty feet, gave them 100 rounds. Surely one or two found a billet!

I realised that this kind of low strafing well behind the Lines was easy hunting, like shooting up red-tab staff cars on our side. And it was safe, nobody had much chance to have a go at me. I followed the road, wide and straight, and sure enough, in a mile or so, caught up a column of lorries and cars. On their way to the Cambrai push, no doubt. I switch-backed along, hosing everything until suddenly the guns stopped. Cocking handles down. No more ammo!

But I'd had enough. My petrol was running low, and I had to get back. The clouds were below 200. I couldn't risk flying over the smoke-shrouded battle at this height, especially with a maniac compass. I decided to chance my luck and get above the clouds, though I'd no idea what height they were. They might go up to 10,000 or more. But I'd got to try. This time I didn't bother about a bearing, I just wanted height. I rose into the cloud at ninety-five and kept her on a straight and steady climb. I had to fly partly by feel, and though I say it myself, you need very gentle reflexes to do this in the unstable Camel. But I did it. I had to. At 4,000 the cloud lightened, and suddenly I was through into brilliant sunshine.

What a contrast with the mist and murk below! Here a beautiful level plain of white lambswool cloud, and not another aeroplane to be seen. I checked the time with the sun's position, found I was going south and swung west. How far should I go? I was taking no more chances. No more landing in Hunland! I flew west at 100 m.p.h. until after twenty minutes I spotted a small gap in the blanket of cloud. I circled over it, could see no trace of war, went through, and at 1,500 feet came clear. It was thickly overcast, but no rain or mist. Lovely countryside, with a broad river winding below. I landed in a field between the river and a fine big château.

Within minutes there were a dozen Frenchmen jabbering away all around me, then along came a lame man who spoke to me in perfect English. Amazingly, he *was* English, the agent for the owner of the château, Baron de Rothschild. I'd come down near Creil, about thirty-five miles from Paris! I couldn't believe it, and felt rather a fool to have strayed so far.

When I got back here, I worked out that when I landed on the other side I was some distance south-east of Cambrai, maybe towards St Quentin. Then when I climbed through the clouds I must have drifted south towards Soissons. Now I'd landed seventy miles south-west of Cambrai. I'm obviously a first-class navigator!

[Such misadventures were by no means rare in really bad weather. The classic example had taken place a fortnight earlier when four Camel pilots of No 3 Squadron, baffled by low clouds and mist, and swept by a strong westerly wind, became hopelessly lost in enemy territory, and were forced to risk a landing to discover their position. They found they were near Namur, over 100 miles east of the Lines. No German troops appeared and three of the Camels—the fourth could not be started—set out to fly a westerly course by compass. They landed when their petrol ran out, only to find themselves prisoners. They had flown 100 miles due *south*, almost to Rheims!]

The Englishman took charge, placed a guard on the plane, took me to the château, contacted the local French aero squadron, and asked them to send a message to 46. Then he showed me around the building, in use as a military hospital, and the grounds, and introduced me to the Baroness (the Baron was away at the war) with whom I had a pleasant lunch in my fug-boots.

Eventually a French flying officer arrived, invited me to fly over to his aerodrome, one of the Air Defence of Paris stations a few miles away, refuel, and stay the night—with maybe a trip to Paris in the evening! Of course, I agreed enthusiastically. He started my engine, and I took off, but a queer fit of cussedness seized the Camel, for she just wouldn't fly to the French aerodrome, which I could practically see, but turned for Izel and the war. I had no map for this part of France, and had to beg my compass to behave, but the Camel was rather foolish about the whole thing, for the weather was worsening, and my petrol was practically exhausted. But we pressed on until suddenly the engine spluttered out. I switched to gravity, and landed in the first decent field near a village.

I'd come down by a little place called Chepoix, where nobody spoke English except the Maire's daughter, the local schoolmistress, who had a smattering. There was no telephone, and after her father had promised to place a guard on the machine, she took me by train to Breteuil where, in the office of the local military, after two hours' telephoning, two French flying officers appeared, who took me in a car to their Mess at Mesnil St Fermin. They belonged to the 218th Escadrille, with Bréguet two-seaters, and were on the move to Peronne to join in the Cambrai push. The C.O., Captain Kahn, and his officers treated me handsomely, giving me dinner in a nice little hotel in Montdidier, and putting me up for the night in their Mess. They also sent a message to 46.

During the evening we unveiled an astonishing coincidence. The Bréguet formation that we ('C' Flight) had seen being chased by V-strutters the previous day, down south of St Quentin, and had protected by diving on the Huns, actually belonged to this escadrille. After we established that, my stock rose high, and I went to bed somewhat inebriated!

Early in the morning a Crossley arrived with my fitter and rigger, and I went back to Chepoix. It was raining much too heavily to fly. I had no money, and had to borrow some from the driver to pay for our four breakfasts—vast omelettes and wine!—in a little estaminet. The rain continued all morning, so again on borrowed money I stood my companions lunch in a café in Breteuil. I also bought a motoring map to get me home.

Back at Chepoix again, with half a bottle of red wine inside me, I decided to have a go, and set off in the rain. I lost my way three times, flying at fifty feet and below, unable to see through the blurred screen, and doing frequent panic swervings to avoid trees and chimney stacks.

After two uncomfortable hours I reached Izel. It was still raining. The aerodrome was deserted, the hangars closed, not a soul was around. I circled the camp at twenty feet to stir everybody up, landed, and taxied to 'C' Flight hangar. People materialised magically and came to me as I switched off and unloaded. First among them was Sergeant-Major Jukes, who called out cheerfully, 'Wrong hangar! You're "B" Flight now, *Captain* Lee!'

While I'd been trapesing round Hunland, I'd been appointed to command 'B' Flight. Later, the Major casually handed me the author-ising signal from III Brigade. I'm keeping it as a souvenir. There'll be a small binge tonight to celebrate, but it will have to be small, as I and five other pilots have to be up at four to do the two-hour drive to Candas to collect new Camels. At ten o'clock I'm on another bombing job—but this time with 'B' Flight!

Saturday, November 24th

Before I describe what has been happening to me during the past two days I'll give the news about the others. First of all, Charles was wounded while trench-strafing in the attack on Bourlon Wood yesterday, while I was still out, and has gone to hospital with a nice blighty. Also yesterday, young Hanafy went down the other side, feared dead, and on the 22nd Atkinson was missing.[1] Also on the 22nd, MacLeod, flying with me, crashed into a tree in the mist, and died of his injuries next day. So, by and large, we're not in a too-cheerful mood.

On the first day of the push, the 20th, the squadron suffered lightly considering the risky weather, but maybe it was this that helped, for we flew too low to be shot at from the ground. Even so, Charles's engine was hit in the Lateau Wood attack, and he came down just behind our advancing troops. Apart from the splintered strut, I got away with a solitary bullet which slit open the back of both legs of my fug-boots—another inch to the north and I'd have joined Charles with a blighty. Smith was wounded and is in hospital. Several people forced-landed because of the mist, but only Sergeant Leigh was hurt, and he's in hospital, too.

The squadron has done much useful work. On zero morning Charles and Ferrie, who led the attack on Awoingt aerodrome, reached their targets, and though Robeson and Thompson, who led the other two jobs, were beaten by the mist and rain, during the day everybody (except me, hobnobbing with a baroness) carried out repeated ground-strafing attacks, mostly on chance targets. There was only limited flying yesterday because of the rain. The prize effort was by Cooper, who went so low to bomb a factory that he hit a metal chimney, and came back with a yard of it dangling from the buckled lower wing.

On the 22nd six of us had a foul trip bringing new Camels from Candas, flying at tree-top level all the way, and by ten o'clock the weather was worse even than on Tuesday, the aerodrome being half shrouded in thick mist. Too difficult for a formation, so I decided to take only MacLeod with me on a low bombing attack on Bourlon village, to be followed by shooting up opportunity targets.

It was rather depressing taking off, with our Military Cross padre seeing us away and wishing us luck with a solemn face. The mist was so dense that I would have cancelled the job if Wing hadn't reported

1. Second Lieutenant S. R. Hanafy was shot down and killed by Leutnant Ronnedes of Jasta 5. Second Lieutenant T. L. Atkinson was shot down and made prisoner of war by Leutnant Rumey, also of Jasta 5.

clearer weather over the Front. We took off in quick succession, but I lost MacLeod at once. Flying at fifty feet, I made for the Arras road to our north, and there the mist thinned a little. Near Arras, Mac appeared, and he then followed me down the Bapaume road until we suddenly plunged into cloud practically to the ground. A chimney stack rushed at me out of the gloom, I banked violently, my wheels missed it by a few yards, I levelled out and edged my way gently eastwards at twenty feet until I was clear. Mac did not appear. I couldn't know that he'd flown into a tree.

After waiting around for him for five minutes, I struck east until I hit Bullecourt, then turned south, where the weather conditions were much better, low cloud still, but no mist. I rose to 1,500 feet, and joined in with a couple of S.E.s that were driving down a Hun two-seater north-east of Havringcourt Wood. I shot off fifty rounds as he came across my front, but stopped when I saw the S.E.s.

I then went over the lines at Bourlon Wood at 400 feet in a convenient bank of cloud, and dived at a group of batteries outside Bourlon village, north of the wood, releasing the bombs at 100 feet. Shells were bursting at the same time, and I couldn't identify all my four explosions, but I'm pretty certain one and probably two landed in the central group. I couldn't help thinking, why am I bombing it if the artillery can shell it?

Sharply levelling out from the dive, I went on low to the north of the village until I hit the straight Arras–Cambrai road, and turned right. There was a column of lorries and other motor transport coming from Cambrai, and I switchbacked along, shooting them up. I looked back—the road was in chaos, lorries in the ditches and on their sides, and everything in confusion. This sort of job is very satisfying.

Cambrai was now just ahead, and I swung south to the Bapaume road, leading me back to Bourlon. I then came up with a column of infantry, about half a mile long, nearing Fontaine, which lies just east of Bourlon Wood. I shot up this column, circled over Fontaine, then turned back, and although the men had already begun to scatter, gave them three more bursts. They made for the shelter of wayside hedges and houses, and several began loosing off at me, but I noticed that at least a score remained lying in the road.

It was then that I spotted, 500 feet above, a plane coming from the

Bourlon direction. I assumed he was British, doing the same job as me, but as he banked I saw the black crosses. He started a flat dive towards me, and I got ready for a scrap, but he turned away, swung round, came back, again began a dive, changed his mind, and shot off to the north. I didn't recognise the type, but from what I heard later, he was one of a bunch of special low-flying planes doing attacks on our troops.

Shells were bursting every half-minute in the area, mostly north of the Cambrai road, and I assumed they were British. As I circled over Fontaine, I glimpsed one crash into a roadside house, which just quietly collapsed to a heap. I then realised that a fierce fight was going on for possession of Fontaine. I saw khaki and field-grey figures clustering close to the walls on either side of the crossroads, firing at one another round corners, but it was all very mixed up, and there was nothing I could do there. So I switched my attention to a group of field-greys filtering off the main road southwards into a large field flanked by a wood with a canal behind it. I dived low and began to spray them, but after one long burst, my guns jammed, first one then the other.

I slid across the field and banked round the wood, keeping as low as I dared while I tried to rectify the jams. Suddenly, when I was at about thirty feet, there was a heart-stopping roar below me, and the plane lifted at least twenty feet vertically. For a few seconds I couldn't see, all the blood in me seemed to shoot up into my head, and I gave myself up as a goner, but seconds later found I was still alive. A shell had exploded directly underneath me. Chunks of shrapnel tore through the fabric of the plane, one piece going clang! somewhere in the engine, which didn't stop but vibrated horribly.

I expected the machine to fall to bits, as it began to wobble violently. The joystick felt loose, with no lateral control and the fore-and-aft like lead. I closed the throttle, switched off, held her off the ground as long as I could, and flopped—I couldn't call it a landing, but at least I didn't turn over—on the large grassy field that was fortunately still beneath me. Fortunately, also, there was next to no wind. She trundled along for fifty yards, while I unbuckled my belt, just in case, then she stopped halfway between the wood I'd just circled and a sunken road.

My first thought was to curse our gunners—I assumed I'd been caught by a short. My second thought was, thank goodness I'm not flying my precious Sopwith-built B2501. My fitter had detected a split in the tail-skid, and I was flying Hootsmon's machine. The third thought was, now to scrounge the watch from its casing!

There I was, sitting in this big field all alone, with nobody in sight, though fitful rifle-fire came from Fontaine, half a mile ahead of me. Otherwise, all seemed peaceful enough, and I was trying to wrench the obstinate casing loose when—crak! crak! crak! crak!—and a sharp rattle of gunfire from my right. Startled, I turned, saw a machine-gun flashing in the trees.

I was out of the cockpit like a jack-in-the-box. I ran as hard as my full flying kit would allow towards the sunken road, keeping the machine between me and the guns, though I could still hear the vicious crak-ak-ak-ak! as bullets passed fairly close to me. They were after me because they were the bunch I'd just been shooting up and they were only 200 yards away. I had nearly 100 yards to run, and with every step was astonished that they didn't hit me. Then the ground dropped away, and I slithered down the bank into the road. I was safe—for the moment. I was gasping for breath—sprinting and flying kit don't go together.

There wasn't a soul to be seen, and I just sat there, getting my wind back and wondering what to do. There was still the crackle of machine-gun and rifle fire from Fontaine. I gingerly stood up, peered over the bank, and saw khaki-clad figures moving around buildings on this side of the village. So they were being driven out.

Suddenly I heard footsteps. I had no gun with me, and didn't know what to expect, so I dropped into a funk-hole by the ditch, one of a line which British or German troops had dug earlier. I kept low until they passed, then looked out—it was a wounded infantryman, arm in a sling. I caught him up and found he was a Seaforth Highlander. The bullet had gone through his shoulder. He said they were being pushed out of Fontaine, the Boche had brought up too many troops. I knew it already, I'd just been shooting some of them up.

As we turned off the road along a hollow which he said led to an advanced dressing station, a Tommy appeared out of a trench on my left, and asked me to speak to his officer. I had no idea any of our troops were there, but, after saying so-long to the Highlander, followed him up the trench into breastworks dug round the curve of a rising field. Here I found myself with the 9th Royal Scots, of the 51st Division. The Company Commander, Captain Maxwell, had seen me come down, and was surprised I wasn't pipped by the Boche opposite. His men had laid quick bets on whether I'd get away with it. From the trench I had a good view of my immense field, with the Camel perched there looking pathetically abandoned, and also of the wood facing us, some 300–400 yards distant, which I now learned was La Folie Wood. From here, too, I could see how the ridge on which Bourlon Wood lies dominates the whole area.

Within seconds of my entering the company dugout, Maxwell produced a bottle of whisky, and gave me a good nip. I needed it! I told him all I could about the German reinforcements coming up from Cambrai, and of my modest efforts to deter them, which didn't amount to much, yet I'd probably killed more Huns in that one column than in all my air fighting. He promised to send a message to my squadron by field phone, and gave me a runner to get me through Cantaing village, up behind us. It was a fitting coincidence that I should come down among the 51st Division. Maxwell was at the gymkhana where the Bristol crashed.

The runner and I had fifty yards of open ground to cross in full view of the Boche gunners in La Folie Wood, and as we dashed across I heard again the crackle of bullets passing too close for comfort. I reached the shelter of the houses in Cantaing absolutely blown once more, but the Scottie was, of course, perfectly fresh. From here, on the crest of the slope, I saw the Seaforths from Fontaine taking up position along the sunken road, so placing my Camel in the centre of no-man's-land.

In the long village street I stopped to rip down a stretch of dangling telephone cable. I'd fled the Camel so precipitately that I'd no time to grab my shoes, and as the ground was soft, my fug-boots kept slipping off my feet. Hence the cable, which I tied tightly round my ankles. But the runner, watching me, became restless, and suggested that we should not dawdle as the Jerries were shelling the village.

He was right. A minute later a shell burst in a house just as we were passing. The house collapsed, and the blast caught us and flung us across the street against the house opposite. Fortunately no harm was done, except bruises, but I did feel that for shells to burst within a few yards of me twice in one morning was too much.

Continuing south-west from Cantaing, I met a scattered stream of reserve troops—scattered because of the shelling—strolling towards the front lines in the most casual way, as though coming from a football match. The advanced dressing station, a corrugated-iron shelter backing on to the bank of the Marcoing–Anneux road, was crowded with wounded waiting to be taken away. After handing round my caseful of cigarettes, I offered to do some stretcher-bearing.

I joined three R.A.M.C. bearers, and, accompanied by a bunch of walking wounded, we set out for the field hospital at Flesquières, nearly two miles away. We were carrying a Seaforth, and I soon began to notice that he was a heavy man. In my flying kit I found the going hard. Halfway there, some approaching troops spotted me and my unaccustomed garb, and one came up and cried to the others, 'Eh, look lads, a bleeding Jerry flier.' 'Bleeding Jerry yourself!' I retorted indignantly, at which our Seaforth laughed so much his wound gave trouble, and we had to rest him on the ground for a few minutes, much to my relief. Before we started off he insisted on giving me his cap-badge as a souvenir.

Having delivered him to the hospital, I was both done in and baffled as to where to go next. I was rescued by a padre, Captain Stuart Robinson, who took me to the rear echelon of the 153rd Brigade, still of the 51st H.D. This was at Metz, some five or six miles away, south of Havringcourt Wood, and we had to walk when we couldn't cadge lifts on gun limbers and supply wagons. At the echelon Mess, the C.O., Major Campbell, gave me hospitality, after which, as I was completely flogged out, I flopped on a bed and was asleep in seconds. Meanwhile another message went to the squadron.

Early next morning I went round the place with Lieutenant Drummond, M.C., of the 6th Black Watch, and scrounged Hun souvenirs from the prisoners' cage, ranging from helmets and knives to a couple of revolvers. Eventually a tender arrived, and I said good-bye to my friends of the 51st.

We had to take a roundabout route home, as the roads behind the newly created salient were packed with traffic of all kinds. We went down to Peronne, and through part of the old Somme battlefield to

Albert, a depressing journey through miles of devastated country, looking even more stricken on the ground than from the air. On either side were thousands of isolated graves, some with improvised wooded crosses, others with reversed rifles topped by helmets—British, French and German. Further on were occasional little cemeteries, where the tidying up has begun, with their orderly rows of white crosses. What a futile waste it all seems.

We didn't arrive at Izel until nine o'clock, after a wearying trip, especially for the driver (he was the same as came to my rescue at Chepoix). Entering the Mess covered with mud, and loaded with souvenirs, I was received with a yell of welcome that for a moment quite moved me. I was too tired to eat, but had a whisky, distributed the souvenirs, told my story in 100 words (rather different from this latter!) and went to bed.

The chaps on the patrols following mine had seen my Camel, now in Hunland, and didn't imagine I could have escaped. Until my message arrived I was posted as missing—the second time in three days. So was MacLeod for a time. Poor old Mac, I can't get over him being killed while flying at my side. We hear that the bad Baron has arrived with his red devils and Fokker Triplanes, and so now I suppose things will get more hectic.

Now that Charles has gone, I've been flying longer in the squadron than anyone else. I feel practically a Boer War veteran. The Major is the only officer who's been longer in the squadron than I have.

Sunday, November 25th

General Trenchard paid us a visit today, and was very complimentary about the good work of the squadron in the advance. After lunch he collected us in the ante-room, and with us all hanging on his every word, told how, when at his H.Q. at dawn on the 20th, he saw the low cloud and the mist, he didn't expect any machines to be able to take the air. When he learned that several squadrons were already in the battle he was very proud and pleased. So much so that after a day of pilots' reports on their work and adventures he set about at ten o'clock that night sending telgrams of congratulations to all the squadrons actively engaged.

After this general talk he had short private chats with half a dozen of us, including me, and was highly interested in my Fontaine landing, and especially in my encounter with the Royal Scots—he is Royal Scots, too. He is a fine man, with a terrific personality, who knows how to impress and inspire us. To have a few words of praise of our work was an enormous encouragement. Trenchard is a leader after the hearts of service pilots, and though we don't like some of the things we have to do, such as D.O.P.s on obsolete machines, everyone in the R.F.C. looks up to him as a great commander.

Of course, every squadron taking part in the show has done useful work, though the casualties have been high. The four squadrons doing low attack work in support of the main tank breakthrough, 46 and 3 with Camels and 64 and 68 with D.H. 5s, have averaged a 30 per cent casualty list. Other squadrons doing artillery observation and air fighting didn't have such losses, but they did their stuff. No 11, for example, are terrifically braced at shooting down their 100th Hun since swopping F.E.2bs for Bristols in June.

The news on the ground is tremendous—it's the most staggering victory of the war—no wonder the church bells rang in England for the first time, though I hope they weren't a little too premature. The tanks might have pulled off a far bigger success, and even reached Cambrai, but for a hold-up at Flesquières, where a single battery knocked out about a dozen of them. It was 64's job to tackle these guns, but they didn't put them all out of action. Nor did we at Lateau Wood, which I hear was taken halfway through the morning by the 12th Division (they were the troops we flew over at twenty feet) but only after sharp fighting, and some loss of tanks.

The big disappointment on the ground was that the cavalry didn't go through, as they and everybody expected when the tank break-through succeeded. One squadron, the Canadian Fort Garry Horse, *did* go through, but they couldn't win the war by themselves. But what a bitter disappointment for the five divisions of cavalry, waiting three years for their big chance to end the stalemate on the ground, and when it comes with a wide-open door they don't take it.

There was no flying today, owing to strong winds and low cloud. Yesterday an absolute gale stopped everything, except in the early morning. At 5 a.m. I took seven pilots to collect new Camels from

Candas, but two crashed on landing, because of the gusty wind. Candas are supplying fifty Camels a day to make good the losses of the squadrons engaged in this push.

I have another early job tomorrow, low bombing of opportunity targets. Sounds easy, but it isn't, as Robinson discovered during the attack on Bourlon Wood on the 23rd. He came back and reported how he'd dived four times to make sure of a hit, and got one bomb right in the middle of a battery. While those of us in the office were saying jolly good show, a phone call came from Wing with a complaint from the gunners that a Camel had repeatedly bombed one of our batteries. Was he one of our pilots?

Wednesday, November 28th

I'm afraid letters haven't been coming regularly again, as I've once more been on a 'gardening' spree. At 7 a.m. on Monday I set out with Ferrie, Robinson and Dusgate on a Ground Target and Bombing Reconnaissance, which meant I had to find the targets and then bomb them and shoot them up.

This is quite tricky in a battle like this, where ground is won and lost and won again every day, for you don't know from hour to hour where our front-line troops are positioned. Bourlon Wood, for instance, has changed hands two or three times. There's no set line, no clearly recognisable no-man's-land, with barbed wire. You may see trenches, but you can only find who's in them by flying low enough to distinguish khaki or field grey. If in doing this you go down to 100 feet or lower, you're an easy target, and dozens of guns will be turned on you. If you stay higher you may not know you're over Boche troops until they open fire at you.

I made first for Fontaine, as I wanted to see my lost Camel, and there it was, squatting sadly in the middle of its field. I wondered who'd won the watch, and my shoes and shaving gear. Even here, from 1,000 feet, although I knew the field was now no-man's-land, I could spot neither Boche nor British front-line trenches with any certainty.

Suddenly Dusgate gave the engine distress signal, and left us. I continued towards the Bourlon ridge, trying from 800 feet to pick up a line of trenches or gun-pits that I could identify. Our bombs were intended for Hun batteries, but where were they? Our latest information, given just before we set out, was that the Germans had re-taken the village last evening, and also part of the wood. I decided to go lower to make sure.

Slowly losing height, I led the way across the straight Cambrai–Bapaume road, with Ferrie and Robby in echelon, all of us weaving constantly to prevent gunners getting too easy a bead on us, and all intently searching the wooded slopes on our right for signs of field grey. I had just decided that some moving figures among the trees along the top of the ridge *were* Boche when I saw flashes among them, from three or four guns. Followed by the two others, I went into a flat dive and opened fire. A few seconds later there was a terrific metallic clang behind, and I felt the thud of bullets. A burst had gone through the petrol tank just behind my back.

I looked over my tail, and my heart positively stopped. Trailing out thirty feet behind me was a wide plume of bluish-white vapour. It was petrol! Pouring out of the tank and being vaporised by the hot exhaust gases from the revolving engine. Exactly as I'd seen happen to planes in air fights just before they burst into flames.

Instantly, I switched off and dipped my nose steeply towards the ground. I didn't care where I came down, scarcely even looked—all I craved for was the solid earth before some spark set everything alight. The ground rushed up. I flattened out, held her off for what seemed a long time until she slowed down to landing speed, touched wheels, ran into a trench, and tipped over into it. I was upside down, hanging on my straps, half concussed—and the petrol was pouring over me. In a sudden panic I unbuckled my harness, dropped head first into the trench, and crawled along it until I was clear.

I climbed out of the trench and took a very deep breath. I was soaked with petrol, but I was alive. Ferrie and Robinson were circling fifty feet above, risking being shot down too. I waved to them to go away, which they did in a very businesslike manner in the direction of the Bourlon ridge.

A shell burst thirty yards away and although it didn't worry me, for I felt safe on the ground, the bombs were still on the machine, very obvious in the upside-down position, and a shell on those would make quite a bang, so I moved away. As I did so, a head appeared out of a trench, ten yards off. 'You all right?' it asked. 'I think so,' I answered, 'so long as you keep your distance with that cigarette. I'm soaked with petrol.'

He climbed out, and other men appeared, and watched me with interest while I look off my flying coat and tunic and vest and flapped them around until the petrol had evaporated. But I stank of petrol for quite a while. At last I went up to them, and found I'd crashed alongside 'D' Battery, 70th Brigade, R.F.A., which was using Boche gunpits occupied also by two large German naval guns. Their dugout, which was fifty steps down, each a foot deep, was like a great tomb, but was generously equipped with bunks and bedsteads and comfortable chairs. Here Captain Brock and his officers made me welcome. They even welcomed the reek of petrol, which they said was a nice change from the peculiar smell that most Boche dugouts have, which comes from the cowhide and horsehide packs that Germans carry.

The usual S.O.S. was despatched to my squadron, and then, as I knew nothing could result for hours, I clambered back into the machine, retrieved my shoes and exchanged them for my fug-boots. I now realised that I'd luckily crashed at a spot between Anneux and Cantaing where there was a depression in the ground, and the machine couldn't be seen by the Huns on Bourlon ridge, which was well over a mile distant. I took a stroll round this little valley with the Brigade Commander, Colonel Daubeny, D.S.O., who gave me lunch, then spent the afternoon with the Brigade Signals Officer.

We walked to Flesquières, and examined the scene at the corner of the château wall where the Hun artillery major and a handful of men had held up the advance early on the 20th by catching the tanks at point-blank range as, one by one, they topped the brow of the slope to his front. It was an amazing sight. In a crescent a few hundred yards long, facing his grave, lay a whole line of disabled tanks. One had advanced to within thirty yards of the battery, but this too was hit and burned out. It was named *Egbert II* and alongside were the graves of the crew.

We returned to 'D' Battery, where towards evening a tender arrived from the squadron's advanced party at Bapaume, jolting unevenly along a track that passed within a few yards of the stricken Camel. But they'd foolishly omitted to bring a trailer and I sent them back to get one, retaining one man, a fitter from 'A' Flight called Edmunds. He was not an armourer, but he defused the bombs and removed them, then set to work to dismantle the plane. I borrowed his tools, and helped, under his instructions.

The usual evening hate began, and one shell killed a 'D' Battery gunner and wounded three—Edmunds and I actually saw the burst, fifty yards away. We worked on even when darkness came, with the help of a torch, which was safe enough because of the fold in the ground. The shelling continued for hours spasmodically. The weather deteriorated steadily, and became much colder until about ten o'clock snow began to fall. We had to give it up, and descended the dugout to find a corner to sleep.

But we were up and around well before dawn, as the battery had to join in a barrage which preceded an attack by the Guards 2nd Brigade on Fontaine. By then the snow had changed to drizzling rain, but it was still cold, with a biting wind. The noise of the attack, which started before dawn but which we couldn't see because of the fold in the ground, went on for several hours, machine-gun and rifle fire, very fierce at times. Tanks took part in the assault, and later in the morning two of them came lumbering along our track, and halted in the dip to put off the Boche gunners shelling them, which did not amuse 'D' Battery at all, for the Boche continued firing blind, and some shots came uncomfortably close. The tank officers said the attack had partly succeeded, but the Guards had been badly mauled. Eventually, the tanks passed on, making for Marcoing.

Shortly a batch of prisoners and some wounded Guardees, all labelled, came by on the way to Flesquières. I talked to one of them, a Grenadier sergeant, with an arm in a sling. He already had four wound stripes on his sleeve, and seemed quite unconcerned about his fifth little dose. He said the Brigade had lost a lot of men, especially the Grenadiers, who'd had two companies practically wiped out by flanking machine-gun fire from La Folie Wood as they advanced against Fontaine—across the field where I landed.

Towards dusk, the mechanics arrived with the trailer. We loaded up, said good-bye to 'D' Battery, and left the place without regrets, for shelling had just started. I took a good load of heavier souvenirs for the chaps (after all, it's not everybody who has the luck to be shot down always near the front line!) such as Boche rifles and grenades. I got back to the aerodrome at 5 a.m. and slept until eleven.

After lunch I did an ordinary patrol at 8,000 with Robeson, Bulman and Blakeley, and much to everybody's surprise returned home with the others. It rained most of the time, and we saw no Huns, though there are plenty around now, including the Circus. It was something of a relief to be on patrol again, instead of doing ground-strafing. I don't like it overmuch, in fact I don't like it at all. Nor does anybody else in the squadron.

Ferrie and Robby said they gave me up for lost when they saw the trail of petrol vapour suddenly stream from my machine. They both went, as I suspected, to shoot up the trenches where the shots came from. I bore no malice against the Boche who'd shot me down, it was good shooting, and I hoped he'd get the Iron Cross, but it was hard to forgive him for smashing my precious Sopwith-built machine, the best in the squadron.

Robeson said, 'You had the luck of the devil not to burst into flames.' I've come to the conclusion that he may be right, and that the devil *is* looking after me, though I'd like to know what for! If I could only be sure he is doing so, I'd be saved a lot of anxiety in these ground-strafing jobs!

Thursday, November 29th

Early this morning I led a patrol of six for over two hours, mostly at 10,000, and mostly just east of the salient. Our job this time was to keep an eye open for the Circus, and there were S.E.s on this job too, but the Baron kept his distance. There was some air activity going on below, but our instructions were to stay up high until the end of the patrol.

The two hours completed, we broke up into three pairs, Thompson and Bulman leading the other two, and Blakeley staying with me, then went down to use up our ammo in trench-strafing. As on Monday, we had little idea of where the opposing lines lay, and again I had to risk going low to find them, but this time I quickly found a mass of field greys tightly packed in what appeared to be support trenches of the Hindenburg Line, well to the west of Bourlon village. I dived and came on them at fifty feet from the north, from behind, but they were on the alert, and let us have it.

You have to rise to at least 200 feet to do any sort of dive, and it's when you're on the crest that you become an easy slow-moving target. It took all I have to dive four times into this pit of flashing guns. Young Blakeley was darned good, diving repeatedly just as though no bullets were coming up at all. Between us we fired 1,400 rounds, so we hope we did *some* damage. It was a pity we didn't have bombs, I reckon there must have been at least a battalion crowded in that one spot. There were other bodies of troops too, spread in open country. When I returned, I reported it as unusual, but whether anyone higher up took any notice, I don't know.

The others found similar groups to the north-west of the wood, and shot them up too, but all our machines were hit, as the Boche was obviously on the look-out.

A couple of hours later I was one of another patrol of eight led by Robeson, but after an hour at 8,000 my engine packed up when we were five miles over, north-west of Cambrai, and I had to stagger back to Wagonlieu. I had a stuck inlet valve. Ten minutes later Dusgate joined me, also with a dud engine. He used his chance to point out to me, as his new flight-commander, that he'd had more than his share of engine trouble lately, and could he please have a new one.

It's nice to be a flight-commander, to be greeted as 'Skipper' and to know I'll be getting more pay, but there's a devil of a lot of work to do compared with being just a pilot. It's not only the returns and other paper work, but having to make decisions on matters I don't know much about, and making sure the new pilots are getting target practice, formation flying, and so on.

We've had half a dozen new arrivals in the past few days, and two have come to 'B' Flight. One of the others, Debenham, is doing a second tour with 46. He was one of the observers in Nieuport two-seaters who left the squadron for England just before I arrived.

By the way, our padre with the M.C. had left us. He couldn't bear the business of seeing us off at the hangars knowing that some of us wouldn't come back, and has returned to a regiment in the Lines. Good for him. That's the sort of padre one could listen to.

November 29th (Diary)

This trench-strafing is becoming rather a strain. In air fighting, what count, apart from having an efficient plane, are things like experience, skill, tactics, good flying, good shooting. Plus luck, of course, though chance is only one of the factors. But trench-strafing is *all* chance, no matter how skilled you are. To make sure of your target you have to expose yourself to the concentrated fire of dozens of machine-guns and hundreds of rifles. Compared with this, archie is practically a joke. Of course, strafing behind the Lines is different, the odds against you aren't nearly so great, and you can usually observe results, which is seldom possible in trench-strafing. I've got to admit it gives me the shakes, with so many guns firing you feel every time you dive that it's bound to be your last.

Even Thompson is feeling it, and nobody in the squadron has more guts than him. He lives in the next cubicle to me, and last night, about midnight, I was awakened by awful screeching noises. It was Tommy. I took a torch and went in to him. He was struggling and sweating and shouting, in the throes of a nightmare. The chaps in the other two cubicles heard, and came in, and we awakened him. He was very shame-faced. He'd just been shot down in flames, he said. Of course, this is the same sort of thing that Ferrie used to do in the cubicle behind me until he moved, and he's as stout as they make them. So it's not wind up, just nervous strain.

[The deep bulge in the Lines created by the breakthrough offered the German High Command an opportunity for a spectacular counter-offensive. At 8 a.m. on the 30th, after a brief but intense bombardment, a massive assault was launched against the British flanks. In the north, the attackers were held except to the west of Bourlon Wood, but in the south a rapid penetration was effected as far as Gouzeaucourt. This dangerous situation was retrieved in a counter-offensive at noon by the Guards Division, in which Gouzeaucourt was recaptured, and the advance held.]

Saturday, December 1st

Once more I have been shot down on the battle front, and am very lucky to be at Izel writing this letter. My companion on the job, Dusgate, is in Hunland, and I don't know whether he's killed or a prisoner.

Yesterday was altogether too exciting for comfort. It began with an ordinary early patrol, with me leading Dusgate, Cooper and Robinson. The clouds were low, about 2,000, and heavy, and there were patches of mist. As we entered the salient just below the cloud base, looking for Huns to fight, I saw that there was great activity around Bourlon, with widespread shelling and smoke, but even more on the southern flank, for the whole area was seething with smoke, shell-bursts and Very lights.

I led the flight down to 800 feet and from there we could plainly see that the Boche had broken through and overrun our forces to a depth of 3–4 miles. Pockets of our infantry, cut off in the sudden advance, were firing lights of every colour as S.O.S. signals. At first there wasn't a lot that we could do. It was difficult to distinguish the Boche from our troops, as they were deployed and our people were scattered. We couldn't tackle this problem in formation, so I gave the signal to break up and attack independently.

Flying at 200 feet, I found that the Boche soldiery were too busy fighting their way forward to give much attention to me, and so when I dived to attack, the job was akin to beating up rear areas. But the trouble was to find groups sufficiently large to attack, and with such fleeting targets you had to be very careful not to put your shots into fleeting targets in khaki!

The problem was worsened by the presence of a couple of dozen or more low flying two-seater Huns[1] flitting to and fro, strafing our troops. They were protected by Albatros fighters up above, scores of them, and fierce scraps were in frequent progress with our machines, mostly S.E.s. As I watched them (instead of getting on with my own job) I saw a V-strutter come down with an S.E. after it—the wings

1. These were Schlachtstaffeln, or battle flights of Halberstadts, for attacking infantry, which were used in force for the first time in this counter-attack at Cambrai.

folded back, the pilot was thrown out and fell with the wreckage barely a quarter of a mile from me. Another loss of life that could easily have been saved with a parachute—not that it matters much with a Hun.

After twenty minutes of shooting up groups of Boche infantry, mostly while they were attacking pockets of resistance, farms and other isolated buildings, north of Gouzeaucourt, I had a shot at a Hun ground-strafer, but the rear gunner was alert, and let me have an accurate burst, as I noted by the tracer. He was too low for me to manœuvre under him, and so I climbed up to see what was happening above.

While I was circling at 4,000, trying to discover the extent of the breakthrough, a D.F.W. came gliding along from the south, its occupants too deeply engrossed in examining the ground to notice me. I turned and gave them a deflection shot at 200 yards, fifty rounds, not expecting much, and was staggered when the machine suddenly dropped into a nose dive, engine on, and went down to hit the ground between Havringcourt and Flesquières.

I was watching it crash when something made me look up, and there were three V-strutters diving down on me from the scrimmage above. I knew I was nearing the end of my ammunition, so I dived down to twenty feet, bolted westwards, and made for the advanced landing ground at Bapaume.

While I was being refuelled, rearmed and bombed up, I was called to the phone—13th Wing wanted to know what was happening. The German attack had taken everybody by surprise and they hadn't much notion of the situation. I didn't know much either, but it was more than they did, and they were glad to have my report.

Thompson and Hootsmon now arrived, and after they'd been re-armed we went off together, but became separated as soon as we went low. Almost at once I found a body of infantry moving in mass along the very road along which, ten mornings ago, Charles had led 'C' Flight in the bombing of Lateau Wood. I flew along the column at 100 feet and released a bomb. The explosion jerked up my tail. With a target like this, from so low a height, I couldn't miss. It was appalling to look back as I swerved away, and see what I can only describe as a hole that the bomb had made in a crowd of human beings.

I circled back and shot them up as I switchbacked along, then returned on a repeat, until only corpses and wounded were on the road. The rest had scattered into the fields at the side, and by now scores of them were firing at me with rifles and machine-guns, so I moved on.

Next, I saw a Camel diving. It was Robinson, who had found a big group of guns lining a hedge, and after making sure that they were Boche, I joined him, got rid of my remaining bombs as well as some long bursts with my gun. Between us we put those batteries out of business for some time. As I was running short of ammo, I turned for Bapaume, and Robby followed, but his engine had been hit, and he forced-landed a few miles short of the landing ground. I pinpointed his position, and went on. I found I'd fired 600 rounds.

The aerodrome was now very busy with Camels and D.H.5s from 3, 64 and 68 (they're Australians) as well as 46, all doing the same job, though mostly on the Bourlon front. Because of the risk of collision with so many machines flying low, Wing sensibly ordered us to fly 100 yards to the right of the Cambrai–Bapaume road when getting to and from the battle areas. Although there was an air of subdued excitement as we waited for our buses to be made ready, nobody spoke much. In fact, there was an oppressive feeling. Almost everyone had been winged in the previous jobs, and I felt that people were inwardly asking, how long can my luck last out.

The third job was a repetition of the other two. I went down to the south again, but it was still difficult to find targets to attack, especially with bombs. There was a big fight going on in and around Gouzeaucourt, but it was the sort of thing you can't join in, as I found last week at Fontaine, so I went further east looking for opportunity targets, the best being a battery, with limbers and wagons, passing through a village, which got three bombs. The fourth bomb went to a large group of infantry waiting by a wood. I directed my ammo against small groups in field grey wherever I could find them. By now I was doing the job mechanically. I was shot at often, and heard the crack of bullets, but nothing hit me that mattered. And all the time, well above, Hun planes and ours were clashing in numerous fights.

At last my ammo ran right out, and I flew clear of the battle area at fifty feet, then on to Izel, for I was hungry. Here we all learned what we'd already seen, that the German breakthrough at dawn, under cover of mist, had produced a very serious situation. They'd attacked on both flanks of the salient, had taken Gouzeaucourt on the south, and were barely being held in the Bourlon area. Our next job was to help stop another breakthrough there.

Because the squadron now has many new pilots who can't be thrown into this ground-attack work, and because Odell, Wilcox, Hughes and Ferrie are on leave, eight of us have to do everything, and the strain of it is beginning to tell. We had a quick lunch, but, as at Bapaume, we hadn't much to say. Personally, I hadn't much spirit for yet another low job, but not a hint could I give of that. I was leading it!

I set out at 2.15, this time with Bulman, Thompson, Cooper, Dusgate and Blakeley. The weather was fairly clear, with cloud at 3,000–4,000. At the salient the air was positively lousy with D-Vs at all levels, but especially over Bourlon. There were also the Hun ground-strafing two-seaters which were being chased off by Camels and S.E.s. It was impossible to stay in formation with bombs on, so again I gave the break-up signal, and off they went to find their own targets, except Dusgate, who, by prior arrangement, stayed with me.

My specified target was a house on the edge of Bourlon village, a H.Q. of some kind. I tried to sneak across the Lines to get there no fewer than seven times, but each time V-strutters and Triplanes came rushing towards us, and we had to turn away. Some had red colourings, which meant Richtofen's Circus, and it was no good trying to fight *them* with bombs on.

By now I was doing the job almost automatically. All this trouble and risk to bomb a house, which might be empty, anyway. I thought, they're bound to get me this time, I can't always be the one to get away with it. But one becomes fatalistic very quickly. I don't even bother to touch wood since we started this trench-strafing racket.

At last, fed up with not being able to penetrate the screen of Hun planes, I went westwards, still followed by the faithful Dusgate, climbed up to 4,000 and flew five miles northwards in the base of the cloud, then approached Bourlon from the north-west. I saw the target, and gave the signal to dive. I'd been told to make four separate attacks, one bomb at a time, to make sure of hitting the house, but I'd instructed Dusgate to release all his four when he saw my first one go, then make his way back across the Lines and wait for me over Havringcourt Wood.

We dived steeply, and I let go at 200 feet. It must certainly have been an important target, for a devil of a lot of machine-gun fire came up at us. As I pulled out of the dive in a climbing turn, I glimpsed Dusgate, also climbing, but then I lost him. I saw the smoke of our bombs bursting—mine was a miss, but his were quite near. But the house hadn't been hit. I had to try again.

I honestly felt quite sick at the prospect. I felt I just hadn't the guts to dive down three more times into that nest of machine-guns, now all alert and waiting for me. I had to do it, but I told myself, only once. And I did it, in a sort of numb indifference. If they got me, they got me. I dived down, to 100 feet, and released all three bombs. Bullets were cracking round me. I swerved violently to the right, and skidded away at twenty feet, where they couldn't follow me. Whether I hit the damned house, I don't know. I wasn't interested it in any more. Marvellously, they hadn't hit *me*, but one bullet had broken the handle of the throttle control, and another had smashed into the Very pistol cartridges, which ought to have exploded and set me alight, but they didn't.

I flew due north to get a breather from the Bourlon mix-up. It was quite peaceful here, so for ten minutes I shot up anything that showed up, mostly transport on the roads. There were no troops for me to go for. Then I climbed up to the cloud base, at 4,000 and made south. I approached the western end of the wood, towards Moeuvres. The ground below and to my left was splashed with shell-bursts, and there were scores of machines swirling around in the air beyond. I wanted to keep clear of them until I'd found Dusgate, and made a line for Havringcourt Wood.

Suddenly a D-V passed across my front from the west, about 200 feet below. As it slid by, I saw the pilot looking out of the further side of his cockpit at the smoke of battle below. He hadn't seen me. I swung steeply down on to his tail, and caught him up so quickly he seemed to be coming back towards me. At twenty yards' range I pressed the triggers. The tracers flashed into his back. The machine suddenly reared up vertically in front of me, and I banked to the right to avoid him. He fell over sideways, and went down in a vertical dive. I swung over and followed him down for a thousand feet, but he was going too fast. He didn't pull out, and crashed west of Bourlon village.

As I was flattening out at under 3,000 there was a sudden crump! of archie. Then crump, crump, crump. Black bursts all round me—a clang in the cowling—a thud somewhere in front. My engine stopped dead. Not even a splutter. A great blast of noise came up from below—exploding shells, guns firing, trench mortars, the rattle of machine-guns, the continuous sharp crackle of rifle fire.

I swung towards the south. It wasn't petrol, there was no smell, but I switched over to gravity to make sure. No result, so I closed the throttle and switched off. There was heavy fighting going on ahead of me, and I was gliding down over the middle of it. I knew the Boche had been attacking here all day, and by now they might have broken through as they had in the south. A dull heaviness flooded over me. Was I for it at last? Was this where my luck ran out? I'd be made a prisoner—if the Boche troops didn't do the same to me as they did to Asher.

I was now at 1,000, gliding steadily down, already being fired at from below. There were Huns flying to my left flank, and any one could knock me down with a single shot. I could do nothing but go ahead, and hope I'd get across. I was zigzagging, looking over the side trying to discover signs of khaki, but the figures I saw scurrying beneath were field grey, no doubt about that.

I was now at 300. The hubbub below came louder and louder. The light was bad, the air smoke-laden. I had to find somewhere to come down, but the ground ahead was a shambles of trees, hedges, guns firing, dumps, trenches. I spotted a short stretch of clear ground off to the right, about the size of a couple of tennis courts. But I was too high, and had to lose height in a side-slip. I held her off to land very slowly. I daren't look sideways—I had to concentrate on the landing. Which side of the Line would I be?

I put her down gently, she trundled to the edge of a trench, and was pulled up by the parapet. Field guns were firing somewhere near me. I sat there tensed, waiting for it, too petrified to look around. For five long, long seconds I just didn't know whether I was a prisoner or not.

Then a couple of tin helmets appeared alongside the cockpit. I sank thankfully into my seat. They were ours, flat and basinlike, not the Boche coal-scuttle.

I got down to the ground, and was quickly surrounded by troops, from whom I learned that I'd come down south of the Bapaume–Cambrai road, west of Graincourt, well under a mile this side of the fighting. The Hun had gained ground here, after fierce fighting, but there'd been no breakthrough. At length, one of the numerous officers around, a gunner, introduced himself as Lieutenant Mills, of 'Q' Anti-aircraft Battery, situated half a mile or so distant, and did I need any help?

We found that the cause of my descent was a chunk of archie, which had gone through the cowling immediately behind the engine, and sliced off the H.T. leads, which were wound tightly round the shaft. There was nothing to be done, the machine would have to be salvaged. I asked Mills to send a signal to the squadron while I decided what to do.

The air above was crowded with planes, and for some time I stood and watched them fighting each other. During half an hour I saw three come down, one a flamer, but none near me. Both British and Boche archie were busy, sometimes overlapping, black and white puffs. I saw something I'd never seen before. A machine was hit by a shell, and blown to fragments. Bits of it fell quickly, such as the engine and pilot's body, but most of the rest seemed to float lazily down like leaves from trees in autumn.

As darkness drew on, the machines gradually thinned out until only odd ones were left. Then about twenty Tripes and V-strutters appeared, in a final sweep of the salient at 3,000. Lieutenant Mills, who had come back again, said they were the Circus. Two of them dropped down, and one dived after a solitary D.H.5 that came from the Cambrai direction, and fired successive bursts at him as they flashed across our front twenty feet up, the D.H. zigzagging along the road to Bapaume, and duly keeping to the right, I hope.

The second Hun came down at my Camel, and put a long burst into it. Mills and I dived into the trench at the first bullet, though he did no damage that I could see. But this little episode persuaded me that I'd had enough for one day. I wanted no more nights in smelly dugouts, nor cadging other people's rations. More important, the Hun might yet launch his breakthrough at dawn, and where would I be then? An additional reason was the shelling that now began.

Mills promised to put a 'Q' Battery guard on the machine, and after abstracting the watch from its case, and a map and my automatic, I set out for Havringcourt in an ambulance belonging to the 4th London Territorials, 47th Division, who were in the thick of the local fighting. Once there, it was dark, and I was soon groping around trying to find the road out of the salient across the nearby Canal du Nord. Nobody I spoke to had any idea.

After a quarter of an hour of wandering up and down the narrow streets I saw a light in a cottage and entered. I had a shock. The scene was one of blood and suffering, in a deadly, sickly smell of ether. Groaning men lay on stretchers against the walls. A couple of absorbed doctors, white coats over their uniforms, attended by R.A.M.C. orderlies, moved swiftly from one man to another, unhurriedly injecting, probing, cutting, stitching. Nobody took any notice of me. I watched fascinated while they cut away at the elbow the mangled remains of a forearm. An orderly placed it on a small heap of other amputated limbs on a ground sheet in a corner, festooned with bloodied lint and bandages.

Outside I drew a deep breath of relief. I thought of that Tommy waking up with no arm. There but for the grace of God . . . ! How the doctors and orderlies can work and live in such primitive conditions was beyond me. I realised that fighting in the air or on the ground isn't the only thing that needs nerve.

I continued on, stumbling into unseen obstructions in the darkness, until I suddenly slipped heavily into a deep trench. I couldn't climb out, so walked along until I came on a large dugout filled with a cheery bunch of R.E.s, who passed me on to Captain Deddes, R.E.s attached 47th Division. He gave me a much needed drink and something to eat, told me I was actually in part of the Hindenburg Line, and said I'd never get away by the Canal du Nord road, which was jammed with traffic, and I'd best go south of the wood.

The roads were pretty full even on this route. I got a lift to Trescault with a motorised machine-gun section on its way to Gouzeaucourt. To Metz on a gun-limber. To Royaulcourt on a kind of baker's cart belonging to the R.E.s. And from there to Bapaume in luxury itself, on the driver's seat of an A.S.C. lorry.

Bapaume was crowded with troops on their way to the salient. At the busy Y.M.C.A., at one o'clock in the morning, I had coffee and biscuits, and telephoned the advanced landing ground for transport. Eventually, a Crossley came, and I reached Izel at three, having been nine hours on the road.

Four hours of sleep, and I was up again to go on patrol at eight. But I'll leave this to my next letter. Thompson did pretty well while I was amusing myself ground-strafing. He had more sense than to use up good bullets that way. He climbed up into the dog-fight levels and shot down two Albatri, both on our side. There's no news of poor old Dusgate, and I'm afraid he's gone down on the other side.

> [Second Lieutenant R. E. Dusgate was a prisoner of war. In a letter sent to me, and still in my possession, his sister stated that he wrote from his prison camp that his engine was hit, like mine, by anti-aircraft fire, and that he landed without injuring himself. But in the German Air Force records he is shown as having been shot down by Oberleutnant Loewenhardt, of Jasta 10, one of the units of Richtofen's Circus. I do not attempt to solve this discrepancy. Dusgate unfortunately died soon afterwards in captivity.]

December 1st (Diary)

The A.A. gunners of 'Q' Battery were keen to show me a flamer which had fallen barely half an hour previously. I was a fool to go. It was a Hun two-seater. The bodies of the pilot and observer were sprawled alongside the ashes of the wreck, their faces just blackened bone, their arms burned off at the elbows, their legs to the knees. It made me sick at the stomach to look at them. That could have happened to me last Monday.

Sunday, December 2nd

I've come to the conclusion that I'm getting fed up with narrow squeaks. I had another one this afternoon, on this confounded trench-strafing. We'd done one show this morning, a C.O.P. of six, led by Robeson, and at 11,000 so darned cold that our guns froze up, and we had to come down to 5,000, where we chased two L.V.G.s to the ground. To conclude the patrol, we went low, as is routine now, to finish up our ammo against Boche trenches. They fired back, but it wasn't fierce. I think they were too cold to care.

We repeated this performance this afternoon, Robey leading me, Cooper and Robinson, and after an hour at 8,000 in atrociously bitter cold, again came low to find trench targets. I duly fired my 600 rounds, but quite frankly this time I really had the wind-up. As I was making my fifth dive on trenches sloping down from the wood to Fontaine, with gusts of rifle fire coming up at me, I felt the thud of a bullet, then my engine petered right out. Not a sound from it—but plenty from below, a hell of a noise, dozens of guns.

I was only 100 feet up, having dived from 500, and I gave myself up as a goner. My mind was a blank, there was nothing I could do except crash. Moving automatically, without any conscious reasoning, I switched on the gravity tank. At once the engine roared into life— wonderful music! I pulled out level, sickeningly close to the ground, barely three feet above a parapet. All I remember noticing was a baby-faced Boche wearing spectacles, mouth open, gaping up at me from a deep trench.

Back home, I found they *had* hit me, an engine bearer, but it was the pressure pump that had packed up, through the cold, I suppose, or the dive. I still don't know what instinct made me switch to gravity, but thank goodness I did. I felt exhausted for quite a time afterwards.

This escape makes me disapprove of trench-strafing more than ever. It's not that I'm against all ground attack work, behind the Lines it can be exhilarating, and you see results. Even yesterday morning's three jobs were all right, the targets were on the move. But at Bourlon the fighting has now settled down, and the Boche are well dug in. To fly along a winding trench, bristling with successive nests of machine-guns and mortars, and rifles by the score, all blasting at you every time you lift up to dive, and fired by people largely hidden and protected by traverses, really makes my hair stand on end.

The strain of waiting for that one bullet with your name on it, knowing that you can't dodge it like you can archie, it quite petrifying. Trench-strafing can be a suicidal job, especially if you're rash, and the staff types who so casually order it can have no conception of what it demands from a pilot. They ought to try it occasionally.

Yesterday my job was, by comparison with today, almost boring. Six of us under Robeson, roaming around east of the salient at 800 in low cloud and mist, and seeing nothing, then shooting half-heartedly at trenches. I was glad to get rid of mine in a couple of long bursts, and go home. The others did the same, except Taffy Hughes, who'd returned from leave only the previous evening, and was still half-conscious. He lost touch with the formation on a turn while we were well over Hunland, wandered round in the mist, suddenly ran into an Albatros, shot it down and saw it crash, though he'd no idea where, then flew west by compass for a quarter of an hour, and luckily landed this side, east of Bapaume.

By the way, the Wing Medical Officer gave me a check-up today, as I've a pain in my tummy which I think is appendicitis, but he says it isn't that at all, but some kind of indigestion, for which he gave me a foul syrupy medicine. I poured it out of my cubicle window. Jock lapped it up with relish, but I've not seen him around since.

Friday, December 7th

There's been nothing very exciting to write about during the past few days. The weather's terribly cold still, with some snow. The fighting on the ground seems to have petered out, and we've finished with trench-strafing and returned to ordinary patrols. But the Hun air forces, including the bad Baron's bunch, have been withdrawn—at any rate, we aren't meeting much opposition.

Two batches of new pilots have arrived during the past few days. They seem a very good lot. Among them are two more Canadians, MacLaren and Falkenburg. Amazing how many Canadians there are in the R.F.C.

We had another Battle of Cambrai casualty today, but a different sort of casualty—a dog. Not Jock, but little Sandy, the melancholy-eyed mongrel that MacLeod adopted and took everywhere with him, except in the air and in the Mess (which is Jock's preserve). Sandy became Mac's shadow, and had no use for anybody else in the squadron. He slept on his bed, waited patiently for him outside the Mess door, trotted after him to the hangar when Mac was on a job, and hung around there until he returned.

On the day Mac crashed, Sandy stayed up at the hangar until it was closed, when the flight-sergeant brought him down to our Mess. For days he's been wandering round the huts and cubicles, refusing food, just looking for Mac. He avoided anybody who tried to stroke him, including me, and has just sickened away. This morning we found him lying outside Mac's old cubicle, almost unable to move. We knew he had to be put out of his misery, but nobody had the heart to do it. At last Robeson took him away into the orchard and put a bullet through his poor little head.

[To eliminate the dangerous sharp salient of Bourlon Wood that the German gains in the south had produced, the British Line was now withdrawn to a position east of Flesquières. This move was completed by December 7th, the final situation showing as much ground lost as gained. So ended the Battle of Cambrai, of which Liddell Hart wrote: 'These eleven days form perhaps the most dramatic of all episodes in the World War.' The most important outcome of the battle was its impact on military strategy, for its lessons pointed the way to both British and German strategy in 1918, and to the German Blitzkrieg strategy of World War II.]

Part Nine

Cambrai Aftermath

Nothing of consequence in the air today. My only job was to lead a patrol of four, and all we did in two hours was to dive on six V-strutters whom we caught attacking two R.E.8s doing art obs north of Bullecourt. The Huns thought it was a trap, and dived away eastwards, and though we followed them down to 2,000 nearly to Douai, and fired half our ammo at long range, nothing happened. Perhaps it was for the best that there was no scrap, as two of my patrol were very new boys.

The chief current happening in the squadron is that Major Babs is going home. On Tuesday morning, when the news came, Robeson and I and a few others assembled in the squadron office to work out a farewell dinner (menu in French!) and binge for the following evening. Just then a D.H.4 landed and the Major went out to see what for. About a quarter of an hour later he came back and sat down in his chair without a word. Nobody noticed anything amiss. Suddenly he exclaimed, 'The bloody fool!' and fainted.

We soon learned what had happened. He was giving the D.H.4's prop a swing to help the pilot start when it kicked back and caught his hand, splitting it between the fingers halfway across the palm. The bloody fool was the D.H.4 pilot for leaving the switch on. We whipped Babs to hospital, but he insisted on the dinner going through, and was back with us next day, arm in a sling.

The dinner and binge were really something, as we combined them with one for Taffy Hughes, who'd been given a flight in 3 Squadron, and for Wilcox and Odell, who've just returned from leave to find they're posted to Home Establishment. They both came overseas after

196

me, but I have to put in an additional spell because I've been promoted.

To make it a really slap-up show we invited people from the other two squadrons, Major Douglas and some of his S.E. pilots from 84 Squadron, at the far end of the aerodrome, and Major Smythies and his types from 64. With three majors around it wasn't so rowdy a party as usual, and it didn't go on too long, as Babs was obviously in pain. There was the customary sing-song, and a mild rough-house. The only amusing incident was when three of us leapt on old Percy Wilcox from behind with the intention of debagging him, and were amazed to find ourselves being flung all over the ante-room. It wasn't Wilcox at all, but Major Douglas,[1] whom we now realise is an excessively wiry type. When he learned it was all a mistake he took it in very good part.

This morning, we were all up early to see Babs off on his journey to Boulogne. With his going, I am now positively the oldest inhabitant among the officers of the squadron. Major Mealing, the new C.O., whose nickname is Standback, is already here trying to settle down to our unorthodox ways. As most of the pilots are new boys, who scarcely knew Babs, he can shape them in the way he likes, without any clinging to the past.

Sunday, December 9th

No flying today because of the weather, which is not a good thing because the newcomers need all the air experience they can get. Robeson and me, and the handful of other pre-Cambrai types, now have the job of rebuilding the squadron with a new C.O. and a set of raw pilots straight from England. We've had eleven in the last fortnight. With the loss of seven people during the show, and the departure of Hughes, Wilcox and Odell, the squadron has been transformed. When I go into the Mess now I scarcely know the names of half of them, though I do try not to adopt the superior attitude of a veteran.

Of course, they're terrifically keen about having a smack at the Hun, and that's as it should be, but we know they have a lot to learn,

1. Major W. Sholto Douglas, afterwards Marshal of the R.A.F. Lord Douglas of Kirtleside.

and it's our job to teach them, just as though they were apprentices. After all, it's not long since I was an apprentice myself, when I would have been grateful for the sort of instruction we're giving. They're nearly all pretty young, but we're pressing them on as quickly as the weather allows, so as to relieve us old stagers of doing all the work. Fortunately, this isn't heavy now, we're under nothing like the pressure that existed when I arrived in the squadron.

The odd thing is that some of them arrive here with the wind-up about Camels, which apparently have a bad name in the training schools in England, through pilots being killed right and left by spinning into the ground. Out here in France none of the old Pup pilots has had any difficulty. The Camel is definitely a woman, and you have to be careful, but once you show you're the boss, she eats out of your hand. (Maybe as a married man I shouldn't have written that!) When the new chaps see how easily most of us do boss the Camel they quickly lose their inhibitions.

December 9th (Diary)

I had proof last night that this darned trench-strafing had begun to get on my nerves. I performed a show like Thompson's—maybe it's catching! Apparently, I was yelling in a nightmare, and *he* had to come into my cubicle and waken *me*. I was shaking and sweating with it. I was diving, diving, into a black bottomless pit with hundreds of machine-guns blasting up endlessly at me. I didn't like it a bit!

Thursday, December 13th

I've got my three pips up at last. The confirmation came this morning, and as soon as my batman knew, he rushed my tunic down to the sergeant fabric worker, who also acts as our tailor. I must say, it's very pleasant to be a real captain at last. But I'm pretty lucky, poor old Wilcox and Odell would have had their promotion soon, like Taffy Hughes, if they'd not been packed off to H.E.

There's not been much serious flying during the past four or five days owing to impossible weather, though we did have indecisive scraps on two patrols of the eight which I led. The trouble is that when half your patrol consists of newcomers, you can't risk a free-for-all dog-fight. Thompson found this today, when he lost Clark[1] during a brief bout with some Albatri. It's all very frustrating. It was disappointment enough, after months of tricky work on Pups, when I'd acquired the experience and skill to make good use of a Camel in a dog-fight, to be switched at once to ground-strafing, but it's nearly as bad now, when we're flying normal patrols again, to have to be wary of combat because most of one's pilots are completely green.

I have a feeling that you may find my letters less interesting than they used to be. The truth is that the spirit doesn't move me at the moment to write long, descriptive tomes. That spell of low strafing has knocked some of the stuffing out of me, I suppose. I don't get the same thrill out of flying, even on Camels, as I used to do. I don't go contour-chasing for fun. I don't sit up high and get that godlike feeling either! And as for trench-strafing, so far from being hawks diving on our prey, we feel more like pheasants driven to the butts!

Thompson goes on leave tonight, and we are giving him a send-off binge, for which I will now stop writing and get dressed. He is taking this letter to post in England.

Added at eleven o'clock

News has just come in.
>Robeson
>Bulman
>Cooper
>Ferrie
>and ME!

have each been awarded the Military Cross!

Friday, December 14th

After the news came through last night we settled down to make a night of it, those who'd already gone to bed getting up at the prospect of a prize party. Following on Thompson's leave binge, it did develop

1. Second Lieutenant A. L. Clark, was shot down and made prisoner by Leutnant Ampel of Jasta 31.

into a major orgy, and no wonder, five M.C.s at a go, when the squadron's only won two in a year!

About one o'clock we visited 64, and found them on the spree, too, as they'd been awarded three M.C.s. Our Sergeants' Mess made it an occasion also, and this morning half of them are still in a daze. The officers aren't feeling too good either, me included, but I led a two-hour patrol at eleven, without meeting any Huns, which was fortunate, for I was still seeing double.

In the afternoon I drove into Arras with Ferrie and Hootsmon to find some Military Cross ribbon. We eventually got it—at a price!—from an old crone in a tiny shop, the front room of a cottage with the roof blown in. They certainly have courage, these elderly civilians, living in a town which is constantly bombed.

Afterwards Ferrie and I flew over to 11 Squadron to congratulate McKeever on his D.S.O., awarded for a stupendous effort during the Cambrai air fighting, when he tackled nine V-strutters singlehanded, and shot down four of them, two to him, two to his observer. He and Ferrie, both Canadians, are very friendly.

Together with the confirmation of my captaincy, the M.C. came through on the 13th. It looks like my lucky number—13th Sherwoods, 13th Wing, R.F.C., 13th Infantry Signals Course, 13 dined at Bruay before we left England, 13 of us arrived in the first batch at Sutton's. But I have a feeling that I mustn't seek it—it has to come to me.

Saturday, December 15th

Poor old Hootsmon was carted off to hospital today, after crashing at No 8 Naval's aerodrome at St Eloi. We'd flown over there to ask some of the Nauticals to dinner, and for some unknown reason he span into the ground right before our eyes. He's pretty badly hurt, I fear. He was less lucky than a newcomer, Walsh, who's crashed two Camels so far, the last after a patrol with me, when he somersaulted on landing, completely smashing the machine, but he emerged unhurt.

I had a letter from Charles Courtneidge, who is in hospital in England, and seems very cheerful about it, except that as he got a bullet in the behind, he can only say, when people ask in what part of his anatomy he was hit, that he was wounded in the Battle of Cambrai.

Charles is, in fact, very unlucky, because being wounded probably cost him a decoration. It hardly seems fair, for he's been doing stout shows on Pups for months, as well as leading the Lateau Wood attack, and other unpleasant Cambrai jobs.

Robeson, with whom I've become pretty close since Babs left, agrees with me on this. He thinks the squadron should have had a D.S.O. to mark the good work done in covering the main tank attack. Robey's a quietly efficient type with a sly sense of humour. He said to me, 'You get shot down three times, you get a captaincy, you shoot down two Huns, you get the M.C.—and that's all you can manage in nearly a fortnight! Why, it's nothing less than slacking!' He also said I looked washed out and should have a rest before I crack up, but I'm not sure whether this wasn't another witticism.

I have put in three of the men for decorations, two in my flight, and one in 'A'. The latter, Edmunds, was with me when my petrol tank was shot through. Of the others, one is Sergeant Dolittle who already has the D.C.M., and who did outstanding work in salvaging crashed machines under fire in the salient, and the other is a transport driver, Leeding, who did the same. I hope they get something, though I have my doubts.

Another futile patrol today, with me leading seven pilots six miles over at 13,000 in thick and cloudy weather, and seeing nothing. Patrols in such conditions are a complete waste of engine time.

I don't know whether Robeson had anything to do with it, and didn't ask, but the Wing M.O. came to see me again this evening, ostensibly about my appendix. He was very chummy, and said that maybe I didn't know it, but I'd had enough. Being shot down three times had done me no good, apart from other things, such as shell-bursts. He told me that even though I wouldn't admit I was on the way to cracking up, my body knew it, hence the tummy pains and other symptoms. I said there was nothing wrong with me that another good binge wouldn't cure.

Saturday, December 22nd

We've not had much excitement lately. The work continues to be mostly training new pilots—formation flying, contour-chasing and target firing. Since last Monday I've done only four patrols, and only the one today saw any serious shooting. I had Edelston, Lambourn and Muir, and we had several long-range brushes with groups of D-Vs, but only got down to fighting with one flight of three, which was below us. I dived from 5,000, again enjoying the way the Camel cuts through the sky, and thought we were going to have a real old-fashioned dog-fight.

I found myself duelling with a silver blue, a very pretty machine. It was the first chance I've had to try the Camel's tight right turn in combat, and it worked amazingly, I was on his tail almost at once. But he'd obviously met Camels previously, and before I'd fired twenty shots he'd reared up, done a half-roll, and vanished behind me. When I came to, the Huns were going east, and we chased after them. I fired 400 rounds, in a succession of bursts, but they drew out of range. The Camel isn't as fast as it feels. It certainly slices through the air like a knife, but the D-V slices quicker.

In the afternoon I led a bunch of the newest newcomers on a practice formation and tour of the Lines—Falkenburg, Watson, Vlasto, Taylor, Kidd and Jenkins. Not very exciting for me, but they needed it. Some of them were skidding and oscillating very unsteadily.

We're having a cold and wintry spell, and several people are down with 'flu, among them the Major and Robeson, both in bed with streaming colds and temperatures. I'm acting squadron C.O., though I think I'd be better off in bed, too. We've run out of wood and coal. Road traffic has stopped because the roads are jammed by drifting snow, which has also blown across the aerodrome and blocked the hangar entrances. Everybody, officers and men (except the sick and palsied!) is constantly up there shovelling snow on to trailers, and carting it away. At least the work makes us warm.

In such weather it takes nearly twenty minutes to get prepared for flying, and even then when we get to 15,000 we're too cold to be of any use for fighting. We now have a new kind of flying gear, called a Sidcot suit, which we clamber into, with thick lining and a fur collar—better than the leather coat and long fug-boots, and much more comfortable in the cockpit.

It is teatime now, I must away and toast. There are four toasting forks, which we use in turn to make a slice, which is then smothered with butter. It's one way of getting warm, because we usually have a decent fire in the Mess, even if there's ice everywhere else. Tea and breakfast are my best meals now, I seem to have gone off lunch and dinner.

Monday, December 24th

I've never forgotten how much I owed to Nobby Scott's talks on tactics, and his demonstrations on patrol, and I'm trying to do the same for my new 'B' Flight fellows. The result is that they're very keen, and improve with every patrol.

Yesterday I led a patrol of four over a snow-covered countryside. What a transformation, especially along the Lines, a beautiful mantle of white covering the pock-marked earth, and the trenches showing up sharply as a maze of black lines zigzagging between scarcely touched white plains—except, of course, where untidy humans had already made their tracks and smudges.

At 4,000 odd we found a yellow-brown L.V.G. around Bullecourt, and chased after him, following him and shooting at long range as he dived down towards Douai, until he landed on the aerodrome at La Brayelle, where A.A. machine-guns held us off. But the pilot was so agitated (or maybe wounded) that he crashed, so we're counting it as a Hun driven down and damaged.

We enjoyed it all hugely, it was rather like having a hunt in the snow at Christmas. But we were very low, and as we climbed, archie started on us quite savagely, and we turned for home, doing various practice formations on the way. Then we did a steep dive between wispy clouds, and came clear just behind an R.E.8. The startled gunner at once let fire, and his tracers flashed among us, then he spotted we were Camels, and waved a friendly apology as we whirled indignantly around him.

I then went down lower and set out on a cross-country practice home, but within a minute, as we were passing south of Arras, my engine spluttered right out. (I afterwards found I'd been hit at La Brayelle.) I was less than 200 feet up. Underneath lay the old Battle of Arras trenches, with not a hope of a landing, and I resigned myself to a crash. Then, as I glided down, I saw, away to the left, an area that had been levelled off to make a football pitch. I made for it, and repeated my Graincourt tennis-court effort. A nearby smoke-stack gave me the wind, I landed gently off a sideslip, and came to a standstill two yards from a mass of barbed wire.

Hundreds of troops appeared from nowhere, but they quickly retreated, because my three companions came down and landed too. Imagine four of us on a football pitch! It certainly showed there was nothing wrong with their piloting. We were now mobbed by soldiery, as there were camps all round us, and thousands rushed to see us, completely packing the football pitch. The excitement was intense. I seized on some M.P.s and N.C.O.s to move them at least to the side-lines, and we managed to get Lambourn and Muir into the air, but Edelston's engine wouldn't start.

I found I'd landed near what was once the village of Mercatel. While we waited for mechanics from Izel we were befriended by officers of the 15th Royal Scots (34th Division, if I remember rightly) in whose Mess we enjoyed some pleasant peaty whisky. Then the 46 Squadron men arrived, with guard, and we went back in their tender.

This morning Edelston and I were up in the dark, and had left before dawn for Mercatel. We took off in mist, flew back at twenty feet in mist, and landed in mist, had early breakfast, then went back to bed. It's been foggy ever since.

One of our great joys these days is a series of lectures we have to listen to, arranged for our edification by 13th Wing. They range from such subjects as 'Recent Operations' and 'Formation Flying' to 'Sanitation' and 'Discipline and Etiquette'. We are, of course, all intensely interested in service etiquette in wartime. The trouble for me is that Wing picked on me to lecture on bomb-dropping, and I have to go round the squadrons in the Wing trying to think of something to say. I started off at 5 p.m. today—Christmas Eve!

Wednesday, December 26th

Yesterday was notable, not just as Christmas Day, with its turkeys and puddings and rich foods (none of which, except the oysters, I could eat because of my so-called indigestion), its church parade, its evening

concert, its various binges, its Very light outburst, but for a real event
—another batch of decorations! Yes, we had three more.

Just before dinner the officers all trooped along to a slap-up champagne dinner which the men were having in a hangar. Then the Major
gave them the news, that three of them had been awarded the Military
Medal! The three I recommended, Sergeant Dolittle, and Leeding and
Edmunds. There was uproar, and everybody was pouring down drink
without a care, whisky, port, champagne, beer, anything that was
handy.

I must say, after being in the squadron so long, I welcomed this
chance to cross the bridge between the men and us. We're cut off from
them, and live in a separate world, simply because they don't fly and
fight, as compared with the P.B.I. and others in the front line, where
officers and men are all in it together. For our other ranks to get three
M.M.s at a go brought them all into the fighting zone, so to speak, and
it did everybody a lot of good.

[These were the only combatant awards gained by other ranks in
46 Squadron throughout the war. In the R.F.C. it was rare for
such decorations to be won by other ranks, other than on flying
duties.]

At last we pulled clear, and went down to the Mess for our own
dinner and our own drinks. Then we staggered up to the hangar again,
this time for the concert, which was excellent, but also for yet more
drinks. How we got through it all, I just don't know. Almost the only
one who was sober was MacLaren, who neither smokes nor drinks.
Because the men knew I'd done the recommending, they plied me
with neat whisky so persistently I was reduced to slyly pouring it to
the ground behind my back. I can't remember much afterwards,
except joining in a mad jamboree with everybody loosing off Very
lights regardless.

Christmas Day was impossible for flying, snow and mist, but unfortunately today was clear, with enormous high cumuli, and I had
to take up a patrol of four at eight o'clock. You can imagine the condition we were in. How we didn't break our necks taking off I don't
know, but after an hour of icy-cold flying we were more than sober.

In fact, I climbed to 11,000 and chased two Albatri around the clouds. We went a long way over after them, and got close enough to fire about 200 rounds, but then they dived into a huge mountain of cloud and disappeared. It was a black storm cloud so they must have had a good time inside.

We had news from Major Babs in England. He was sent to hospital, refused to stay there, tried to sneak out, and had his trousers locked up. He threatened to run around the streets in his pyjamas, and we think they were probably locked up too, which must have baffled him.

Friday, December 28th

I spent all yesterday in bed with abdominal pain, which didn't matter because snowstorms and high winds stopped all flying. The M.O. came in the afternoon, and insists it's due to nervous strain, but I said there's nothing wrong with my nerves if I can pull off a successful emergency landing from 200 feet on to a football pitch.

This morning I had a patrol laid on, and duly got up for it, but felt too ropey even to take breakfast, except a cup of hot milk. When Robinson said I looked too groggy to fly, and offered to lead the patrol, I was thankful, and went back to bed. Three hours later he and Lambourn burst into my cubicle with the news that they'd shot down a Pfalz two-seater in flames. They came across it south-west of Cambrai, and fired at 300 yards, not expecting much, and were amazed when it suddenly dived down, alight, and crashed just west of Havringcourt.

I slept most of the day, and after dining on my usual milk and brandy, settled down to write this. But I can't stay here, there's a binge developing in the Mess to celebrate Robby's flamer. I can hear him yelling 'Cheerio, Chokololovitch!', his favourite war-cry. I can't bear it any longer, so now I shall get up and dress and join them, maybe a drop of booze will do me good.

Sunday, December 30th

I felt much better yesterday, and led a patrol of four, for two hours, mostly at 7,000. The weather was clear, and about four miles over I spotted two L.V.G.s at 4,000 and we dived steeply on them. I again got the thrill of streaking down at 130 mph in a nearly vertical dive, very different from the protesting throbbing of the Pup. We pulled up underneath the rearmost machine, and fired at it one after another from below and behind. The pilot jinked furiously, and the observer put in some very hot shots, but we should have got them easily, our shooting must have been atrocious.

After 100 rounds my right Vickers jammed, and by the time I'd knocked the cocking handle down the Hun had dived steeply east. His companion had vanished earlier. I was furious at missing what should have been a gift, especially after Robby's long-range effort. Four of us should have got them both, but we made a mess of it, and didn't even get one—'driven down' doesn't rate for much. We'll have to have a small tactical inquest on this little show.

Walsh crashed again today, in a wood near Amiens, in a new Camel he'd just collected from Candas, but this time he killed himself. He was flying in misty weather, and it was the sort of thing any of us might have done over the past few weeks—as MacLeod did. Taylor could have done the same when he also collected a new machine, he too lost his way in mist, and crash-landed in the Scarpe valley— fortunately on this side of the Lines.

Tuesday, January 1st, 1918

At 11.55 last night I stood with Major Mealing, Robeson, Captain Thom (the new R.O.) and some of the old-timers outside the Mess, waiting for the New Year. Scattered in the orchard around us were the others, Colt in one hand, Very pistol in the other. We waited in the darkness for the Major, who kept an eye on his watch with a torch.

Twelve o'clock! The Major fires a red Very light, and instantly all the others go soaring up into the air. Then comes a fusillade of shots as the automatics are emptied, also upwards! Then hoots and catcalls, followed by prolonged cheering. As it peters out we hear a similar din coming from 64 next door.

We go into the Mess, drink toddy, sing *Auld Lang Syne*, yell 'Cheerio 46!' and 'Cheerio, Chokololovitch!' We're visited by some of the chaps from 64, go through it all again, and eventually stagger off to bed. It's 1918, and we're all still alive!

New Year's Day, I was up early for a patrol at eight, but a visit to the hangars showed that the mist was much too thick for flying. After lunch, the Major asked me not to fly any more, as he's recommended me for H.E. The M.O. has reported that I am run down physically, and won't be able to do any more useful flying until I've had a good spell of leave.

Now that the decision has been made, I think maybe they're right. While I was on leave, I had that queer urge to get back here, and as I mentioned before, when I arrived at the Mess it seemed like coming home. But now things have changed so much, so many chaps have gone, and half the people in the Mess are strangers. I've been longer in the squadron than anybody (a month longer than Ferrie, who's next) and now I realise I've had enough. I feel a sort of waning of the spirit, and I shan't grumble if I'm now for home.

Ferrie is to take over from me, and I couldn't wish for a better successor. He'd been warned that he was getting a flight in No 3, but now that I'm off pretty soon the Major's holding him here.

I spent a lazy and interesting hour going through my log-book. I find I've done 386 hours solo, plus 12½ hours dual. I've done 260 hours in France, of which 222 were over the Lines. I've done 118 patrols and ground strafings, been reported missing four times, had 56 combats, and shot down 11 Huns, 5 by me solo, the rest shared. Not wonderful compared with people like Ball, Bishop, Collishaw and McCudden, and I'm miles from being an ace, but at least I'm not a pigeon any longer, in fact I think I can consider myself practically a hawk!

Thursday, January 3rd

I'm terribly depressed this evening. Ferrie has been killed. He led his patrol out this afternoon, had a scrap, came back leading the others, then as they were flying along quite normally in formation, his right wing suddenly folded back, then the other, and the wreck plunged vertically down. A bullet must have gone through a main spar during the fight.

The others went after him and steered close to him in vertical dives.

They could see him, struggling to get clear of his harness, then half standing up. They said it was horrible to watch him trying to decide whether to jump. He didn't, and the machine and he were smashed to nothingness.

I can't believe it. Little Ferrie, with his cheerful grin, one of the finest chaps in the squadron. God, imagine his last moments, seeing the ground rushing up at him, knowing he was a dead man, unable to move, unable to do anything but wait for it. A parachute could have saved him, there's no doubt about that. What the hell is wrong with those callous dolts at home that they won't give them to us?

Monday, January 7th

There's no point in posting this letter, I'll be home before it could get there, but I'm writing it to round off the scores and scores I've written, and shall take it with me when I leave for England tonight.

They gave me a whale of a farewell last evening. Gallons of booze. Too many speeches. All the old songs—*So Early in the Morning*, *The only, only Way*, *Haven't Got a Hope in the Morning*, as well as songs from the shows—*Some Girl Has Got to Darn His Socks*, *If You Could Care for Me*, *Three Hundred and Sixty-Five Days*, *Here Comes Tootsie*, *Hello, My Dearie*, *I'm Lonesome for You*. The new boys have learnt them very quickly. These are tunes I shall never forget, they're part of 46, part of me.

Thompson is taking over 'B' Flight—and he'll be every bit as good as Ferrie would have been. Poor old Ferrie. And Asher. And Armitage, MacLeod and McDonald and Eberlin and Kay and all the others who didn't have my kind of luck. Yes, I've been darned lucky, but at Cambrai I used it all up, and I couldn't have expected any more.

And so it's all over, and I'm for home. But I'm not saying goodbye—I may come back, like Debenham. So it's just Cheerio, Forty-Six —to me the most wonderful squadron of them all.

Postscript

What happened to those I left behind?

Robeson, on promotion to major to command No 24 Squadron, was relieved as O.C. 'A' Flight by 'Chaps' Marchant, who was on a second tour, and who soon won the M.C. Luxmore also returned for a second tour, but to No 54 Squadron, where as a flight-commander he gained the D.F.C. P. W. S. (Georgie) Bulman was wounded late in January, but in March came back as a flight-commander to No 3 Squadron, where he was awarded a bar to his M.C. Another early winner of the M.C. was H. N. C. Robinson, with also the Croix de Guerre.

The squadron's star was Donald MacLaren, the non-smoking, non-drinking Canadian from Vancouver, who after three quiet months to learn the trade, started shooting down Huns freely when the German attack began in March. He became the squadron's top ace, obtaining fifty-four victories in six months, and ended his time in 46 as acting C.O., with the D.S.O., M.C. and bar, D.F.C., and two French decorations. He was fifth in the roll of British aces.

The second star Hun-hunter was G. E. Thompson, with twenty-one victims, for which he held the D.S.O. and M.C. He was killed soon after posting to Home Establishment, and in the way he always dreaded, his plane bursting into flames seconds after take-off at Portmeadow. Others who were soon killed in flying accidents were Percy Wilcox, who crashed early in 1918 at Martlesham Heath, and Nobby Scott at Shoreham.

Among the numerous casualties before and during the March fighting were A. L. Kidd, F. C. Bailey, J. W. Muir, E. Smith and W. J. Shorter, all killed, G. D. Jenkins and several others wounded, and R. H. Edelston, G. D. Falkenburg and A. L. T. Taylor, prisoners of war.

And me? After a spell of leave, and some months of instructing on Camels at Joyce Green, I was posted to do a second tour, this time on Salamanders, the new armoured plane for ground strafing. The war ended before the squadron could get to France. Charles Courtneidge, after spending the last year of the war on flying instruction, followed his father and sister into the theatre. We met occasionally between the wars. He died shortly before World War II broke out. Normie Dimmock also became a flying instructor, and was awarded the A.F.C.

After the war Major Babington rose high in the R.A.F., becoming in the fulness of time Air Marshal Sir Philip, K.C.B. He and I were the only two members of 46 of 1917 vintage who elected to remain in the new Service, though Dimmock returned to it later, and several came back to serve through World War II. 'Chaps' Marchant, who died a few years ago, went into the family business, but he also set about organising the squadron annual reunions that have taken place ever since.

The 50th reunion dinner, held while this book was nearing completion, was attended by ten of the 1916–18 old-timers, as well as by seventy-five other officers, all of whom, except a handful of guests, served in the squadron between the wars, during World War II, and subsequently, among these the members of the present-day squadron.

Appendix A

The Failure in High Command

In October 1909 the Secretary of State for War, Mr R. B. Haldane (later Viscount Haldane) appointed a highly qualified civil engineer, Mr Mervyn O'Gorman, as Superintendent of the Royal Aircraft Factory at Farnborough. He did this because he believed that aeroplanes could be designed efficiently only under 'scientific' governmental supervision. His belief was to be bitterly paid for in flesh and blood.

O'Gorman was an able engineer, but he was also an ambitious empire-builder, who considered that the role of the Factory should be to sponsor a standard government aeroplane. He was in a strong position, for as he had direct access to Haldane, he could outmanoeuvre any officer who disagreed with him. But there were few who did. Most of the senior Royal Flying Corps officers at the War Office regarded the flying machine as merely an aerial extension of cavalry reconnaissance, for which they demanded a stable vehicle which could be flown 'hands off' while the pilot examined the ground, wrote notes and drew maps, and they were satisfied that O'Gorman had an aeroplane that filled the bill.

This was the Blériot (later British) Experimental, which was slow, unmanoeuvrable, heavy on the controls and difficult to arm with a machine-gun, but O'Gorman won authority to develop and standardise it because it was inherently stable, and it was backed by General Henderson, head of the Directorate of Military Aeronautics, and by other senior officers, among them General Sykes and General Sefton Brancker, who as a notably unskilful pilot saw only virtue in a machine that practically piloted itself. None of these officers can escape his share of responsibility for the failure of the High Command to provide the R.F.C. with aeroplanes fit to fly and fight in.

Supporting O'Gorman's aim of creating a Government monopoly in the construction of military aeroplanes, the Directorate restricted the growth of private manufacturing, to the extent of equipping the Corps in part from French firms. When war began Britain thus lacked a flourishing aircraft industry, such as existed in France and Germany, and no military aeroplanes were in production stage other than the current Factory B.E.—the B.E.2c.

On O'Gorman's urgent recommendation the Directorate rashly agreed that this machine should be standardised and produced in quantity. Meticulously detailed drawings for its manufacture were prepared by the Factory, and issued to contractors, many of whom had never made any aeroplane part before. In the course of time over twenty firms were engaged in turning out the B.E.2c, 2d and 2e, and B.E.12, but before they were successively in production they were already obsolescent, so swift were advances in the design of aircraft under the spur of war.

Every subsequent aircraft produced by the Factory, with the exception of the F.E. pusher-fighters, was a development of the basic, stable B.E., and every one except the last, the S.E.5, was fundamentally inefficient for military use. The B.E.s were by far the most ineffective and vulnerable aeroplanes to fly in France. Their replacement, the cumbersome R.E.8, was little better, and at first even worse, for it was so dangerous that many service pilots refused to fly it. No 52 Squadron, the first to be equipped with it in France, had so many fatal crashes that the pilots asked, and were allowed, to revert to B.E.2cs. Another R.E.8 squadron, No 59, lost ten machines and crews in one day in 'Bloody April'.

It is significant that of Richtofen's 80 British and French victories, 46 were supplied by the Factory—29 B.E.s and R.E.8s, 14 F.E.s and 3 S.E.5s. The S.E.5a, a compacted and more manœuvrable B.E.12, with a powerful engine, proved capable of meeting German fighters on level terms, and it was the Factory's only real success.

The inability of the B.E.s to fight, or even to defend themselves, was shown when the Fokker monoplanes began to shoot them down by the dozen, but because the consequent casualties were minute compared with those of the ground battles, they were regarded as of no importance by the War Cabinet, though not by Trenchard, in command of the R.F.C. in the field. But towards the end of 1915 public attention was called to them by Noel Pemberton-Billing, M.P., who described the B.E.s as 'Fokker fodder', and condemned the R.F.C. High Command for failing to supply their pilots with worthy aeroplanes. He was supported by other members of both Commons and Lords, who declared that 'our pilots are being murdered rather than killed'.

The Government was forced to order a judicial enquiry, which began in May 1916 under Mr Justice Bailhache. His report, published in November, whitewashed the senior R.F.C. officers responsible, but blamed the supply organisation. O'Gorman became the scapegoat, and a few months later resigned. Pemberton-Billing's accusations were dismissed as extravagant, but they were to be proved to the hilt in 'Bloody April'.

Even before then it had become clear that the control of design and production by a bureaucratically run 'Factory' had utterly failed, and that aeroplanes were urgently needed that could fight as well as fly. The R.F.C. pundits turned to the aircraft industry they had so stupidly stifled, only to find that every firm of note was committed by contract to the R.N.A.S.

Fortunately for British aviation, the Admiralty had, from the beginning, declined to be tied to the Factory for its machines, and backed by the vigour and long-sightedness of the First Lord, Winston Churchill, had entrusted the aircraft industry in both Britain and France with the production of airframes and engines to meet specific naval requirements. Such firms as Short, Sopwith, Bristol, Airco (de Havilland), Vickers, Rolls-Royce had already turned out much better aeroplanes and engines than any of the Factory's products.

Because the R.N.A.S. had contracted for more machines than it could use, a number of types, such as Sopwith two-seaters, were switched to the R F.C. But because the whole industrial complex for aircraft manufacture had been bedevilled by the War Office's long neglect, and the Factory's jealous embargoes, there were constant delays which kept machines from reaching the Front until they were obsolescent. The pressure was partly eased by the purchase of surplus French aircraft, such as the Spad, Nieuport and Morane monoplane.

In spite of these drastic expedients, the senior officers of the R.F.C. Supply Directorate, none of whom had any experience of air combat, except in the most gentlemanly way with carbines and revolvers, still clung to the inherently stable products of the Factory. The episode of the Sopwith Pup was a typical example of this attitude. The Pup, with Admiralty agreement, was offered to the R.F.C. in February 1916, but on O'Gorman's advice preference was given to his so-called fighter, the B.E.12. When the B.E.12 abjectly failed, with the usual loss of life, against the Albatros D-II, the R.F.C. was reduced, in November, to borrowing No 8 Naval Squadron, whose Pups promptly dealt with the D-II. The Pup did not reach the R.F.C. until the R.N.A.S. tired of it at the end of 1916.

The Supply Directorate, while decreeing that the Factory, too committed by its rigid organisation for any rapid major change, should continue to devote its extensive supply facilities to producing proved 'duds', now entered into competition with the R.N.A.S. for the products of the airframe and engine firms of Britain and France. So began the phase of rivalry between War Office and Admiralty for the supply of materials, engines and labour, characterised by indiscriminate purchasing, attempts to corner vital components, and friction between both staffs and subordinates, all of which led to inefficiency, delays, and wasteful competition, in which the R.F.C. invariably came off worst.

These destructive disputes and manœuvrings continued until the Royal Air Force was formed in April 1918, but the inefficiency did not disappear. To describe the wretched story of the incredible blunders of the air supply organisation during the last year of the war, the disastrous hasty contracts, the faulty co-ordination of effort, the ill-judged control of material and labour, the mass production of untried, defective engines, would run far beyond the capacity of an appendix.

Almost the only light that shone during the long period of neglect, incompetence and folly in the supply of aircraft for the R.F.C. was the undismayed courage of those sent out every day to face death in aeroplanes that should have been thrown on the scrap-heap many months before.

Appendix B

Trenchard's Strategy of the Offensive

After the Battle of Messines air activity had to slacken because of the R.F.C.'s heavy losses in April and May, which forced General Trenchard, on June 10th, to instruct his Brigade Commanders 'to avoid wastage of both pilots and machines, for some little time. My reserves at present are dangerously low, in fact, in some cases, it barely exists at all. . . . It is of the utmost importance, however, that the offensive spirit is maintained.'

General Trenchard was right to sustain an offensive spirit. Where he erred was in identifying this with an offensive strategy which was, in effect, a territorial offensive. To him, as to his staff, and most of his senior commanders, for a British aeroplane to be one mile across the trenches was offensive: for it to be ten miles over was more offensive.

Influenced perhaps by naval doctrines—'seek out and destroy the enemy' and 'our frontiers are the enemy coasts'—he applied them to the air, not appreciating that they were largely irrelevant in a three-dimensional sphere. In the air fighting of World War I, despite the siege-like situation on the ground, it was not a fighter aeroplane's position in relation to a line of defences that measured the offensive spirit but the aggressive will of its occupants to attack the enemy wherever he was encountered, at whatever odds.

The pursuit of a territorial offensive strategy of distant patrols, together with the handicap of a prevailing westerly wind, resulted in a large proportion of aircrew disabled by wounds, or put out of action by faulty engines or gun jams, falling into enemy hands. That the High Command should uphold such avoidable wastage in 1917, when the R.F.C. was desperately short of aeroplanes, aero-engines and trained pilots, is hard to fathom.

These direct losses were augmented by the wear and tear on pilots and planes in chasing the mirage of air ascendancy over the Lines by continuous standing patrols of fighters along the whole British front, regardless of the needs of the tactical situation, ground or air. While we thus dissipated our strength, more often than not merely beating the empty air, the Germans, in their so-called defensive strategy, concentrated forces superior in numbers or equipment and engaged our scattered Line Patrols in turn, and our Distant Offensive Patrols as and when it suited them. The result was that in 1917 British air losses were at times nearly four times as great as the German.

Though the real criterion of an offensive policy was not place but aggressiveness, even this was useless without efficient aeroplanes. The most rashly aggressive pigeon won't get far with a hawk. Important as was the offensive spirit in the air war, technical superiority was more vital, not least because it conferred the initiative.

For the High Command to persist, despite the toll in life and material, in continuously patrolling the Lines and in sending obsolescent machines deep into German-held territory, was incomprehensible even at the time. In retrospect, such obduracy seems as irrational as Haig's unyielding adherence to attrition, and the no less stubborn Admiralty resistance to escorted convoys.

Appendix C

Why No Parachutes?

Nothing more mystified the pilots and observers of the R.F.C., R.N.A.S. and R.A.F. during 1917–18 than the dour refusal of their High Command to provide them with parachutes. During the half-century that has followed, no question has more puzzled air historians on every level.

Because no specific reason was ever established for their refusal, a convention has grown up over the years, erected on the gossip and half-truths of the day, that the decision against parachutes was taken first because no reliable parachute then existed, and second because so convenient a facility for escape might invite pilots to abandon their aircraft without a determined fight.

The first reason was unquestionably given by those responsible, but it was untrue. The second was a slur on the flyers who daily risked their lives in France, and one which has since provoked indignation among the survivors of those who were there. But it is an invention. That some such notion was in the air as a rumour is not to be denied, but it was not based on an official attitude.

I have made a close examination of all the War Office files dealing with parachutes during 1914–18, files not previously open for inspection except under ban of official censorship, and nowhere have I found any specific statement by any officer or official on which could be pinned the calumny that parachutes would encourage unnecessary abandonment of aircraft.

Another convention that has emerged in recent years is the habit of attributing the official denial of parachutes to one man, and one man alone, General Trenchard. This trend is based partly on a passage in his biography, by Andrew Boyle, which states that Trenchard's attitude to parachutes 'was characteristically spartan. His balloon observers, being defenceless, were issued with them, but not his airmen.'

This statement is too vague to hold the significance placed on it. In the early and middle stages of the war Trenchard was not the dominating figure he afterwards became. Even if he had been emphatically against parachutes he could not have imposed his bias over two years on other R.F.C. officers of similar or higher seniority. Moreover, as Commander in the Field, and later Chief of the Air Staff, he would have been much too occupied with weighty day-to-day problems of high direction to be able to intervene frequently in this one question of technical equipment.

In none of the War Office files mentioned have I found evidence that he was in any way responsible for the denial of parachutes. On the contrary, his name is conspicuously absent from the list of senior R.F.C., R.N.A.S. and R.A.F. officers at the War Office and Air Ministry who between them did collectively smother the development of the parachute.

The argument put forward by some of these officers that no reliable parachute existed was merely evidence of ignorance. Parachutes were in regular use before the war at fairs, displays and country shows in Europe and the United States, in exhibition jumps from free balloons, carried out by both men and women, and only rarely with accident.

In these parachutes the weight of the falling jumper pulled the canopy from a container attached to the basket of the balloon and immediately opened it. To attach so bulky a container to the early aeroplanes, fragile and underpowered, occurred to no one until March 1912, when a successful jump from 1,500 feet was made in America. The feat was repeated in England in May 1913, when a pull-off fall was made from 2,000 feet over Hendon aerodrome.

In 1908, in America, a different kind of parachute had been introduced, for free fall, in which the parachute was attached as a pack to the jumper, and opened by him by a ripcord and handle as he fell. This new contrivance was employed only for balloon jumps until October 1912, when a similar pack was used in a free-fall jump from a Wright aeroplane, again in the U.S.A. This dramatic advance, which was repeated at shows and displays through the States, held no significance for any of the supposedly alert minds engaged in developing the infant flying services of both the U.S.A. and the then much more militant nations of Europe.

It is thus indisputable that two years before the war there existed a free-fall pack parachute of proven performance, which though perhaps immature by modern standards, could have been taken up by any of the powers and developed alongside the then equally immature aeroplane.

Although, after World War I broke out, observation kite balloons were provided with the traditional showman's type of free-balloon parachute, not only were the 1912 free-fall drops from aeroplanes completely forgotten, but nobody in authority gave a thought to the possibility of adapting the reliable balloon-type parachute for use from aeroplanes.

However, the initiative had already been taken by a civilian, Mr E. R.

Calthrop, a retired engineer, who had developed a new design of parachute for the simple, altruistic purpose of saving lives. This unconvincing motive, together with the unhappy name he gave to it, 'Guardian Angel', were enough to damn it in the eyes of most service people, but the Guardian Angel, though not a free-fall, and far from perfect by later developments, was a sound, well-thought-out proposition, more compact and quicker in action than the old-fashioned Spencer parachutes supplied to kite-balloon observers.

But Calthrop's invention, perhaps because his approach to inflated official-dom was not always sufficiently tactful, was regarded by the War Office and Admiralty with dislike, and every high-level advance on his part for tests and trials was brusquely rebuffed.

War Office files show that even in May 1914, before the war began, Cal-throp, whose parachute had already been successfully tried out at Barrow-in-Furness with the co-operation of Vickers, invited the R.F.C. and R.N.A.S. at Farnborough to test it also. Captain E. M. Maitland of the R.F.C., who had done a 7,000-foot parachute jump from an airship the year before, was quite prepared to test it, but there is no evidence that any result followed from this or similar invitations made to both War Office and Admiralty.

Later, in October 1915, at the Royal Aircraft Factory, the enterprising Superintendent, Mervyn O'Gorman, one of the few people alive to the potentiality of the parachute, and with an experienced balloon jumper on his staff, proposed to experiment with a Calthrop. 'I have fitted this to an aero-plane for preliminary trials with a dummy', he wrote to the Directorate of Military Aeronautics, seeking approval for the modest expenditure involved.

'Do you wish experiments of this nature to be proceeded with?' minuted the Assistant Director of M.A. 'No, certainly not!' wrote General Henderson, G.O.C. of the R.F.C. What Daimler's Chief Engineer, A. E. Berriman, called 'some very interesting experiments' were thus abruptly halted. A year later a junior staff officer had the effrontery to suggest that permission might now be given for the experiments to be resumed, but his nose was rubbed in Hender-son's 'Certainly not!'

Undeterred, Calthrop persevered in his efforts to gain official approval, but he was up against influences both practical and intangible. That the primitive aeroplane of 1915–16 could not carry the weight of a parachute without some sacrifice of performance was an objection every pilot understood and accepted though not perhaps to the degree expressed by a gallant R.N.A.S. officer, Commander Boothby, who wrote: 'We don't want to carry additional weight merely to save our lives.'

The intangibles were much less acceptable to the fighting airman. He could not easily tolerate the customary Whitehall opposition to change, to new notions, which existed at high levels in even the young and vigorous R.F.C. and R.N.A.S. Nor did he appreciate the attitude of some senior officers, influenced no doubt by the traditions of the sea, who believed that the occupants of a stricken aeroplane should dive to their deaths with a stiff upper lip, in the manner of the captain of a sinking ship.

A further intangible was the sheer ignorance of those members of the Air Board who lacked experience of air combat except in the carbine era. Even so fine an officer as General R. M. Groves could write: 'Smashed aircraft generally fall with such velocity that there would hardly be time to think about the parachute.' At the time this sentence is written, some 200,000 airmen have saved their lives by parachutes because they managed to find time to think.

Another member of the Air Board, Lord Sydenham, wrote: 'The point is, could pilots make use of the Guardian Angel parachute at the moment when it becomes clear that their machine had come to grief?' Lord Sydenham was not an airman, and his qualifications to adjudge on this question were outstanding only in the negative. The sixty-nine-year-old peer's soldiering days had ended over twenty years earlier, and his two previous public appointments had been Superintendent of the Royal Carriage Factory and Chairman on the Royal Commission on Contagious Diseases.

The Air Board decision on October 1916 was that it should await further developments. But developments by whom? The hoary process of passing the buck was now in operation. In January 1917 the secretary of the Board wrote: 'I gather from General Brancker that there is at present no idea of using parachutes in connection with heavier-than-air craft.' This was thought unnecessary because the R.N.A.S. was now experimenting with parachutes for use in airships.

But at the time that the Board, and the higher officers of the technical directorates, were holding down the Guardian Angel, trials of it were being held by junior officers at Orfordness Experimental Station, where during January successful jumps were made by Captain C. F. Collet from a B.E.2c. No member of the Air Board took any interest in the reports submitted, and not for a full year were the tests resumed at the same station.

But in France General Trenchard heard of the trials, and despite his many preoccupations as Commander in the Field, suggested that they be continued in France. They were not continued anywhere. On January 16th he asked for twenty black Calthrop parachutes for dropping spies from aeroplanes behind the German lines, and the records show that they were delivered to No 2 Aircraft Depot between January and March. Trenchard was at least not blindly opposed to parachutes.

Yet successive members of the Air Board continued to rebuff Calthrop's efforts. In May he made yet another approach, and after referring to the Orfordness trials and the spy-dropping operations, suggested that if his parachutes could not be used by squadrons in France they might at least be employed in training schools. General L. E. O. Charlton's decision in the column of the minute sheet was simply 'No!' Calthrop persisted 'in view of the many deaths from the burning of pilots'. '*Not* many', commented Charlton.

Calthrop had heard of the suggestion that possession of a parachute might 'impair a pilot's nerve when in difficulties, so that he would make improper use of his parachute, with the result that more machines would be crashed'. He argued that surely an airman at the Front, knowing he could use his parachute in emergency, 'would attempt to achieve more', but this rational view, which was to be borne out a thousand times in World War II, inspired no reaction.

Among the stock attitudes adopted by members of the Directorate and the Air Board to account for their hostility to parachutes, additional to such notions as that a falling airman would lose consciousness, was the one advanced by the Board's secretary, Major Baird, M.P., in the House of Commons, when he stated that 'pilots did not desire parachutes for aeroplanes'. This view was based on that held by those senior R.F.C. and R.N.A.S. officers who had never experienced fierce lethal air combat, nor witnessed the desperate need of comrades falling to their death in broken or burning planes. Such as Groves, when he wrote: "The heavier-than-air people all say that they flatly decline a parachute in an aeroplane as a life-saving device worth carrying in its present form'. The people he referred to were not the pilots of B.E.s and R.E.s, or Nieuport and Sopwith two-seaters, or F.E.8s and the other death-traps then being flown in France.

Such statements were evidence of the wide gulf that existed between the fighting ranks of the R.F.C., the pilots and observers in France up to, but not often including, the squadron commander's grade of major, and the ranks who were too senior to fight, and who never experienced post-Fokker air fighting in any form.

The truth was that from early 1917, especially during and after the 'Bloody April' losses, there were few fliers with any experience of air fighting who were not obsessed to some degree, though usually secretly, with the thought of being shot down in flames. The top-scoring British ace Mannock was the classic example. To all these a parachute would have been a stiffener to strain and morale. But their views did not go beyond the level of the squadron or wing commanders, who feared that to support such attitudes would expose them to criticism for tolerating morale-weakening influences.

Another stock attitude was that the Guardian Angel was not efficient enough.

Under Government auspices it could have been developed and improved quickly and at trifling cost, and a reliable free-fall parachute would undoubtedly have been evolved within a few months. But the active-service flier did not want to wait for perfection. He wanted something quickly, that would offer a hope of escape, much as a lifebelt offers hope to a seaman from a sinking ship. Even if the parachute were not infallible it would offer a sporting chance, which was better than a death that was certain.

At length, by the end of 1917, a Parachute Committee had been formed on the recommendation of General Maitland, to examine whether or not parachutes should and could be provided. The secretary, Major Orde-Lees, was a keen and experienced parachutist, but not most of those with whom he worked. 'I doubt whether the practicable application of the Guardian Angel parachute is possible during war', wrote the Controller of the Technical Directorate, who then added: 'I think that one parachute should be sufficient to rescue both pilot and observer.'

But in France parachutes at last found support from a high-ranking officer, General Longcroft, commanding the 3rd Brigade, R.F.C., one of the senior officers who was not too senior to fly fighting machines and to make parachute descents. He wrote that 'I and my pilots keenly desired parachutes, and recommend the Calthrop method of fitting the pack to the top of the fuselage'. The official argument against this proposal was that 'it would impose a dangerous strain on the pilot', which was apparently considered worse than being killed. Persisting, Longcroft argued that the principal use of the parachute would be to get clear of a burning plane. He added that he had heard the objection that pilots might jump prematurely, but, as a practical parachutist, he did not believe it. His letters went into the pending tray.

By now the French and Italians, and, as was shortly to be shown, the Germans, were all well advanced in experiments in parachutes, and in January 1918 the Air Board was at last driven into giving Calthrop an order, but mainly, as Brigadier-General MacInnes noted later, 'to keep the firm alive'. Subsequently, Calthrop was permitted for the first time to publicise his invention, and he then disclosed that many flying officers had approached him to supply and fit a parachute at their own expense, but that the Air Board would not countenance any such demonstration of poor morale. After all, Major Baird had officially stated that pilots did not want parachutes.

But ideas were changing, though not to the extent of producing action. 'The question of parachutes now requires more consideration than has been given to it in the past', wrote Commander W. Forbes-Sempill, D/D.A.T.S. in April 1918. 'I think it is no exaggeration to say that everyone agrees that parachutes should be provided on aircraft.'

This view was given a fillip in mid-1918 when the Germans started using free-fall parachutes in France, so provoking a Press and public reaction which Whitehall could not ignore. In September, as a result of tests made in France with S.E.5s and Snipe, a request for 500 Calthrop parachutes was submitted. Except for one minor modification, they were exactly the same as the model standardised in July 1916. But they were never employed in action. The war ended without any parachute being used by the British in France, except for the dropping of spies.

The War Office files show clearly that for this dereliction, no one man, nor even any specific group of men, can in fairness be indicted. It was the collective official mind actuated by intangible prejudice which was responsible. As Calthrop wrote with understandable bitterness in January 1919: 'No one in high quarters had any time to devote to investigating the merits of an appliance whose purpose was so ridiculously irrelevant to war as the saving of life in the air.'

Index

70 71 72 73 10 9 8 7 6 5 4 3 2 1

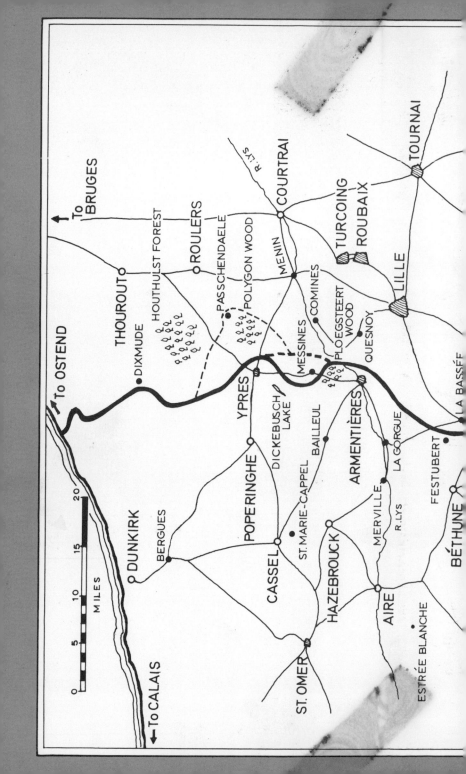